AF805857

Comparative Study on Patent Claim Interpretation: The United States and China

Zhe Peng

Comparative Study on Patent Claim Interpretation: The United States and China

知识产权出版社有限责任公司
Intellectual Property Publishing House Co., Ltd.

Springer

Zhe Peng
School of Law
Shandong University
Qingdao, Shandong, China

ISBN 978-981-96-0835-5 ISBN 978-981-96-0836-2 (eBook)
https://doi.org/10.1007/978-981-96-0836-2

Jointly published with Intellectual Property Publishing House
The print edition is not for sale in China (Mainland). Customers from China (Mainland) please order the print book from: Intellectual Property Publishing House.
Co-publisher's ISBN: 978-7-5130-7417-9

Translation from the Chinese Simplified language edition: "中美专利权利要求解释比较研究" by Zhe Peng, © Intellectual Property Publishing House Co., Ltd. 2021. Published by Intellectual Property Publishing House Co., Ltd. All Rights Reserved.

© Intellectual Property Publishing House 2025

This work is subject to copyright. All rights are solely and exclusively licensed by the Publisher, whether the whole or part of the material is concerned, specifically the rights of translation, reprinting, reuse of illustrations, recitation, broadcasting, reproduction on microfilms or in any other physical way, and transmission or information storage and retrieval, electronic adaptation, computer software, or by similar or dissimilar methodology now known or hereafter developed.
The use of general descriptive names, registered names, trademarks, service marks, etc. in this publication does not imply, even in the absence of a specific statement, that such names are exempt from the relevant protective laws and regulations and therefore free for general use.
The publishers, the authors, and the editors are safe to assume that the advice and information in this book are believed to be true and accurate at the date of publication. Neither the publishers nor the authors or the editors give a warranty, express or implied, with respect to the material contained herein or for any errors or omissions that may have been made. The publishers remain neutral with regard to jurisdictional claims in published maps and institutional affiliations.

This Springer imprint is published by the registered company Springer Nature Singapore Pte Ltd.
The registered company address is: 152 Beach Road, #21-01/04 Gateway East, Singapore 189721, Singapore

If disposing of this product, please recycle the paper.

Preface

The significance of claims cannot be emphasized too much in patent infringement litigation. As the former Chief Judge of the U.S. Court of Appeals for the Federal Circuit in 1990 stated, "the name of the game is the claim".[1] In current U.S. and Chinese patent law, claims define the scope of patent rights. Interpreting claims to determine the scope of a patent is the first and crucial step in patent infringement. In the United States, where claim interpretation is a separate step in litigation, many infringement cases are settled once claim interpretation is decided by a court.

Because of the tremendous significance of the claims, they are typically drafted with special care to define the subject matter of patent protection definitely and clearly.[2] However, the meaning of claim terms is still disputed from time to time in litigation. Litigators attempt to convince the court to adopt an interpretation of the terms in favor of their own clients. The literal scope defined by clarifying the meaning of the claim terms, together with the scope defined by the application of the doctrine of equivalents, determines the scope of patent protection resulting from claim interpretation in patent infringement litigation.[3]

The United States has a long history emphasizing the role of the patent system in promoting technological innovation and economic growth. Similarly, China has been working on a transition from a manufacture-based economy to an innovation-based economy and published the Outline of National Intellectual Property Strategy, which emphasizes the significance of patents in making this transition. To promote patent and innovation policy, patent claims should be interpreted to maintain a fine balance between two

---

[1] Giles S. Rich, *The Extent of the Protection and Interpretation of Claims-American Perspectives*, 21 International Review of Industrial Property and Copyright Law (ICC), 497, 499 (1990).

[2] James R. Barney, *An Empirical Analysis of District Court Claim Construction Decisions*, 2011 Stanford Technology Law Review 1 (2011).

[3] Claim interpretation is also a crucial step in patentability determination (e.g., patent prosecution and invalidation). This study focuses on the claim interpretation in infringement litigation.

competing interests: (1) giving incentives to further innovations for inventors and (2) securing legal certainty for the public.[4]

This study is a comparative study of claim interpretation in the United States and China with a focus on the function of the rules. Because the U.S. patent law and Chinese patent law have very different conceptual frameworks and U.S. and Chinese courts define some rules for claim interpretation differently, it is easy to conclude that the protection scope resulting from claim interpretation is very different between these two countries. However, these differences may be artificial and the rules may function similarly to lead to a similar scope of protection. The U.S. and Chinese law defines a few of rules of claim interpretation in very similar expressions. However, those rules do not always function in the same way. Therefore, this study addresses the question whether the rules of claim interpretation function similarly or differently in the United States and China.

In order to answer this question, this study examines information from various sources. This research focuses on different legal materials in the U.S. section and Chinese section, because the two legal systems operate differently. To examine the rules in the United States, this research mainly focuses on cases and statutes, while using literature including treatise, law review and journal articles and books as a secondary reference. In contrast, to examine the rules in China, this research examines a variety of sources, including cases, statutes, judicial interpretations, policy documents and transcripts while using literature as a secondary reference.

Similar to the United States, cases and statues are still a focus for understanding claim interpretation in China. But in addition to cases and statutes, there is a unique source of law in China. This source of law is called "Judicial Interpretation", which provides some significant rules in claim interpretation.[5] The instructions from the higher levels become important guidelines for judges in adjudicating cases. When a new judicial interpretation is issued, a representative from the Supreme People's Court of China will be interviewed by the media and will give an official explanation to the media about the background and purpose of the new rules. The interview transcript is published by the Supreme People's Court's website and newspaper.

Since 2008, the Supreme People's Court of China has held an annual Intellectual Property Judicial Conference, which is attended by Chinese judges nationwide. The conference enables judges to discuss the cutting-edge issues in intellectual property cases and resolve conflicting views. The transcripts of the major presentations are published in the China Intellectual Property Protection Yearbook. Both the interview transcripts and conference transcripts are viewed by judges and attorneys not only as aids to understand the policy but also as instructions on how to implement the law. The Supreme People's Court and other patent-related governmental institutions

[4] Toshiko Takenaka, *IP Boom or IP Bashing?—Current Trends in IP Legislation and Case Law*, 21 Japan Spotlight 23 (2006).

[5] Sup. People's Ct, The Rules on Citing Normative Documents (关于裁判文书引用法律、法规等规范性法律文件的规定) (2009). *See* Peter H. Corne, *Creation and Application of Law in the PRC*, 50 American Journal of Comparative Law 369, 409 (2002).

also periodically issue policy documents. Those policy documents do not provide instructions for adjudication, but explain the general policy trend.

Based on the cases, statutes and other related materials, this study explains how the United States and Chinese claim interpretation rules function to determine the scope of patent protection and how these rules reflect patent policy. Contrary to the common view in the Western world that China is reluctant to protect patent rights,[6] Chinese patent claim interpretation rules function very similarly to those in the United States. This study will discuss Chinese rules, which are adopted from United States, as well as rules which look different but function in the same way as U.S. rules, thus resulting in the same protection scope.

Moreover, Chinese claim interpretation has gone through an evolutionary process, which is similar to the U.S. patent law history. In the late 1990s, the U.S. courts started to give more weight to the public notice function of patent claims and legal certainty with the protection scope resulting from claim interpretation.[7] Following the U.S. trend, Chinese courts have also moved in the same direction to emphasize legal certainty.

Qingdao, China Zhe Peng

[6] Xuan-Thao Nguyen, *The China We Hardly Know–Revealing the New China's Intellectual Property Regime*, 55 St. Louis University Law Journal 773 (Lead Article) (2011).

[7] *See e.g., Hilton Davis Chem. Co. v. Warner-Jenkinson Co., Inc.*, 62 F.3d 1512, 1530 (Fed. Cir. 1995). supplemented, 64 F.3d 675 (Fed. Cir. 1995) and rev'd, 520 U.S. 17, 117 S. Ct. 1040, 137 L. Ed. 2d 146 (1997) and adhered to, 114 F.3d 1161 (Fed. Cir. 1997) supplemented, 64 F.3d 675 (Fed. Cir. 1995) and rev'd, 520 U.S. 17, 117 S. Ct. 1040, 137 L. Ed. 2d 146 (1997) and adhered to, 114 F.3d 1161 (Fed. Cir. 1997).

Contents

Chapter 1
U.S. Claim Interpretation: Procedural Law

1.1 U.S. Court System in General: Lawyers, Judges, Technical Experts

1.1.1 *Claim Interpretation by Judges*

In the *Markman* case, the Supreme Court decided that it is the judge, rather than the jury, who shall interpret the literal scope of a patent claim.[1] Prior to *Markman*, the use of jury trials had been increased in patent infringement litigation. In 1996, the Court's decision in Markman was heavily based on functional considerations, including the suitability of interpretation issues for determination by judges and the importance of uniformity in the treatment of a given patent.[2]

The practice of identifying claim interpretation as a question of law, and thus resolving claim interpretation by a judge, had been a practice in existence in the district court and Federal Circuit before the *Markman* case.[3] In *Markman*, in the federal district court of first instance, the jury found infringement, but the district court judge disagreed and entered a judgment of no infringement.[4] The patentee, *Markman*, appealed to the Federal Circuit and then appealed to the Supreme Court, insisting that the constitution requires that the outcome of the case should be up to the jury to decide.[5]

---

[1] Markman v. Westview Instruments, Inc., 517 U.S. 370, 116 S. Ct. 1384, 134 L. Ed. 2d 577 (1996) (Markman II).

[2] Ibid., at 377, 116 S. Ct. at 1389, 134 L. Ed. 2d 577 (1996).

[3] See e.g., Kraus v. Bell Atlantic Corp., 716 F.Supp. 182, 184 (E.D.Pa.1989); Becton Dickinson and Co. v. C.R. Bard, Inc., 922 F.2d 792, 797 (Fed.Cir.1990); Markman v. Westview Instruments, Inc., 772 F. Supp. 1535, 1536 (E.D. Pa. 1991) aff'd, 52 F.3d 967 (Fed. Cir. 1995) aff'd, 517 U.S. 370 (1996) (Markman I).

[4] Markman, at 377, 116 S. Ct. at 1389, 134 L. Ed. 2d 577 (1996).

[5] Ibid.

© Intellectual Property Publishing House 2025

Z. Peng, *Comparative Study on Patent Claim Interpretation: The United States and China*, https://doi.org/10.1007/978-981-96-0836-2_1

Markman owned U.S. Reissue Patent No. 33,054 for his "Inventory Control and Reporting System for Drycleaning Stores" and brought an infringement suit against Westview and Althon Enterprises, an operator of dry-cleaning establishments using Westview's products (collectively, Westview).[6] Part of the dispute hinged upon the meaning of the words in the patent claim.[7] The case was tried before a jury.[8] A witness produced by Markman testified about the meaning of the claim language before the jury. The jury found an infringement of Markman's independent claim 1 and dependent claim 10.[9] Nevertheless, the District Court granted Westview's deferred motion for judgment as a matter of law, rejected Markman's argument on the meaning of the claim terms and found no infringement.[10]

One of the disputed claim terms was "inventory", a term found in Markman's independent claim 1, which stated that Markman's product can "maintain an inventory total" and "detect and localize spurious additions to inventory". The district court judge rejected Markman's expert's definition of inventory, which limited the definition of inventory to only include cash.[11] Instead, the court determined the term "inventory" in Markman's patent encompassed "both cash inventory and the actual physical inventory of articles of clothing".[12] Consequently, the defendant's device did not infringe, because it functioned merely to record an inventory of receivables by tracking invoices and transaction totals, rather than to record and track an inventory of articles of clothing.[13] Markman appealed and both the Federal Circuit and the Supreme Court affirmed.

The Supreme Court's analysis began with a constitutional law analysis. Based on the historical test, the Seventh Amendment of U.S. constitution does not guarantee a right to jury trial for claim interpretation.[14] The Seventh Amendment provides that "[i]n Suits at common law, where the value in controversy shall exceed twenty dollars, the right of trial by jury shall be preserved[...]".[15] In order to determine whether a trial decision should be made by a jury, the Supreme Court used the "historical test", which asked two questions: (1) whether the cause of action was tried at law at the time of the [nation's] founding; (2) if the action in question belongs in the law category, if the particular trial decision must fall to the jury in order to preserve the substance of the common-law right as it existed in 1791 when the Seventh Amendment was ratified.[16] The patent claim was not mentioned by statute in the United States until

[6] Markman, 517 U.S. at 374, 116 S. Ct. at 1388, 134 L. Ed. 2d 577.

[7] *Ibid.*

[8] Markman, 517 U.S.at 370.

[9] Ibid.

[10] Ibid.

[11] Markman, 772 F. Supp. at 1537–1538.

[12] Ibid.

[13] Ibid.

[14] Markman, 517 U.S. at 377, 116 S. Ct. at 1388–1390, 134 L. Ed. 2d 577.

[15] U.S. Const., Amdt. VII.

[16] Markman v. Westview Instruments, Inc., 517 U.S. at 376. See also Tull v. United States, 481 U.S. 412, 417 (1987).

the Patent Act of 1836 and was not required by statute until the Patent Act of 1870.[17] Consequently, the Supreme Court held that there was no clear historical precedent in 1791 for practice of claim interpretation.[18]

Since the U.S. Constitution does not require a jury trial for claim interpretation, the Court made its conclusion mainly based on functional and practical considerations. The Court believed that judges are in better positions than juries to interpret the claims for two reasons. First, claim interpretation is similar to interpreting the language in legal documents (e.g., contracts and statutes), and thus, judges have better training and experience.[19] Second, legal consistency will be better served if judges interpret the claims, since judges follow precedents.[20]

The U.S. courts emphasized that claim interpretation is special and involves highly technical legal issues and thus requires particular legal training and practice.[21] The courts and patent office had developed special and sophisticated doctrines relating to the form and scope of claims.[22] As a result, patent claim issues had become complex and highly specialized.[23] The *Markman* Court, by citing *Parker v. Hulme*,[24] found that a judge, due to his training and discipline, is more likely to give a proper interpretation to such instruments than a jury.[25]

In response to Markman's argument that a jury is necessary to determine the credibility of expert testimony on the meaning of the disputed term, the Court held that judges are still in a better position in a credibility determination with respect to claim interpretation. The jury has a good capability to determine demeanor,[26] to sense the "mainsprings of human conduct",[27] or to reflect community standards.[28] However, in claim interpretation, it is a rare case that a credibility determination is to choose between experts whose testimony was equally consistent with a patent's internal logic.[29] In sum, the Court found, the credibility determination should be taken into consideration within the necessarily sophisticated analysis of the whole document.[30] Notwithstanding its evidentiary underpinnings, claim interpretation is

---

[17] JANICE M. MULLER, AN INTRODUCTION TO PATENT LAW 273 (2006).

[18] Markman, 517 U.S. at 376.

[19] Ibid.

[20] Ibid., at 390–91.

[21] Parker v. Hulme, 18 F. Cas. 1138, 1140 (C.C.E.D. Pa. 1849). cited by Markman 517 U.S.at 388–90.

[22] William Redin Woodward, Definiteness and Particularity in Patent Claims, 46 Michigan Law Review 755 (1948).

[23] Ibid., at 765.

[24] Parker, 18 F. Cas.at 1140.

[25] Markman, 517 U.S. at 376.

[26] Miller v. Fenton, 474 U.S. 104, 116, 106 S. Ct. 445, 451, 453 (1985).

[27] Commissioner v. Duberstein, 363 U.S. 278, 289 (1960).

[28] United States v. McConney, 728 F.2d 1195, 1204 (C.A.9 1984) (en banc).

[29] Markman, 517 U.S. at 376.

[30] Ibid. See also Bates v. Coe, 98 U.S. 31, 38 (1878); cf. U.S. Industrial Chemicals, Inc. v. Carbide & Carbon Chemicals Corp., 315 U.S. 668, 678 (1942).

similar to judges' other responsibilities in the normal course of a trial.[31] In conclusion, a judge is in a better position to ascertain whether an expert's proposed definition fully comports with the specifications and claims and so will preserve the patent's internal coherence.[32]

The district court's opinion in the *Markman* case exemplifies that a court examines the meaning of a claim term asserted in an expert's testimony by looking at the patent itself and considering the patent's internal logic. In response, the patentee's witness' assertion that "inventory" only includes cash and does not include physical inventory of articles of clothing, the district court conducted an analysis of the claim language itself: "to read the word inventory otherwise would lead to 'semantic antics' in reading the claim that the [...] system can detect and localize spurious additions to inventory as well as spurious deletions therefrom. It is difficult to visualize a system that would detect and localize spurious dollar deletions and additions to inventory".[33] Thus, the district court rejected the interpretation asserted by the patentee's witness.

Another functional consideration to allocate all issues of claim interpretation to a judge is to uphold the uniformity of treatment of a given patent.[34] Allowing a judge instead of a jury to decide claim interpretation promotes uniformity among district courts through application of *stare decisis*. The Court used the word "promote" and cautiously noted "though it will not guarantee" uniformity. There are many other factors that could impact uniformity, but at least a hearing before a judge will increase the opportunity of interjurisdictional uniformity. A judge can take precedents established by judges in other jurisdictions into consideration. The court cited previous cases as a reminder of the importance of consistency in claim interpretation. "Finally, we see the importance of uniformity in the treatment of a given patent as an independent reason to allocate all issues of construction to the court. As we noted in General Elec. Co. v. Wabash Appliance Corp., 304 U.S. 364, 369, 58 S.Ct. 899, 902, 82 L.Ed. 1402 (1938), '[t]he limits of a patent must be known for the protection of the patentee, the encouragement of the inventive genius of others and the assurance that the subject of the patent will be dedicated ultimately to the public'".

a. Magistrate Judges

A U.S. magistrate judge is a judicial officer of a district court and is appointed by majority vote of the active district judges of the court to exercise jurisdiction over cases when parties agree to have a magistrate judge.[35] In a patent case, a magistrate judge can be assigned either to participate either in discovery only, in the interpretation of discovery procedures, or to handle the entire claim interpretation.[36]

---

[31] Markman, 517 U.S. at 376.

[32] Ibid.

[33] Markman, 772 F. Supp. at 1535.

[34] Markman 517 U.S. at 390–91.

[35] The Federal Judiciary: Frequently Asked Questions, http://www.uscourts.gov/faq.html (last visited Aug. 14, 2008).

[36] David L. Schwartz, Practice Makes Perfect? An Empirical Study of Claim Construction Reversal Rates in Patent Cases, 107 Michigan Law Review 223, 247 (2008).

The number of magistrate judges participating in claim interpretation is small. A statistical study shows that there have been 485 trial court judges whose decisions on claim interpretations had been reviewed by the Federal Circuit, and of those cases, only 32 of them involved magistrate judges. In the 743 claim interpretations' cases collected in this study, only 19 cases were entirely handled by magistrate judges without oversight by a district court judge.[37] Existing research does not show a significant difference between the performance of magistrate judges and district court judges.[38]

b. Patent Pilot Program

Most district courts use random drawings to assign patent cases, to assure an equitable distribution of caseloads and avoid judge shopping.[39] In response to the demand for more specialized district court judges in the patent area, in January 2011, Congress passed Public Law No.111–349, which establishes a pilot program. It was introduced by Representative Darrell Issa (R-CA) with co-sponsors Representatives Howard Coble (R-NC), Hank Johnson, Jr. (D-GA) and Adam B. Schiff (D-CA).[40] The Director of the Administrative Office of the U.S. Courts selected 14 district courts in June 2011 to participate in the 10-year pilot program, including Central District of California, Northern District of California, Southern District of California, Southern District of Florida, Northern District of Illinois, District of Maryland, District of Nevada, District of New Jersey, Eastern District of New York, Southern District of New York, Western District of Pennsylvania, Western District of Tennessee, Eastern District of Texas and Northern District of Texas.

The program aims to enhance patent expertise by designating judges to handle patent law cases. Public Law No. 111–349 requires that a selected district with at least 10 judges have at least three designated patent judges, and a selected district with fewer than 10 judges have at least two designated patent judges. The program will compare the reversal rates and disposition times between designated judges and non-designated judges over the 10-year period and determine if specialization improves patent practice.

The co-sponsor Johnson said that the program will "create a cadre of judges who gain advanced knowledge of patent and plant variety protection through more intensified experience in handling the cases, along with special education and career development opportunities".[41] However, some research shows that in the past, those judges who handled more patent cases do not necessarily have a low reversal rate in claim interpretation.[42] It is hard to predict the success of the pilot program.

---

[37] Ibid., at 284.

[38] Ibid., at 249.

[39] The Federal Judiciary: Frequently Asked Questions, http://www.uscourts.gov/faq.html (last visited Aug. 14, 2008).

[40] H.R. 628, 111th Cong (2011).

[41] Pilot Program to Enhance Expertise in Patent Cases, United States Courts website (February 2011). http://www.uscourts.gov/News/TheThirdBranch/11-02-01/Pilot_Program_to_Enhance_Expertise_in_Patent_Cases.aspx.

[42] Schwartz, Supra note 36, at 249.

1.1.2 Lawyers

U.S. attorneys are required to earn a law degree in order to take the bar exam. Thus, all attorneys practicing patent law have a formal legal education. A Bachelor's of Science (B.S.), at minimum, is required to take a specialized patent bar exam in order to practice patent prosecution. However, entrance to the patent bar is not required to litigate patent infringement cases. Therefore, an attorney who litigates claim interpretation always has a law degree but does not necessarily have a scientific degree. However, many attorneys involved in patent litigation have scientific degrees.

In many states in the United States, continuing legal education (CLE) participation is a mandatory requirement for attorneys to maintain their licenses to practice law.[43] Continuing legal education is professional education for lawyers that takes place after bar admission.[44] CLE requirements include a certain number of credit hours over a period intervals and sometimes involve specific hour requirements for special topics, such as ethics. In order to fulfill the CLE requirement, attorneys who practice patent law are motivated to attend courses or seminars on relevant topics.

1.1.3 Technical Experts

a. Party Appointed Expert Witness

Rule 702 of the Federal Rules of Evidence provides: "If scientific, technical, or other specialized knowledge will assist the trier of fact to understand the evidence or to determine a fact in issue, a witness qualified as an expert by knowledge, skill, experience, training, or education, may testify thereto in the form of an opinion or otherwise". Some district courts even believe that expert witnesses are practically a requirement in patent litigation.[45] The trial judge has discretion to permit the use of experts.[46]

Expert witnesses translate the patent specification from the terminology only understood by those skilled in technical language into terms comprehensible to

---

[43] Continuing legal education, Wikipedia article, http://en.wikipedia.org/wiki/Continuing_legal_education.

[44] Ibid.

[45] See e.g., Eldon Industries, Inc. v. Vanier Mfg., Inc., 14 U.S.P.Q.2d (BNA) 1075, 1076, 1990 WL 160,220 (C.D. Cal. 1990).

[46] Salem v. U. S. Lines Co., 370 U.S. 31, 35, 82 S. Ct. 1119, 8 L. Ed. 2d 313 (1962); Acoustical Design, Inc. v. Control Electronics Co., Inc., 932 F.2d 939, 18 U.S.P.Q.2d (BNA) 1707, 1709 (Fed. Cir. 1991).

courts.[47] "Since the issues of claim interpretation are matters of law, the expert testimony is limited to aiding the court in understanding the technology".[48] The expert's credentials and experience are important factors for litigants to consider.[49] Also, an expert witness ability to educate individuals with little or no patent knowledge is very important.[50]

b. Court-Appointed Expert Witness

For tasks like claim construction, courts may select evidentiary court-appointed experts,[51] procedural special masters,[52] or common-law technical advisors.[53]

The court-appointed expert is based on FRE 706: "(a) Appointment. The court may on its own motion or on the motion of any party enter an order to show cause why expert witnesses should not be appointed and may request the parties to submit nominations. The court may appoint any expert witnesses agreed upon by the parties and may appoint expert witnesses of its own selection. An expert witness shall not be appointed by the court unless the witness consents to act [...] A witness so appointed shall advise the parties of the witness' findings, if any; the witness' deposition may be taken by any party; and the witness may be called to testify by the court or any party. The witness shall be subject to cross-examination by each party, including a party calling the witness".[54] The Advisory Notes suggest the qualification requirement for expert witnesses: "[T]he contention is made that court appointed experts acquire an aura of infallibility to which they are not entitled".[55]

1.2 Jurisdiction

Claim interpretation, as a part of patent infringement litigation, is usually conducted in federal district courts of first instance. When the America Invents Act (AIA) was enacted on September 16, 2011, all patent cases were assigned to federal courts instead of state courts.[56] In the past, it was more complex to determine whether a case with a patent issue would go to federal court. According to the old law regarding

---

[47] Learned Hand, Historical and Practical Considerations Regarding Expert Testimony,15 Harvard Law Review 40 (1901).

[48] National Presto Industries, Inc. v. West Bend Co., 76 F.3d 1185, 1190, 37 U.S.P.Q.2d (BNA) 1685, 1688 (Fed. Cir. 1996).

[49] John Gladstone Mills, Donald Cress Reiley, III, Robert Clare Highley, Patent Law Fundamentals (2012) § 20:105.

[50] Ibid.

[51] Fed. R. Evid. 706.

[52] Fed. R. Civ. P. 53.

[53] Dolly Wu, Patent Litigation: What About *Q*ualification Standards for Court Appointed Experts?, 2010 Boston College Intellectual Property and Technology Forum 91,501(2010).

[54] Fed. R. Evid. 706.

[55] Fed. R. Evid. 706. See Wu, Supra note 53, at 91,501.

[56] SEC. 19 (a).

subject matter jurisdiction, federal courts have jurisdiction over disputes "arising under" the patent laws.[57] It is how the plaintiff pleads the action, rather than the nature of the underlying dispute, that dictates which court has jurisdiction.[58] The Supreme Court defined "well-pleaded claims" to explain under what kinds of situations a patent-related dispute "arises under" patent law.[59] If a plaintiff establishes that federal patent law creates the cause of action or that the plaintiff's right to relief necessarily depends on resolution of a substantial question of federal patent law, patent law is a necessary element of a well-pleaded claim and thus the case is subject to federal jurisdiction.[60] If a plaintiff complained of patent infringement, it is a case arising under the Patent Act and therefore is under the federal district courts' jurisdiction.

In general, the Federal Circuit has jurisdiction over all patent infringement cases appealed from the district courts and International Trade Commission (ITC).[61] Since Appeals are not taken to the regional circuits in which the district court resides, the Federal Circuit effectively becomes a specialized appellate court, as the only appellate court with jurisdiction to hear patent infringement cases on appeal.

In the past, there was one exception to federal jurisdiction for claim interpretation.[62] When a patent infringement issue is brought only via counterclaim, the federal circuit does not have jurisdiction over that counterclaim.[63] However, this is an extremely rare case and there has only been one patent infringement case that falls into this jurisdictional hole.[64] However, according to the American Invent Act, the Federal Circuit now has jurisdiction over all patent cases without exception.[65]

---

[57] 28 USC 1338.

[58] KIMBERLY P. MOORE PAUL R. MICHEL, & RAPHAEL V. LUPO PATENT LITIGATION AND STRATEGY (2008) Some patent related cases, e.g., breaching of a licensing agreement, do not have basis in Patent Act, are subject to state court jurisdiction because the complaint is pleaded under state contract law.

[59] Chrisitanson v. Colt Indus. Operating Corp., 486 U.S. 800, 801, 7 USPQ2d 1109 (1988).

[60] Ibid.

[61] 28 U.S.C.A. § 1295 (West).

[62] Holmes Group, Inc. v. Vornado Air Circulation Sys., Inc., 535 U.S. 826 (2002).

[63] Ibid.

[64] Schinzing v. Mid-States Stainless, Inc., 415 F.3d 807, 811 (8th Cir. 2005). See Schwartz, Supra Note 36 at 265.

[65] American Invent Act SEC. 19 (b).

1.3 Evidence: Intrinsic Evidence Versus Extrinsic Evidence

1.3.1 Conflict Precedent Before Phillips

There are two categories of potential sources of evidence that can be used to interpret the claims: intrinsic evidence and extrinsic evidence.[66] Intrinsic evidence includes the patent document itself (claims, specifications) and the patent's prosecution history.[67] Extrinsic evidence broadly refers to any other type of evidence that does not fall into intrinsic evidence, including expert testimony, inventor's testimony, dictionaries, treaties, articles, etc.[68] *Phillips en banc* case established a methodology that intrinsic evidence should be given more weight than extrinsic evidence.[69]

The hierarchy[70] of the case mainly means the different weight given to each type of evidence, instead of the sequence of steps used by the judge in consulting various types of evidence.[71] Also, it does not exclude the use of extrinsic evidence. *Phillips* authorized the district court to consider extrinsic evidence,[72] but warned that extrinsic evidence is biased in nature[73] and reliance on extrinsic evidence will undermine the public notice function of patents.[74]

Before *Phillips*, two Federal Circuit cases in 2002 reflect the split between the literalist approach and the contextual approach.[75] The literalist approach gives greater reliance to extrinsic evidence, e.g., *Texas Digital*.[76] Literalists emphasize the ordinary meaning, which is often based on dictionary definitions; the meaning can only be changed by clear, contrary evidence in a patent's specification and prosecution history. The contextualists tend to give more weight to intrinsic evidence, with a balanced focus on the customary meaning in the relevant prior art, the patent specification and other evidence, e.g., *Teleflex*.[77] This dispute in methodology led to an *en banc* decision in Phillips to clarify the hierarchy of evidence.

---

[66] AMY LANDERS, UNDERSTANDING PATENT LAW 259 (2008).

[67] Vitronics Corp. v. Conceptronic, Inc., 90 F.3d 1576, 1582–83 (Fed. Cir. 1996).

[68] Ibid., at1584.

[69] Phillips v. AWH Corp., 415 F.3d 1303 (Fed. Cir. 2005) (en banc).

[70] ROBERT L HARMON, PATENTS AND THE FEDERAL CIRCUIT (2011).

[71] Phillips, 415 F.3d at 1303, citing Vitronics, 90 F.3d at 1582.

[72] Ibid., at 1317.

[73] Ibid., at 1319.

[74] Ibid.

[75] DONALD S. CHISUM, CHISUM ON PATENTS §18.03 (2012).

[76] Texas Digital Systems, Inc. v. Telegenix, Inc., 308 F.3d 1193 (Fed. Cir. 2002), cert. denied, 538 U.S. 1058 (2003). See Jennifer R. Johnson, Out of Context: Texas Digital, the Indefiniteness of Language, and the Search for Ordinary Meaning, 44 IDEA 521 (2004); Ruoyu Roy Wang, Texas Digital Systems v. Telegenix, Inc.: Toward A More Formalistic Patent Claim Construction Model, 19 Berkeley Technology Law Journal 153 (2004).

[77] TeleFlex, Inc. v. Ficosa North America Corp., 299 F.3d 1313 (Fed. Cir. 2002). See Also Astrazeneca AB v. Mutual Pharmaceutical Co., Inc., 384 F.3d 1333, 1337, 72 USPQ2d 1726 (Fed.

1.3.2 *Phillips* En Banc *Decision*

Philips' patent was directed to building modular, which can be used to build prisons and security institutions.[78] The parties disputed the meaning of "baffle" in the asserted patent claim: "building modules adapted to fit together for construction fire, sound and impact resistant security barriers and rooms for use in securing records and persons, comprising in combination, an outer shell ... sealant means ...and further means disposed inside the shell for increasing its load bearing capacity comprising internal steel baffles extending inwardly from the steel shell walls". The district court read the term "baffle" with the limitation that the baffles are oriented at acute or obtuse angles, other than 90 degrees from the wall face, because the district court found the claim is a "means plus function" claim and thus the scope of the claim should be limited to the disclosed embodiment.

On appeal, a panel of Federal Circuit judges was divided.[79] The majority sustained the district court's summary judgment of non-infringement, and the dissenting judges would have reversed the summary judgment of non-infringement.[80] The majority, although it found that the claim was not a "means plus function" claim, upheld the restricted reading of "baffle" based on its reading of the specification.[81] The panel noted that the specification repeatedly refers to the ability of the claimed baffles to deflect projectiles.[82] Also, the specification describes the baffles as being "disposed at such angles that bullets which might penetrate the outer steel panels are deflected".[83] In addition, the panel observed that baffles oriented at 90 degrees to the wall were found in the prior art.[84] Based on this information in the specification, although nowhere in the patent is it explicitly explained what the right angel is, the panel concluded "that the patentee regarded his invention as panels providing impact or projectile resistance and that the baffles must be oriented at angles other than 90"[85] degrees. The panel added that the patent specification "is intended to support and inform the claims, and here it makes it unmistakably clear that the invention involves baffles angled at other than 90" Id. at 1214 degrees. The panel therefore upheld the district court's summary judgment of non-infringement.

The dissenting judge also consulted the specification, but concluded that "baffle" should be given the full scope of its ordinary meaning, because nothing in the

---

Cir. 2004) (first case used the term "clear disavowal": [Teleflex is] "the first case to use the formulation 'expressions of manifest exclusion or restriction, representing a clear disavowal of claim scope' [...].").

[78] Claim 1 of the '798 patent, Phillips., 415 F.3d at1303.

[79] Phillips, 363 F.3d at 1207.

[80] Ibid.

[81] Ibid., at 1212.

[82] Ibid., at 1310.

[83] Ibid. citing '798 patent, col. 2, ll. 13–15; see also id. at col. 5, ll. 17–19 (baffles are "disposed at angles which tend to deflect the bullets").

[84] Phillips, 415 F.3d at 1310.

[85] Phillips, 363 F.3d at 1213.

specification redefined the term "baffles" or constituted a disclaimer specifically limiting the term to less than the full scope of its ordinary meaning.[86] The dissenting judge argued that the specification "merely identifies impact resistance as one of several objectives of the invention".[87] Also, the majority of the panel agreed that the ordinary meaning of baffle is "something for deflecting, checking, or otherwise regulating flow".[88] Thus, the dissenting judge concluded that "baffle" is not limited to those with an angle other than 90 degrees, and the summary judgment should be overturned.

The Federal Circuit decided to take this case *en banc* and affirmed the majority's contextualist rationale, but adopted the broader interpretation in accordance with the dissenting judge.

1.3.3 The Hierarchy of the Evidence

The *Phillips en banc* court clarified that the intrinsic evidence, such as the claim itself, specification and prosecution history, is superior to extrinsic evidence.[89] Extrinsic evidence is evidence outside of the official administrative record of the patent procedure.[90] The extrinsic evidence identified by the Phillips en banc Court included expert testimony, treatise, dictionaries, etc. Although the Federal Circuit had previously found that dictionaries hold a "special place" and "may sometimes be considered along with the intrinsic evidence",[91] the *Phillips en banc* court nevertheless categorized dictionaries as merely extrinsic evidence.

The *Phillips en banc* court restated the superiority of intrinsic evidence and the inferiority of extrinsic evidence. Claim interpretation should start with the claim itself,[92] and also consider other claims in the patent.[93] By referring to *Vitronics*, the *Phillips en banc* court repeated that the specification "is always highly relevant to the claim construction analysis. Usually, it is dispositive; it is the single best guide to the meaning of a disputed term".[94] In addition, the prosecution history "can often inform the meaning of the claim language by demonstrating how the inventor understood the invention and whether the inventor limited the invention in the course of prosecution,

---

86 Ibid., at1217.

87 Ibid.

88 Ibid., at 1216–17.

89 Phillips, 415 F.3d at 1315.

90 MULLER, Supra Note 17, at 338.

91 Belll Atl. Network Servs., Inc. v. Covard Commc'ns Group Inc., 262 F.3d 1258, 1267 (Fed. Cir. 2001).

92 90 F.3d at 1582.

93 Ibid.

94 Ibid.

making the claim scope narrower than it would otherwise be".[95] The *Phillips en banc* court expressed its mixed opinion on extrinsic evidence. On one hand, it admitted that extrinsic evidence "can shed useful light on the relevant art".[96] On the other hand, the court explained that extrinsic evidence is "less significant than the intrinsic record in determining 'the legally operative meaning of claim language'".[97]

In particular, the court addressed the biased nature of expert testimony. It also pointed out that extrinsic evidence does not necessarily reflect the perspective of a person skilled in the art.

1.3.4 How to Understand the "Hierarchy"

The *Phillips en banc* court emphasized that the hierarchy of evidence is the weight that a judge gives to the different types of evidence, rather than the order a judge consults the evidence.[98] This statement can be understood in light of the instructions set in *Vitronics*, which was reaffirmed by *Phillips en banc*. *Victronics* instructs that a judge may admit and use extrinsic evidence for the purpose of understanding the invention.[99] Meanwhile, it also limited the use of extrinsic evidence to interpretation "in those cases where the public record unambiguously describes the scope of the patented invention, reliance on any extrinsic evidence is improper",[100] and "extrinsic evidence…may not be used to vary or contradict the claim language".[101]

However, the instructions in *Vitronics* are not necessarily inherently clear. The dissenting opinion in *Cybor* questioned the logic of the understanding and interpretation and distinction by asking "what is the distinction between a trial judge's understanding of the claims and a trial judge's interpretation of the claims to the jury? Don't judges instruct the jury in accordance with their understanding of the claims"?[102]

A possible explanation of the "understanding vs. interpreting" distinction is that these concepts come into play at different stages of the claim interpretation process. *Victronics*' statement that intrinsic evidence alone will be sufficient to resolve any claim interpretation issue in most cases is valid if a certain precondition is met: a judge already possesses sufficient scientific knowledge to understand the claims,

---

95 Ibid. Citing Vitronics, 90 F.3d at 1582–83 ("The purpose of consulting the prosecution history in construing a claim is to 'exclude any interpretation that was disclaimed during prosecution'").

96 Phillips, 415 F.3d at 1317.

97 Ibid., at1317, citing C.R. Bard, Inc. v. U.S. Surgical Corp., 388 F.3d 858, 862 (Fed.Cir.2004), quoting Vanderlande Indus. Nederland BV v. Int'l Trade Comm'n, 366 F.3d 1311, 1318 (Fed.Cir.2004); See also Astrazeneca AB v. Mutual Pharm. Co., 384 F.3d 1333, 1337 (Fed.Cir.2004).

98 Phillips, 415 F.3d 1303, 1324.

99 Vitornics, 90 F.3d 1576, 1584.

100 Ibid, at 1583.

101 Ibid, at1584.

102 Cybor Corp. v. FAS Technologies, Inc., 138 F.3d 1448, 1474–75 (Fed. Cir. 1998) (Rader Dissent).

specifications and prosecution history. In order to meet this precondition, a judge usually needs to obtain basic knowledge through expert testimony and other extrinsic evidence.[103] In the first stage, a judge learns the necessary knowledge through expert testimony, etc., by using extrinsic evidence. In the second stage, a judge with the necessary knowledge is able to analyze the intrinsic evidence to reach a conclusion; this is the "interpretation".

The dissenting opinion continued to question that "what happens when that learning influences a trial judge's interpretation of the claim term? Are trial judges supposed to disguise the real reasons for their interpretation? How will this perverse incentive to 'hide the ball' improve an appellate review"?[104]

Vitronics establishes that a judge does not need to cite extrinsic evidence to support its conclusion on interpretation.[105] If a judge does need to cite extrinsic evidence, he or she needs to provide a legitimate reason. According to *Victronics*, the legitimate reason is that a judge still cannot choose between different interpretations by consulting intrinsic evidence. *Vitornics* opinion did not use the term "cite". Instead, it uses "rely on".[106] But as a practical matter, the only way for the appellate court (and the public) to know if a judge relied on certain evidence is to see if the judge cited that evidence to support the conclusion in the opinion.

In a perfect world, where a judge can obtain the necessary knowledge in order to understand a patent, a judge will obtain objective, accurate and correct information. Regardless of what resource the judge obtained such knowledge, the interpretation should be the same and thus there is no need to disclose the source of such information. But in a real world, none of the sources from which a judge can obtain information is absolutely free from bias. The expert testimony is biased in nature. The dictionaries and treatises may contain different perspectives and definitions and do not necessarily accurately reflect "the understanding of a skilled artisan in the field of the patent".[107] Thus, it is very true that "the learning influences a trial judge's interpretation of the claim term", and it will be helpful to improve the transparency of claim interpretation to encourage judges to fully disclose all the information he or she consulted and how such information influenced his or her interpretation. It is detrimental to allow a judge to "hide the ball".[108] Thus, if the instructions set in case law are confusing to a Federal Circuit judge, the instructions definitely need further clarification.

---

[103] Markman, 52 F.3d at 986.

[104] Cybor Corp., 138 F.3d at 1474–75.

[105] Vitronics Corp., 90 F.3d at 1576.

[106] Ibid., at 1583.

[107] Phillips, 415 F.3d at 1318.

[108] Cybor Corp., 138 F.3d at 1474–75.

1.4 First Instance: Two-Step Analysis

There are two steps of patent infringement determination: (1) interpret the disputed claims and (2) compare the claims to the accused infringing device, method, or process.[109] If all-elements in the patent claim can be found in the accused device, method, or process, it is a literal infringement. If one or more of the elements of the patent claim cannot be found in an infringing device, method, or process, but has "equivalent (s)" which are not insubstantially different from the element (s), it is an infringement under doctrine of equivalents.

The two steps are separate because of the different roles played by judges and juries. Claim interpretation is a question of law[110] and decided by judges.[111] Comparing patent claims to the accused infringing technology is a question of fact, which is decided by a jury.[112] The Federal Circuit established judges' obligation to instruct the jury on the meaning of the words used by an inventor in a claim, making it necessary to interpret the disputed claim before the jury trial.[113] In civil law countries where there is no jury trial, the two-step distinction is not always necessary.

However, the Federal Circuit refused to mandate claim interpretation procedures or timing.[114] Thus, district courts have developed different approaches to resolve claim interpretation, including the *Markman* hearing. A *Markman* hearing is a mini bench trial focusing on claim interpretation, which is conducted before the jury trail.[115] The hearing takes place before a judge; the parties may argue their interpretation of the disputed claim and present evidence and expert witnesses.[116] A judge in the Federal Circuit sat by designation in a patent trial and conducted a model patent trial which included a two-day *Markman* hearing to receive evidence, including testimony.[117] Some courts do not determine claim interpretation until the last day before the jury is instructed.[118] At that time, most evidence and arguments have already been presented to the jury.[119] Some courts resolve claim interpretation according to

---

[109] See Ultra-Tex Surfaces, Inc. Hill Bros. Chemical Co. 204 F3d 1360, 1363 (Feb. Cir. 2000).

[110] Festo Corp. v. Shoketsu Kinzoku Kogyo Kabushiki Co., Ltd., 344 F.3d 1359 (Fed. Cir. 2003).

[111] Markman, 517 U.S. at 370, 116 S.Ct. at 1384, 134 L.Ed.2d 577.

[112] "The jury trail is a matter of right and will be granted if either party demands one in accordance with the requirements of rule 38 of the Federal Rules of Civil Procedure". MOORE, Supra 58, at 814.

[113] Elf Atochem N. North America, Inc. v. Libbey –Owens-Ford Co. 894 F. Supp. 844 (D. Del. 1995).

[114] Amegan Inc. v. Hoechst Marion Roussel, Inc., 126 F. Supp.2d 69, 57 USPQ2d 1449 (D. Mass. 2001).

[115] MOORE, Supra 58, at 257.

[116] Ibid.

[117] See Loral Fairchild Corp. v. Victor Co. of Japan, Ltd, 906 F.Supp. 789, 802 (E.D.N.Y. 1995).

[118] Ibid., at 802.

[119] See e.g., Johns Hopkins Univ. v. CellPro, Inc., 894 F. Supp. 819, 829–27 (D. Del 1995).

the paper record without a hearing.[120] If the meaning of a claim is clear to the district judge by evaluating the documents, including the patent itself and the prosecution history, the judge may conclude that a *Markman* hearing is unnecessary.[121]

The *Cybor* pointed out that having a separate hearing for claim interpretation at an early stage of litigation means deciding the central issue at a potentially premature stage.[122] Claim interpretation is a learning process for judges.[123] The trial judge, after learning new information during the infringement trial, may find that earlier determination on claim interpretation is not accurate.[124] The same situation may arise with appellate judges; for example, in one instance, the Federal Circuit found that a claim interpretation, which had been affirmed in an earlier appeal, was wrong.[125]

1.5 Second Instance: Appellate Review Standard

The U.S. Supreme Court clarified that appellate review standard on patent claim construction in *Teva case*,[126] which ended the debates in decades over de novo standard and clearly erroneous standard. The U.S. Supreme Court declared that the ultimate claim construction remains an issue of law that is to be reviewed by the Federal Circuit under de novo standard; meanwhile, "subsidiary factual matters" in claim constructions must be reviewed on appeal for "clear error" rather than de novo, unless the district court reviews only intrinsic evidence to the patent.[127]

The debates over de novo standard and clearly erroneous standard can be traced back to *Markman*. After *Markman* Federal Circuit judges were divided on the issue of whether claim interpretation is a purely legal question and thus should be reviewed

[120] Elf Atochem N. North America, Inc. v. Libbey –Owens-Ford Co. 894 F. Supp. 850, 37 USPQ2d 1065 (D. Del. 1995).

[121] E.g., Revlon Consumer Products Corp. v. Estee Lauder Companies, Inc., 00 CIV.5960 RMB AJP, 2003 WL 21,751,833 (S.D.N.Y. July 30, 2003), Aspex Eyewear, Inc. v. E'Lite Optik, Inc., No. Civ.A. 398CV2996, 2002 WL 1,751,381 at *11 n. 6 (N.D.Tex. Apr.4, 2002); Rogers v. Desa Int'l, Inc., 166 F.Supp.2d 1202, 1204–05 (E.D.Mich.2001); Electronic Planroom, Inc. v. McGraw-Hill Cos., 135 F.Supp.2d 805, 832 n. 25 (E.D.Mich.2001); Interactive Gift Express, Inc. v. Compuserve Inc., 95 Civ. 6871, 1998 WL 247,485 at *1 n. 3 (S.D.N.Y. May 15, 1998), vacated on other grounds, 256 F.3d 1323 (Fed.Cir.2001); Brosnan v. Rollerblade, Inc., No. C97-0782, C97-3258, 1998 WL 209,155 at *3 (N.D.Cal. Apr.27, 1998); LRC Elec., Inc. v. John Mezzalingua Assocs., Inc., 974 F.Supp. 171, 181–82 (N.D.N.Y.1997).

[122] Cybor Corp., 138 F.3d at 1474.

[123] Ibid.

[124] Ibid.

[125] See CVI/Beta Ventures, Inc. v. Tura LP, 112 F.3d 1146, 1157–58, 1160 n. 7, 42 USPQ2d 1577, 1585, 1587 n. 7 (Fed.Cir.1997) (finding error in a claim construction that had been affirmed in an earlier appeal), cert. denied, 522 U.S. 1109, 118 S.Ct. 1039, 140 L.Ed.2d 105 (1998). Cited in Cybor Corp., 138 F.3d at 1474.

[126] Teva Pharmaceuticals USA, Inc. v. Sandoz, Inc., 135 S.Ct. 831 (2015).

[127] *Ibid.*, at 841.

de novo. The Federal Circuit resolved this issue by reviewing Cybor[128] *en banc* and the majority voted to adopt the de novo standard of review. The majority interpreted *Markman II*[129] as conclusive that claim interpretation is a purely legal issue. However, some judges disagree and believe that the majority in *Cybor* is inconsistent with the policy considerations in *Markman II*.[130] Although the inconsistency in case law was resolved, disagreement among judges continued, until Teva.

1.5.1 A Split Among Federal Circuit Judges After Markman II

The Supreme Court decision in *Markman* did not provide a clear answer to the question of whether claim interpretation is a purely legal question and whether it should be reviewed de novo. Federal Circuit judges understood the ruling of *Markman II* in different ways. In *Markman I*, the Federal Circuit held that claims should be interpreted by judges and that the basis of claim construction is purely a matter of law.[131] Thus, a district court's claim interpretation shall be reviewed de novo on appeal.[132] The Supreme Court affirmed the Federal Circuit's conclusion that claims shall be interpreted by judges.[133] But the Federal Circuit judges cannot reach a consensus on the issue of whether the Supreme Court also agreed with its reasoning: that claim interpretation is a matter of law. As cited in *Cybor* (1998), after the Supreme Court's *Markman II* decision, panels of Federal Circuit judges used the de novo review standard.[134] Meanwhile, other panels of Federal Circuit judges considered some claim interpretation findings to be factual in nature and thus applied the clearly erroneous standard.[135] Those panels, who applied the clearly erroneous standard, also believed that their decisions are consistent with *Markman II*.

---

[128] Cybor Corp., 138 F.3d at 1456.

[129] Markman, at 517 U.S. at 370, 116 S.Ct. at 1384, 134 L.Ed.2d 577.

[130] Cybor Corp, 138 F.3d at 1448 (dissent).

[131] Markman v. Westview Instruments, Inc., 52 F.3d 967, 979, 34 USPQ2d 1321, 1329 (Fed.Cir.1995) (en banc) (Markman I).

[132] Markman, 52 F.3d at 981.

[133] Markman, 517 U.S. at 370, 116 S.Ct. at 1384, 134 L.Ed.2d at 577.

[134] See Serrano v. Telular Corp., 111 F.3d 1578, 42 USPQ2d 1538 (Fed.Cir.1997); Alpex Computer Corp. v. Nintendo Co., 102 F.3d 1214, 40 USPQ2d 1667 (Fed.Cir.1996); Insituform Techs., Inc. v. Cat Contracting, Inc., 99 F.3d 1098, 40 USPQ2d 1602 (Fed.Cir.1996); General Am. Transp. v. Cryo-Trans, Inc., 93 F.3d 766, 39 USPQ2d 1801 (Fed.Cir.1996).

[135] Eastman Kodak Co. v. Goodyear Tire & Rubber Co., 114 F.3d 1547, 1555–56, 42 USPQ2d 1737, 1742 (Fed.Cir.1997); Serrano v. Telular Corp., 111 F.3d 1578, 42 USPQ2d 1538 (Fed.Cir.1997), (Mayer, J., concurring); Wiener v. NEC Elecs. Inc., 102 F.3d 534, 539, 41 USPQ2d 1023, 1026 (Fed.Cir.1996); Metaullics Sys. Co. v. Cooper, 100 F.3d 938, 939, 40 USPQ2d 1798, 1799 (Fed.Cir.1996).

1.5.2 Cybor*: Uniform Federal Circuit Case Law*

Two years after the Supreme Court issued its decision in *Markman*, the Federal Circuit judges ordered that *Cybor* be decided *en banc* to resolve the conflicting precedent. The Federal Circuit judges concluded that claim interpretation is subject to the de novo review standard because it is a purely legal issue.[136] This is consistent with what the Federal Circuit found in *Markman I*. In *Cybor*, the majority of Federal Circuit judges agreed that *Markman I* is valid and consistent with *Markman II*. By disavowing any contrary language in previous Federal Circuit opinions, *Cybor* eradicated any inconsistencies in the review standard in the Federal Circuit.[137]

Unlike most U. S. cases where the development of the legal doctrine is closely related to the factual pattern of the individual cases, the lawmaking in *Cybor en banc* decision is not factually based. The disputed U.S. Patent No. 5,167,837 (the '837 patent) in *Cybor* discloses a device and method for accurately dispensing industrial liquids. The district court found that Cybor infringes all claims of the '837 patent.[138] On *en banc*, the judges unanimously agreed that the standard of review, regardless of whether the de novo or clearly erroneous standard is applied, does not affect whether the findings of the trial court are affirmed in their entirety.[139] Thus, this is purely a discussion of the law without the factual context of the disputed case. The analysis of the majority opinions relied heavily on the interpretation of Supreme Court's decision in *Markman II* in order to reach this conclusion.[140]

Federal Circuit acknowledged that the Supreme Court framed its reasoning differently from the Federal Circuit.[141] However, the majority still believed that the Supreme Court agreed that claim interpretation is a legal issue[142] since the Court stated that "treating interpretive issues as purely legal will promote (though not guarantee) intrajurisdictional certainty".[143] Also, the sentence "treating interpretive issues as purely legal will promote (though not guarantee) intrajurisdictional certainty [...] under the authority of the single appeals court"[144] is quoted by the Federal Circuit as a demonstration of endorsement of the Federal Circuit's role of providing national uniformity.

The *Cybor* majority disagreed with some previous Federal Circuit opinions that the Supreme Court had asserted that claim interpretation is based on factual underpinning.[145] The Supreme Court previously stated that "construing a term of art after

---

[136] Cybor, 138 F.3d at 1451 (Fed. Cir. 1998).

[137] Ibid., at 1456.

[138] Ibid., at1454.

[139] Ibid., at 1473.

[140] Ibid., at 1451–1456.

[141] Ibid., at 1455.

[142] Ibid., at 1455.

[143] Markman, 517 U.S. at 390, 116 S. Ct. at 1396, 134 L. Ed. 2d 577.

[144] Cybor, 138 F.3d at 1455.

[145] Ibid.

receipt of evidence" is a "mongrel practice",[146] and that the issue may "fall [...] somewhere between a pristine legal standard and a simple historical fact",[147] However, the *Cybor* majority does not think that these words suggest that there are any questions of fact in claim interpretation; instead, this phrase is merely a recognition that the question of "fact or law" in claim interpretation is not simple or clear cut. By quoting the Supreme Court's constitutional analysis, the issue "falls somewhere between a pristine legal standard and a simple historical fact, the fact/law distinction at times has turned on a determination that, as a matter of sound administration of justice, one judicial actor is better positioned than another to decide the issue in question"[148] the majority opinion in *Cybor* concluded that the Supreme Court decided whether claim interpretation is a question of fact or law, instead of classifying it as having components of both fact and law.[149]

1.5.3 Disagreements Continued After Cybor

Since *Cybor* was not appealed to the Supreme Court, it is not clear if the Supreme Court would agree with *Cybor's* interpretation of *Markman II*. The dissenting opinion suggested that the majority's interpretation of *Markman II* is incorrect.

The dissenting opinion quoted *Markman II*, which has a different interpretation from the majority opinion. According to the opinion, "mongrel practice" means that the Supreme Court understood claim interpretation as a mixed question of law and fact, rather than a purely legal question.[150] The decision, which reserved claim interpretation for judges, is merely a policy and functional choice and not because claim interpretation is a purely legal issue.[151]

Also, the dissenting opinion believed that the *Cybor* majority opinion is inconsistent with the policy considerations in *Markman I* & II.[152] *Markman II* emphasized the value of uniformity in claim interpretation, explaining that this is an important reason to give the power to interpret claims to judges.[153] *Markman I* promised to provide more certainty in claim interpretation. However, the de novo standard resulted in a high reversal rate, which undermines the policy to promote certainty established in *Markman II*.[154]

146 Markman, 517 U.S. at 378, 116 S. Ct. at 1390, 134 L. Ed. 2d 577.

147 Ibid.

148 Ibid.

149 Cybor, 138 F.3d at 1455.

150 Cybor, 138 F.3d at 1473.

151 Ibid., at 1477–78.

152 Ibid., at 1477.

153 Ibid.

154 Ibid.

In *Amgen* (2006), seven out of twelve judges expressed their willingness to revisit *Cybor*.[155] Four Federal Circuit judges expressed a desire to overturn *Cybor*. Three other Federal Circuit judges noted that they would also reconsider *Cybor* but did not believe that *Amgen* was the appropriate case in which to do it.[156] In their opinion, the appropriate case would be "the typical case in which the language of the claims, the written description, and the prosecution history on their face did not resolve the question of claim interpretation, and the district court found it necessary to resolve conflicting expert evidence to interpret particular claim terms in the field of art".[157]

The "appropriate case" to resolve the standard of review issue as described by the three judges in *Amgen* recalls what the Supreme Court stated in *Markman I*. The Supreme Court held that it is a rare case that two conflicting expert testimonies are equally consistent with a patent's internal logic and cannot be resolved by comparing the expert testimonies with the intrinsic evidence.[158] In other words, it rarely happens that a court needs to choose between external evidence merely by making a credibility determination.[159]

The rare case described by the Supreme Court is just the "appropriate case" referred to by the three judges in *Amgen*. If the Federal Circuit has not found such an appropriate case, that means that the Supreme Court is correct: this kind of case is indeed rare.

However, just because there is no case requiring a creditability determination does not mean that challenging the de novo standard is not necessary. Besides making a creditability determination, aren't there other issues in claim interpretation that could be identified as factual, or at least mixed? The Supreme Court in *Markman II* did not conclude that claim interpretation itself is a purely legal issue.[160]

1.5.4 The Supreme Court Teva Decision

In order to resolve the review standard issue, Supreme Court ruled *Teva* case in 2015. *Teva* is a case on patent validity. However, the appellate review standard established by *Teva* applies to all claim interpretation cases, including those on validity and infringement issues. As a consequence of this landmark case, the parties shall pay more attention to extrinsic evidence they use on the first instance of patent litigation, since reversing a trial court's holding on extrinsic evidence became more difficult after *Teva*.

---

155 Amgen Inc. v. Hoechst Marion Roussel, Inc., 469 F.3d 1039 (Fed. Cir. 2006) (en banc).

156 Ibid.

157 Amgen, 469 F.3d at 1045.

158 Markman, 517 U.S. at 376, 116 S. Ct. at 1389, 134 L. Ed. 2d 577.

159 Ibid.

160 Ibid.

In *Teva*, the parties litigated the meaning of a claim term "molecular weight".[161] There are three different ways to calculate molecular weight, as argued by Sandoz.[162] In Sandoz's view, since Teva's patent claim does not say which method of calculation should be used, the claim's phrase "molecular weight" is indefinite, and the claim fails to satisfy the critical patent law requirement.[163] The trial court, after taking evidence from expert testimony as extrinsic evidence, concluded that the patent claim was sufficiently definite.[164] The trial court found that in context a skilled artisan would understand that the term "molecular weight" referred to molecular weight as calculated by one of the methods "peak average molecular weight".[165]

The case was reversed on appeal. On appeal, the Federal Circuit found that the term "molecular weight" was indefinite and consequently held the patent invalid.[166] In reaching this conclusion, the Federal Circuit reviewed de novo all aspects of the trial court's claim construction, including the trial court's determination of subsidiary facts.[167]

Teva filed a petition for certiorari. The Supreme Court granted that petition to clarify the standard of review on claim interpretation. While confirming that claim interpretation is not for a jury but exclusively for the court, the Supreme Court pointed out that the *Markman* case did acknowledge that the interpretation of a claim term has "evidentiary underpinnings".[168] Accordingly, when the Court held in *Markman* that the ultimate question of claim construction is for the judge and not the jury, the Court did not create an exception from the ordinary rule governing appellate review of factual matters.[169] In some cases, the trial court will need to look beyond the patent's intrinsic evidence and to consult extrinsic evidence in order to understand for example, the background science or the meaning of a term in the relevant art during the relevant time period. In cases where those subsidiary facts are in dispute, courts will need to make subsidiary factual findings about that extrinsic evidence. These are the "evidentiary underpinnings" of claim interpretation discussed in *Markman*. And this subsidiary fact-finding must be reviewed for clear error on appeal, according to Rule 52(a).[170] Thus, the Supreme Court held that the ultimate claim construction remains an issue of law that is to be reviewed by the Federal Circuit without deference, subordinate issues of fact decided by a district court are entitled to deference according to Rule 56(a)(6) of the Federal Rules of Civil Procedure and are not to be overturned unless clearly erroneous.[171] When the

---

[161] Teva Pharms. USA, Inc. v. Sandoz, Inc., 135 S. Ct. 831, 835 (2015).

[162] Ibid., at 836.

[163] Ibid.

[164] Teva Pharms. USA, Inc. v. Sandoz Inc., 810 F. Supp. 2d 578, 595 (S.D.N.Y. 2011).

[165] Ibid., at 596.

[166] Teva Pharms. USA, Inc. v. Sandoz, Inc., 723 F.3d 1363, 1369 (Fed. Cir. 2013).

[167] Ibid., at 1373.

[168] Teva, 135 S. Ct., at 835.

[169] Ibid., at 838.

[170] Fed. R. Civ. P. 52.

[171] Teva, 135 S. Ct., at 834.

trial court reviews only evidence intrinsic to the patent, the judge's determination is solely a determination of law, and the court of appeals will review that construction de novo.[172]

1.6 Procedures for Determining the Doctrine of Equivalents

In the United States, the procedure used to determine the expanded patent scope under the doctrine of equivalents is different from the literal interpretation of the claims.

Unlike the literal interpretation of patent scope, expanding the doctrine of equivalents is an issue of fact to be submitted to a jury in a jury trial with proper instructions and to be decided by a judge in a bench trial.[173] The doctrine of equivalents is a question of fact.[174] The Federal Circuit emphasized in Warner Jenkinson *en banc* that the doctrine of equivalents is just like other issues of fact.[175] If it is determined by a judge at the trial level, the appellate review standard is clearly erroneous.[176] If the issue is determined by a jury verdict at the trial level, the appellate review standard is lack of substantial evidence.[177] The evidence necessary to find an infringement under the doctrine of equivalents, according to Federal Circuit, can be made in "any form", including testimony of experts or others versed in the technology, documents and disclosures of the prior art.[178]

---

172 Ibid.

173 Hilton Davis Chem. Co. v. Warner-Jenkinson Co., Inc., 62 F.3d 1512 (Fed. Cir. 1995) supplemented, 64 F.3d 675 (Fed. Cir. 1995) and rev'd, 520 U.S. 17 (1997) and adhered to, 114 F.3d 1161 (Fed. Cir. 1997).

174 Ibid.

175 Ibid.

176 Ibid.

177 Ibid.

178 Ibid.

Chapter 2
Chinese Claim Interpretation: Procedure Law

2.1 Chinese Court System in General

2.1.1 Trial by Judges

In contrast to the *Markman* hearing in the United States, usually there is no separate procedure for claim interpretation in China. Since China follows a civil law system, China does not have jury trials and does not need to have a separate hearing for claim interpretation. The Supreme People's Court (SPC) suggested that claim interpretation should be conducted first and should then be compared to the scope to the properly interpreted claim to the accused device later, which is consistent with the practice in the United States.[1] But in practice, most judges do not separate the steps of claim interpretation and infringement determination, which is similar to the practice in Japan and Germany.[2] In other words, a judge usually has already reviewed all the information about the accused device before starting claim interpretation. It is very common that a judicial opinion begins by comparing the difference between the patented invention and the accused device and then discusses the disputed claim terms in the context of the comparison.

[1] Supreme Court case Zuigao Renmin Fayuan Minshi Shenpanting Guanyu Wangchuan yu Hefei Jichu Maoyi Youxian Zeren Gongsi deng Zhuanli Qinquan Jiufen An de Han (最高人民法院民事审判第三庭关于王川与合肥继初贸易有限责任公司等专利侵权纠纷案的函) [Wangchuan v. Hefei Jichu Trade LL.C], ipr. China court (Sup. People's Ct. Feb. 2, 2001). (When comparing the patented technology and accused infringing product, it should firstly determine the scope of patent, and after that, proceed to compare the differences and similarities between the disputed technical solutions, by forensic center, etc.) (在将神电公司技术与王川专利进行相同或者等同判定时，首先要确定专利的保护范围，然后才是通过技术鉴定等方式来比较争议技术方案的异同).

[2] See comparative study on claim interpretation in Toshiko Takenaka, Interpreting Patent Claims: The United States, Germany and Japan, 17 IIC Studies (1995).

© Intellectual Property Publishing House 2025

Z. Peng, *Comparative Study on Patent Claim Interpretation: The United States and China*, https://doi.org/10.1007/978-981-96-0836-2_2

2.1.2 Lawyers

Since 2017, taking a bar exam in China requires a law degree, which could be Bachelor of law, Master of law, or Juris Master. The difference between Master of Law or Juris Master is that the former requires that the bachelor degree has to be Bachelor of Law and the later accepts applicants with a bachelor degree in any major. Thus, some lawyers majored in science or engineering in their undergraduate studies and studied law in graduate education. Also, before 2017, a bachelor degree in any major was sufficient to take a bar exam. This also gives people with scientific background opportunities to become lawyers.

Thus, Chinese attorneys who practice patent law include people with different educational backgrounds: those who have both legal education and scientific education, those who only have legal education and those who only have a scientific education.

2.1.3 Technical Experts in Claim Interpretation

Technical experts have played a significant role in defining the scope of patents in China. Even though many courts intend to appoint more judges with technical backgrounds in IP Tribunals, judges' technical expertise is still generally insufficient for them to understand the various technologies involved in patent cases.[3] With a limited number of judges working on patent cases, it is difficult to have judges educated in all fields of technology.

The United States has only two types of experts in patent cases: (1) court-appointed experts and (2) party-appointed experts. In China, there are four kinds of technical experts who can help judges: jurors, consultants, forensic experts and expert witnesses. Jurors and consultants are "internal" experts, meaning that they are hired by the court and work closely with judges. They are supposed to be neutral. Forensic experts and expert witnesses are "external" experts, who are usually chosen by the litigating parties. Their opinions are treated as evidence and accepted upon examination. Forensic experts are chosen by consensus of the parties and they are supposed to be neutral. Each party can provide its own expert witnesses, and expert witnesses may testify against one another.

In the United States, party-appointed expert witnesses are the most frequently used technical experts, while court-appointed experts or neutral experts are less frequently used. In China, court-appointed or neutral experts are more frequently

[3] See the speech note of the Vice President of Supreme People's Court of China jianming Cao (曹建明), Zai Quanguo Fayuan Zhishi Chanquan Shenpan Gongzuo Huiyi Shang de Jianghua (在全国法院知识产权审判工作会议上的讲话) [The Speech at National Intellectual Property Trial Conference], (National Intellectual Property Office ed., Intellectual Property Press) [知识产权年鉴, 国家知识产权局编] (2006).

used. Currently, the forensic centers[4] are the most frequently used option. Courts in Beijing use jurors more frequently[5] while those in Shanghai mainly rely on consultants.

Jurors who participate in patent trials are usually scientists, engineers and even patent examiners. They are paid a reasonable compensation for transportation and loss of working time from the court budget.[6] According to feedback received from judges, assistance from jurors is very effective in resolving technical difficulties.[7]

According to the Chinese Civil Procedure Law, jurors may be ordinary people selected by the courts to participate in the collegial panel. In the first instance, the court has the option of including both judges and jurors or exclusively judges in the collegial panel.[8] The juror will perform the same function as judges, deciding both issues of fact and law.[9] Using jurors in patent trials generally follows the rules of

---

4 Beijing High People's Court Intellectual Property Trial Tribunal, Practice of Beijing Courts on Intellectual Property Law Trial, in Reference for Intellectual Property Trial (知识产权办案参考) Intellectual Property Law Center of China Social Academy ed. (中国社会科学院知识产权中心，北京市高级人民法院知识产权庭主编) (2001). The Third Civil Divison of Beijing High People's Court (北京市高级法院民三庭), Suggestions and Thoughts on Intellectual Property Judicial Protection (关于知识产权司法保护机制中有关主要问题及其意见和建议), in China Intellectual Property Judicial Protection Website (中国知识产权司法保护网. (2005) http://www.chinaiprlaw.cn/file/200510105865.html.,). See also The Intermediate People's Court Of Jining (济宁市中级人民法院), A Research on Intellectual Property Judicial Enforcement in Shandong Province: from A Civil Litigation Perspective, 22 Shandong Trial 44 (2006) (关于山东省知识产权司法保护的调研——以知识产权民事审判为视角, 22 山东审判 44, (2006)). See also Jiancheng Yang, Patent Forensic Report in Intellectual Property Trial, 2 Reference for Intellectual Trial 34, (2001) (杨建成, 知识产权审判中专利鉴定问题研究, 2 知识产权办案参考 34, (2001)).

5 Beijing High People's Court, Supra Note 4.

6 Guanyu Wanshan Renmin Peishenyuan Zhidu de Jueding (关于完善人民陪审员制度的决定) [the decision of improving institution of juror] [Standing Comm. Nat'l People's Cong., May 1st, 2005], art 18.

7 Ming Chang (常鸣), Beijing Yizhongyuan Yinru Zhuanjia Peishenyuan Duiwu Chengxiao Xianzhu (北京一中院引入专家陪审员队伍成效显著) [Experts jurors work well in Beijing First Intermediate People's Court] (2010), at http://www.chinacourt.org/html/article/201002/22/396132.shtml. See also The Third Civil Division of Beijing High People's Court, Suggestions and Thoughts on Intellectual Property Judicial Protection, China Intellectual Property Judicial Protection Website. (2005) at http://www.chinaiprlaw.cn/file/200510105865.html. (北京市高级人民法院民三庭, 关于知识产权司法保护机制中有关主要问题及其意见和建议，中国知识产权司法保护网). See also The Intermediate People's Court of Jining, A Research on Intellectual Property Judicial Enforcement in Shandong Province: from A Civil Litigation Perspective, 22 Shandong Trial 44 (2006) (济宁市中级人民法院，关于山东省知识产权司法保护的调研——以知识产权民事审判为视角, 22 山东审判 44, (2006)). See also Jiancheng Yang (杨建成), Patent Forensic Report in Intellectual Property Trial, 2 Reference for Intellectual Trial 34 (2001) (知识产权审判中专利鉴定问题研究, 2 知识产权办案参考 34, (2001)).

8 Guanyu Renmin Peishenyuan Canjia Shenpan Huodong Ruogan Wenti de Guiding (关于人民陪审员参加审判活动若干问题的规定) [Several rules about the jurors' participate in trial] (Sup. People's Ct., Nov. 23, 2009) Zhonghua Renmin Gongheguo Falü Quanshu (中华人民共和国法律全书) (P.R.C.), art 2.

9 Guanyu Wanshan Renmin Peishenyuan Zhidu de Jueding (关于完善人民陪审员制度的决定) [the decision of improving institution of juror] [Standing Comm. Nat'l People's Cong., May 1st, 2005], art 1. Guanyu Renmin Peishenyuan Canjia Shenpan Huodong Ruogan Wenti de Guiding

civil procedure, but there are some exceptions concerning the selection procedure for using technical experts as jurors.

In the past, there were no formal requirements regarding juror selection, and courts had the flexibility to invite any technical expert to participate in patent cases. In 2004, the law was changed; now jurors must be selected randomly from a pool of jurors who are mainly ordinary people, meaning that the court loses the chance to choose experts as jurors.[10] In 2009, the new judicial interpretation from the SPC made an exception, namely that if the case requires a juror with specialized knowledge, the courts can select jurors from a pool with that specialized knowledge.[11] Thus, after a short interruption, the technical juror was restored.[12]

Requesting a report from a Forensic Center is another frequently used method for judges to obtain technical assistance.[13] Compared to the jurors, who only receive limited compensation to participate in patent cases, the Forensic Center is a commercial provider of technical assistance. The parties request the Forensic Center's assistance by mutual agreement, and the cost is shared by the parties.[14] In rare cases, where neither of the parties requests a forensic report but the judge believes that it is necessary to obtain such a report to understand the facts, the judge can make the request and the cost is covered by the court. The Forensic Center hires scientists and engineers from research institutes or industry, many of them working as forensic experts as part-time jobs.[15]

Because the Forensic Center is a commercial organization providing a broad choice of experts, it has been a popular option.[16] However, it is also under fierce

(关于人民陪审员参加审判活动若干问题的规定) [Several rules about the jurors' participate in trial] (Sup. People's Ct., Nov. 23, 2009) Zhonghua Renmin Gongheguo Falü Quanshu (中华人民共和国法律全书) (P.R.C.), art 7–10.

[10] Guanyu Wanshan Renmin Peishenyuan Zhidu de Jueding (关于完善人民陪审员制度的决定) [the decision of improving institution of juror] [Standing Comm. Nat'l People's Cong., May 1st, 2005], art 14.

[11] Ibid., at 5.

[12] Ming Chang (常鸣), Beijing Yizhongyuan Yinru Zhuanjia Peishenyuan Duiwu Chengxiao Xianzhu (北京一中院引入专家陪审员队伍成效显著) [Experts jurors work well in Beijing First Intermediate People's Court] (2010), at http://www.chinacourt.org/html/article/201002/22/396132.shtml.

[13] E.g. Supreme Court case Zuigao Renmin Fayuan Minshi Shenpanting Guanyu Wangchuan yu Hefei Jichu Maoyi Youxian Zeren Gongsi deng Zhuanli Qinquan Jiufen An de Han (最高人民法院民事审判第三庭关于王川与合肥继初贸易有限责任公司等专利侵权纠纷案的函) [Wangchuan v. Hefei Jichu Trade LL.C], ipr. China court (Sup. People's Ct. Feb. 2, 2001). See example of forensic report in claim interpretation Ningbo Shi Dongfang Jixin Zongchang v. Jiangyin Jinling Wujin Zhipin Youxian Gongsi (宁波市东方机芯总厂与江阴金铃五金制品有限公司) [Ningbo Dongfang Jixin Zongchang v. Jiangyin Jinling Wujin Zhipin Youxian LL.C],ipr. China court [Sup. People's Ct. Mar. 6, 2002.

[14] E.g., Zhishichanquan Susong Anjian Jianding Guize (知识产权诉讼案件技术鉴定规则) [Forensic rule of intellectual property cases] (Jiangsu High People's Ct., 2001), art 3, 7, 29.

[15] Jiancheng Yang (杨建成), Zhishi Chanquan Shenpan Zhong Zhuanli Jianding Wenti Yanjiu (知识产权审判中专利鉴定问题研究) [Patent Forensic Report in Intellectual Property Trial], 2 Zhishi chanquan banan cankao (知识产权办案参考) 34 (2001).

[16] Ibid.

criticism regarding its credibility and other negative considerations.[17] There is no supervision or auditing of the forensic centers and there are no clear guidelines to evaluate the qualifications of forensic reports.[18] Moreover, the forensic experts rarely attend the hearings; thus, there is limited opportunity to challenge their credibility through cross examination.[19] There is a strong concern that the forensic report, which does not have stronger legal credibility than other evidence, will be accepted by judges without careful examination and thus lead to injustice.[20] In addition, many forensic reports reach conclusions beyond the factual issues or conclusions pertaining to legal issues such as claim interpretation and infringement.[21] This raises concern that judicial power has been passed to the unsupervised Forensic Center.[22]

Some courts also hire technical experts as consultants.[23] There is no formal procedure for the selection, and the form of communication between judges and consultants is informal. This approach is preferred by the courts in Shanghai.[24] The consultants' opinions are not available to the public and there is no procedure to prevent a conflict of interest from arising. Thus, the use of consultants has fallen under a great deal of suspicion.[25]

---

[17] The Intermediate People's Court of Jining, A Research on Intellectual Property Judicial Enforcement in Shandong Province: from A Civil Litigation Perspective, 22 Shandong Trial 44 (2006) (济宁市中级人民法院，关于山东省知识产权司法保护的调研——以知识产权民事审判为视角，22山东审判44 (2006)) See also Jiancheng Yang, Zhishi Chanquan Shenpan Zhong Zhuanli Jianding Wenti Yanjiu (知识产权审判中专利鉴定问题研究) [Patent Forensic Report in Intellectual Property Trial], 2Zhishi chanquan banan cankao (知识产权办案参考) 34 (2001).

[18] Ibid.

[19] Ibid.

[20] Ibid.

[21] See an article co-authored by two judges Hailong Sun (孙海龙) & Jianjun Yao (姚建军), Qinquan Wenti Wanquan Bu Yinggai Jianding (侵权问题完全不应该鉴定) [Forensic Certificate should absolutely not be used in Infringement Determination], 02 China Patent and Trademark (中国专利与商标) 57 (2010).

[22] Ibid. See also The Intermediate People's Court of Jining, A Research on Intellectual Property Judicial Enforcement in Shandong Province: from A Civil Litigation Perspective, 22 Shandong Trial 44 (2006) (济宁市中级人民法院，关于山东省知识产权司法保护的调研——以知识产权民事审判为视角，22山东审判 44 (2006)). See also Jiancheng Yang, Patent Forensic Report in Intellectual Property Trial, 2 Reference for Intellectual Trial 34, (2001) (杨建成, 知识产权审判中专利鉴定问题研究, 2 知识产权办案参考 34 (2001)).

[23] Guanyu Kaizhan Zhuanli Shenpan Gongzuo de Jige Wenti de Tongzhi (关于开展专利审判工作的几个问题的通知) [Announcement on several issues in patent trial work] (Sup. People's Ct., Feb. 16, 1985) Zhonghua Renmin Gongheguo Falü Quanshu (中华人民共和国法律全书) (P.R.C.).

[24] Shanghai Shi Gaoyuan Jianli Zhishi Chanquan ZhuanJia Ku (上海市高院建立知识产权专家库) [Shanghai High People's Court established IP expert group], Wenhui bao (文汇报), Dec. 2, 2009.

[25] The Intermediate People's Court of Jining, A Research on Intellectual Property Judicial Enforcement in Shandong Province: from A Civil Litigation Perspective, 22 Shandong Trial 44 (2006) (济宁市中级人民法院，关于山东省知识产权司法保护的调研——以知识产权民事审判为视角，22 山东审判44 (2006)). See also Jiancheng Yang, Patent Forensic Report in Intellectual Property Trial, 2 Reference for Intellectual Trial 34, (2001) (杨建成, 知识产权审判中专利鉴定问题研究, 2 知识产权办案参考 34 (2001)).

Expert witnesses are also allowed under the Chinese Civil Procedure Law. However, in practice, this approach is less frequently used than recourse to the forensic centers.[26] One reason is that the witnesses usually will not agree to attend the hearing. This is not a problem in patent cases but is a common problem in all other civil litigation. Another reason is that without help from internal experts whose position is neutral, judges may not be able to decide between conflicting expert testimonies.[27]

Since 2008, the SPC strongly discouraged using the forensic center and encouraged the use of expert witnesses. The SPC instructed the lower courts to only request forensic reports when the technical issues could not be otherwise understood. The SPC did not provide any specific guidelines for the use of expert witnesses.[28] Without remedying the underlying issues of relying upon expert witnesses in the overall litigation system, it is almost impossible to expect that expert witnesses will be used frequently in patent litigation merely because of the SPC's instruction. Also, implementation of the SPC's instruction on reducing the use of the forensic centers depends on whether judges can obtain sufficient assistance from internal experts. When judges cannot understand the technical facts and there are no internal experts, such as jurors or consultants, to help the forensic report remains an option.

2.2 Evidence

The 2009 Judicial Interpretation by SPC held that evidence can be used as a reference in claim interpretation. Evidence such as descriptions and attached drawings, prosecution history and other related claims (intrinsic evidence) should be considered first.[29] If the meaning of the claim terms is still not clear, the literature in public domain (e.g., reference books, textbooks) and the common knowledge of "a person having ordinary skills in the art of invention" (PHOSITA) in the art can be used as

[26] Xintian Yin, who is one of the legislators drafting patent statutes, pointed out, according to cases published Beijing courts, court had used forensic institute too much and used expert witness too little. 2000 (尹新天, 专家点评, 北京知识产权审判案例研究 (北京市高级人民法院民三庭 ed. 2000). Xintian Yin, "Expert Commentary", in Beijing Intellectual Property Cases Study (Beijing High People's Court, Tribunal No.3 ed., 2000).

[27] The Intermediate People's Court of Jining, A Research on Intellectual Property Judicial Enforcement in Shandong Province: from A Civil Litigation Perspective, 22 Shandong Trial 44 (2006) (济宁市中级人民法院, 关于山东省知识产权司法保护的调研——以知识产权民事审判为视角, 22 山东审判 44 (2006)). See also Jiancheng Yang, Patent Forensic Report in Intellectual Property Trial, 2 Reference for Intellectual Trial 34, (2001) (杨建成, 知识产权审判中专利鉴定问题研究, 2 知识产权办案参考 34 (2001)).

[28] Cao, supra note 3.

[29] Guanyu Shenli Qinfan Zhuanliquan Jiufen Anjian Yingyong Falü Ruogan Wenti de Jieshi (关于审理侵犯专利权纠纷案件应用法律若干问题的解释) [Explanations of Issues regarding to Application of Law on Patent Infringement Trial] (Promulgated by Sup. People's Ct., Dec. 29, 2009, effective Jan.1, 2010), (Chinalawinfo) (China).

secondary evidence (extrinsic evidence).[30] If the description can clarify the meaning, the judges do not have to consult another reference.[31]

Two articles of the Judicial Interpretation (2009) referred to PHOSITA. In Article 2 of Judicial Interpretation (2009), it says that a claim should be interpreted in light of PHOSITA's understanding of the written description.[32] Thus, the general methodology is that the judges should interpret the patent from a PHOSITA perspective. In Article 3, of Judicial Interpretation (2009), the concept of PHOSITA was used in a different way.[33]Article 3 of the Judicial Interpretation (2009) defines the hierarchy of the evidence. When the description and prosecution history are not sufficient to resolve the claim interpretation dispute, secondary evidence like treatises, dictionaries and "the understanding of PHOSITA"[34] can be consulted. In this situation, PHOSITA is referred to as one kind of external evidence. There is actually no such evidence that can inherently determine the PHOSITA understanding. The treatises, dictionaries and the experts' publications and testimonies may provide different definitions of a term. The PHOSITA understanding must be determined by a judge needs by consulting all of the available evidence. Therefore, the "PHOSITA understanding" in Article 3 should be understood as "any other evidence which can prove the understanding of PHOTISTA".

2.3 Jurisdiction

Courts are the main forum to litigate patent infringement cases in China.[35] There are no specialized patent courts like the U.S. Federal Circuit in China. Unlike the United States, where all patent infringement cases are appealed to one court, none of the Chinese appellate courts has exclusive jurisdiction over patent case. Although there are a couple of intellectual property courts in cities like Beijing and Shanghai, there is no patent court. According to the Chinese Civil Procedure Law, a significant number of patent infringement cases will not have the opportunity to be appealed to the

[30] Ibid.

[31] Zuigao Renmin Fayuan Zhishi Chanquanting Fuzeren Jiu ⟨Guanyu Shenli Qinfan Zhuanliquan Jiufen Anjian Yingyong Falü Ruogan Wenti de Jieshi⟩ Da Jizhe Wen (最高人民法院知识产权庭负责人就《关于审理侵犯专利权纠纷案件应用法律若干问题的解释》答记者问) [Public Interview with the Chief of the Intellectual Property Tribunal of Sup. People's Ct. Explanations of Issues regarding to Application of Law on Patent Infringement Trial, with Respect to ⟨Explanations of Issues regarding to Application of Law on Patent Infringement Trial⟩], China court (Sep.18, 2010, 19: 40 pm); http://rmfyb.chinacourt.org/public/detail.php?id=134762.

[32] Guanyu Shenli Qinfan Zhuanliquan Jiufen Anjian Yingyong Falü Ruogan Wenti de Jieshi (关于审理侵犯专利权纠纷案件应用法律若干问题的解释) [Explanations of Issues regarding to Application of Law on Patent Infringement Trial] (Promulgated by Sup. People's Ct., Dec. 29, 2009, effective Jan.1, 2010), (Chinalawinfo) (China).

[33] Ibid.

[34] Ibid.

[35] Fernado, supra note 18, at 26.

Chinese Supreme Court. Thus, the provincial level appellate courts—High People's Courts—have the final authority for many patent infringement cases. This causes wide variations in the practice of claim interpretation among the many provinces.

Although China does not have a specialized patent court, the court system still provides specialization in patent law through another mechanism. Patent cases are handled by a specialized division of the courts of general jurisdiction. The specific units that handle patent cases are the Intellectual Property Tribunals or Collegial Panels.[36] Most cases are heard by an Intermediate People's Court and can be appealed to a High People's Court. On both factual and legal issues, the standard of appellate review is similar to de novo. Under Chinese Civil Procedure Law, judges resolve both factual and legal issues at the trial level.[37] On appeal, the higher courts review both factual and legal issues. The standard of review is whether the facts are clear, whether application of the law is correct and whether there has been an abuse of procedure that may have impacted the judgment.[38]

China's judicial system contains courts of general jurisdiction as well as courts of specific jurisdiction.[39] Patent trials are conducted by a court of general jurisdiction. The general jurisdiction framework is constructed as a system of "four tiers and two instances".[40] The "two instances" rule specifies that parties involved in civil litigation, including patent infringement cases, are allowed one trial and only one appeal.[41] The four tiers are: (1) the Supreme People's Court (SPC); (2) the High People's Courts (HPC); (3) the Intermediate People's Courts (IPC); and (4) the Primary People's Courts (PPC).[42] The SPC is the highest court in the nation and supervises all courts, including the courts of special jurisdictions.[43] Below this court are the HPCs,[44] of

---

[36] Jiang Zhipei (蒋志培), Zuigao Renmin Fayuan Zhishi Chanquan Ting de Sheli he Fazhan (最高人民法院知识产权庭的设立和发展) [The Establishment and The Development of The Intellectual Property Tribunal of Supreme People's Court], in Zhishi Chanquan yu Gaige Kaifang Sanshi Nian (知识产权与改革开放三十年), (Zhishi Chanquan yu Gaige Kaifang Sanshi nian ed. 2008).

[37] Minshi Susong Fa (民事诉讼法) [Civil Procedure Law Court], (promulgated by the Standing Comm. Nat'l People's Cong., Apr. 7, 1991, effective Apr. 7, 1991, June 27 Amended 2017) 1991 STANDING COMM. NAT'L PEOPLE'S CONG. GAZ. (China).

[38] Ibid.

[39] There are courts with specific jurisdictions, which handle maritime, military, and railway cases. See CHINA INTERNET INFORMATION CENTER, China's Judiciary, Zhong guo wang (中国网), at http://www.china.org.cn/english/Judiciary/31280.htm.

[40] See Fayuan Zuzhi Fa (法院组织法) [Court Organization Law], 2006, arts. 2, 12 (P.R.C.). See also ROBERT SLATE, Judicial Copyright Enforcement in China: Shaping World Opinion on TRIPS Compliance 31 North Carolina Journal of International Law and Commercial Regulation. 665 (2006).

[41] See Fayuan Zuzhi Fa (法院组织法) [Court Organization Law], 2006, arts. 2, 12 (P.R.C.).

[42] See the statistics in Renmin Fayuan Jianjie (人民法院简介) [The Introduction of People's Courts], Zuigao Renmin Fayuan Wang (最高人民法院网) (2010), at http://www.court.gov.cn/jgsz/rmfyjj/.

[43] Donald C. Clarke, Power and Politics in the Chinese Court System: The Enforcement of Civil Judgments, 10 Columbia Journal of Asian Law 1, 7 (1996).

[44] Daniel C. K. Chow, The Legal System of the People's Republic of China 200 (2003).

which there are thirty one,[45] one for each province, autonomous region and centrally administered city.[46] Below the HPCs are 409 Intermediate Level People's Courts (IPCs).[47] These courts are established just below the provincial level in prefectures, provincially administered cities, and within centrally administered cities.[48] At the lowest level are the roughly 3117 PPCs that exist at the county level.[49] With those numbers, it is easy to conceptualize that the judiciary in China is a huge system and that its units spread out across a broad geographical area.

Generally, patent jurisdiction is limited to the SPC, HPCs and selected IPCs (71 out of 409).[50] Patent infringement cases are mainly litigated in the HPCs and the 71 IPCs. Although selected PPCs have jurisdiction in regard to other intellectual property cases, patent matters are not included. One exception is that, in 2009, for the first time, a PPC was designated to handle patent cases, which the Supreme People's Court considered a pilot program.[51]

---

[45] See the statistics in Renmin Fayuan Jianjie (人民法院简介) [The Introduction of People's Courts], Zuigao Renmin Fayuan Wang (最高人民法院网) (2010), at http://www.court.gov.cn/jgsz/rmfyjj/.

[46] Renmin Fayuan Jianjie (人民法院简介) [The Introduction of People's Courts], Zuigao Renmin Fayuan Wang (最高人民法院网) (2010), at http://www.court.gov.cn/jgsz/rmfyjj/. China is divided into twenty-three provinces. China is divided into twenty-three provinces. DAVID T. WANG, Judicial Reform in China: Improving Arbitration Award Enforcement by Establishing a Federal Court System, 48 Indiana International & Comparative Law Review 649, 652 (2008). According to Jessica Zoe Renwald, Foreign Investment Law in the People's Republic of China: What to Expect from Enterprise Establishment to Dispute Resolution, 16 Indiana International & Comparative Law Review453, 455 (2006).

An autonomous region is a minority entity and has a higher population of a particular minority ethnic group. Like Chinese provinces, an autonomous region is a first-level administrative subdivision of China and has its own local government. There are five autonomous regions in China: Guanxi, Inner Mongolia, Ningxia, Xinjiang, and Xizang (Tibet).Id. A centrally administered city is a special municipality directly controlled by the central government, as compared to the local government. There are four such municipalities: Beijing, Shanghai, Tianjin, and Chongqing.

[47] See the statistics in Renmin Fayuan Jianjie (人民法院简介) [The Introduction of People's Courts], Zuigao Renmin Fayuan Wang (最高人民法院网) (2010), at http://www.court.gov.cn/jgsz/rmfyjj/.

[48] A provincially administered city is a city the government of the province sits. Each province is then subdivided into prefectures, counties, and cities. In addition, each county may also be subdivided into townships, national minority townships, or towns. DAVID T. WANG, Judicial Reform in China: Improving Arbitration Award Enforcement by Establishing a Federal Court System, 48 Santa Clara Law Review 649, 652 (2008). According to Peter H. Corne, Creation and Application of Law in the PRC, 50 The American Journal of Comparative Law 369, 388–89 (2002).

[49] See the statistics in Renmin Fayuan Jianjie (人民法院简介) [The Introduction of People's Courts], Zuigao Renmin Fayuan Wang (最高人民法院网) (2010), at http://www.court.gov.cn/jgsz/rmfyjj/.

[50] This number is by the end of 2008. The number of IPCs with patent jurisdiction keeps growing. See Yonghui Chen & Xiaoxi Xie, Quanguo Fayuan Zhishi Chanquan Shenpan Gongzuo Qude Xinjinzhan (全国法院知识产权审判工作取得新进展) [The new improvement of national courts in intellectual property trial], Renmin Fayuan Bao (人民法院报) Dec. 1. 2008.

[51] Wei Huang (黄伟), Yiwushi Fayuan Chengwei Quanguo Shouge Ke Shenli Zhuanli Jiufen An Jiceng Fayuan (义乌市法院成为全国首个可审理专利纠纷案基层法院) [The Yiwu Court

Most patent cases are litigated in the selected intermediate courts as first instance and in high courts as second instance. Only a small number of cases reach the Supreme Court. Most patent cases start from IPCs as the first instance.[52] However, a few patent cases are handled by the HPCs due to the "huge amount of damage"[53] or "the severe impact to the society".[54] The SPC allows each HPC to determine what level of "damage" or "impact to society" rises to this level. Therefore, the amount of damage, which determines where the case can be litigated, varies from one jurisdiction to another. According to the "two instances" rule, most cases will end in the HPCs, while a small number of cases that start from the HPCs can be appealed to the Supreme Court. In special instances, the Supreme People's Court can take a case, regardless of whether it is in appeal or has already reached a final judgment.[55] This is called the supervision procedure and is intended to correct obvious mistakes.[56] Consequently, the HPCs are in a better position than the SPC to understand the cutting-edge issues involving patents and thus to perform the law-making task.

Although the patent jurisdiction rule limits the number of courts that can handle patent cases, the number is still huge.[57] The National Intellectual Property Strategy (2008) suggests that the system should "concentrate jurisdiction on technology related cases"[58]; apparently this plan has not yet been implemented. The growing number of IPCs with patent jurisdiction[59] and the first PPC designated with patent

---

becomes the first basic which trails patent disputes], Zhongguo Zhishi Chanquan Bao (中国知识产权报) Jul. 17th 2009.

[52] Zhipei Jiang (蒋志培), Patent Litigation in China, 9 Fed. Cir. B.J. 479, 482 (1999–2000).

[53] The starting amount to try a patent case in a HPC is one million. Guanyu Tiaozheng Difang Geji Renmin Fayuan Guanxia Diyishen Zhishi Chanquan Minshi Anjian Biaozhun de Tongzhi (最高人民法院, 关于调整地方各级人民法院管辖第一审知识产权民事案件标准的通知) [The announcement on adjusting the standard of local courts' jurisdiction over the first instance civil intellectual property cases] (Sup. People's Ct, Jan 28, 2010, Feb.1, 2010) Zhonghua Renmin Gongheguo Falü Quanshu (中华人民共和国法律全书) (P.R.C.).

[54] Zhipei Jiang (蒋志培), Patent Litigation in China, 9 Fed. Cir. B.J. 479, 482 (1999–2000).

[55] Civil procedure Law, art. 204.

[56] Ibid.

[57] Zhongguo Shehui Kexueyuan Zhishi Chanquan Zhongxin, Zhongguo Zhishi Chanquan Zhifa Tixi de Zuotian Jintian he Mingtian (中国知识产权执法体系的昨天今天和明天) [The yesterday, Today, and Domorrow of the Chinese Intellectual Property Law Enforcement], in Zhongguo Zhishi Chanquan Baohu Tixi Yanjiu (中国知识产权保护体系研究) [The Study on Chinese Intellectual Property Protection System] (2008).

[58] Guojia Zhishi Chanquan Zhanlüe (国家知识产权战略) [Outline of the National Intellectual Property Strategy] (St. Council, June 5th, 2008), Zhonghua Renmin Gongheguo Falü Quanshu (中华人民共和国法律全书) (P.R.C.).

[59] In 2006, the number was 62, and in 2008, it becomes 71. See Zhongguo Shehui Kexueyuan Zhishi Chanquan Zhongxin, Zhongguo Zhishi Chanquan Zhifa Tixi de Zuotian Jintian he Mingtian [中国知识产权执法体系的昨天今天和明天, The yesterday, Today, and Tomorrow of the Chinese Intellectual Property Law Enforcement], in Zhongguo Zhishi Chanquan Baohu Tixi Yanjiu [中国知识产权保护体系研究, The Study on Chinese Intellectual Property Protection System 2008]. See also Jing Wang (王静), "Tui er bu xiu xin xi zhishi chanquan Zeren Buyiyang de Faguan Jiang Zhipei—Jianzheng Gaige Kaifang Yilai Zhongguo Zhishi Chanquan Shenpan" (退而不休心系知识产权 责任不一样的法官蒋志培——见证改革开放以来中国知识产权审判) [Retirement But

jurisdiction indicates patent jurisdiction is expanding, rather than contracting into specialized courts.

The multiple appellate jurisdictions contribute to the inconsistency of claim interpretation. Different courts have interpreted one patent in different ways and find different scopes of protection.[60] However, multiple jurisdiction is not the only cause of resulting inconsistencies. Even in the same jurisdiction, the court does not necessarily follow examples established in previous cases. In *Zhou Lin* (1996)[61] and *Zhou Lin* (2005),[62] although the patent in question was the same and the accused infringing products were similar, the same trial court found infringement in the 1996 case and found non-infringement in the 2005 case.[63] In the judicial opinion, the court neither referred to the 1996 case nor explained why the finding was different.

2.4 First Instance—One-Step Analysis

Chinese courts do not have a jury and thus have no need to distinguish the role of the judge and jury at trial. Thus, the basis for two-step analysis does not exist in China. Unlike the U.S. litigation procedure, there is no separate hearing for claim interpretation in Chinese patent infringement litigation. The SPC, in some of its judicial opinions, emphasized that when determining patent infringement, claim interpretation should be a separate step which is conducted before comparing a patent to an accused infringing product.[64] But it is still common practice that Chinese judicial opinions do not distinguish between claim interpretations and comparisons.

In *Wang Chuan* (2000), the SPC discussed several issues related to determining patent infringement and pointed out "when determining literature infringement or infringement under the doctrine of equivalents, first the literal scope of patent right should be determined, and after that, the disputed technologies shall be compared by forensic certification or other approach", and "the protected scope of invention or utility patent is based on the content of claims".[65]

Not Laying Back: Judge Zhipei Jiang Witnessed The History of China Intellectual Property Trial], Fa zhi wang (法制网) (2009), at http://www.legaldaily.com.cn/2007fxy/2009-03/19/content_1056467.htm.

[60] Jiang Zhipei (蒋志培), Zai Quanguo Fayuan Zhishi Chanquan Shenpan Gongzuo Huiyi Shang de Jianghua (在全国法院知识产权审判工作会议上的讲话) [The Speech at National Intellectual Property Trial Conference], (Zhishi Chanquan Chubanshe 2003).

[61] Zhoulin v. Beijing Aomei Guang Jidian Lianhe Kaifa Gongsi, Beijing Huaao Dianzi Yiliao Yiqi Youxian Gongsi (周林诉北京奥美光机电联合开发公司,北京华奥电子医疗仪器有限公司) [Zhoulin v. Beijing Aomei Guangjidian Lianhe Kaifa LL.C., Beijing Huaoa Electronic Medical Device LL.C.], ipr. China court (Beijing Hig. People's Ct., Mar. 22, 1996).

[62] Ibid., See also Zhoulin v. Xingyun Shiye (Chengdu) Youxian Gongsi Deng (周林诉兴运实业) [Zhoulin v. Xingyun Shiye LL.C., etc.] ipr. China court (Beijing Interm. Ct. Jun. 24, 2005).

[63] See more discussion in the section of doctrine of equivalents.

[64] Cao, supra Note 3.

[65] Cao, supra Note 3.

The *Wang Chuan* case was accepted by the SPC under the Trial Supervision Procedure, which allows the SPC to review a case after it has already received a final decision by a court of second instance. According to the Civil Procedure Law, a case can only be appealed to a court of second instance and cannot consequently be appealed to a higher court. In *Wang Chuan*, the litigants appealed to the High People's Court. In this situation, the SPC may only accept the appeal when there is an obviousness mistake or serious abuse of procedure. A Trial Supervision case will attract the lower courts' attention and impact their approach to claim interpretation. However, some lower court does not strictly follow this two-step requirement.

It is still common practice for judicial opinions to mix the comparisons and claim interpretations together. Judges first separate the claim into technical features and then compare the technical features to those of the accused technology. During the comparison, judges identify the terms of claims which have multiple meanings and are disputed by the parties and decide the meaning in order to determine infringement.[66]

2.5 Second Instance: Appellate Review Standard

In China, the appellate procedure regarding claim interpretation does not raise an issue of whether or not claim interpretation is a pure legal question. Appellate judges review both factual and legal questions without deference to the first instance court's opinion. The Chinese appellate review standard of claim interpretation is similar to the de novo review standard in U.S. law. As discussed previously, U.S. courts have debated whether claim interpretation is a question of law or fact in order to determine the proper standard of appellate review. In China, the standard of review for both legal and factual issues are the same, and thus, Chinese courts do not raise the issue of standard of review in claim interpretation.

The Chinese Civil Procedure Law applies to all patent infringement cases. According to the Civil Procedure Law, the appellate court reviews both factual and legal issues.[67] The review standard is "the facts are clear" and "the application of law is correct".[68]

Although the statute mentioned factual issues and legal issues separately, that language does not make a difference in the appellate review process. If the "legal application is mistaken", the appellate court shall reverse. If the "factual question is

[66] Yan Wenjun (闫文军), Zhuanliquan de Baohu Fanwei: Quanli Yaoqiu Jieshi he Dengtong Yuanze Shiyong (专利权的保护范围:权利要求解释和等同原则适用) [Yan Wenjun, Scope of Patent Protection: Interpretation of Claim and Application of Doctrine of Equivalents] (Falü Chubanshe 2007).

[67] Article 151 Civil Procedure Law of the People's Republic of China (2007 Amendment).

[68] Ibid.

not clearly answered or the factual finding is not well supported by the evidence", the appellate judge can either choose to remand or reverse.[69]

2.6 Procedures for Determining Doctrine of Equivalents

The appellate review standard concerning the doctrine of equivalents is the same as that of claim interpretation in China. Unlike the U.S. law, in which the doctrine of equivalents is a factual issue and reviewed under the clearly erroneous standard on appeal, Chinese appellate courts review the doctrine of equivalents without any deference to the trial decision.

---

69 Ibid.

Chapter 3
U.S. Claim Interpretation: Substantive Law

3.1 Source of Law

The U.S. statutes provide very limited guidance for claim interpretation in 35 U.S.C.§271 & §112(f). The Supreme Court and Federal Circuit have undertaken most of the responsibility to develop the rules.

3.1.1 Statutes

The primary statute concerning U.S. patent law is Title 35 of the U.S. Code (U.S.C.), which was enacted by an Act of Congress on July 19, 1952, and most recently revised by passing the Leahy-Smith America Invents Act on September 16, 2011.

In contrast to China and many other civil law countries, which have a statute to state that a claim defines the scope of a patent, 35 U.S.C. does not provide general guidance for claim interpretation. 35 U.S.C.§271 addresses patent infringement, but does not directly address claim interpretation. 35 U.S.C.§112 provides the requirement for specification and specifically states a rule for interpreting a means-plus-function claim: "an element in a claim for a combination may be expressed as a means or step for performing a specified function without the recital of structure, material, or acts in support thereof, and such claim shall be construed to cover the corresponding structure, material, or acts described in the specification and equivalents thereof".[1]

[1] 35 U. S. C. §112.

© Intellectual Property Publishing House 2025

Z. Peng, *Comparative Study on Patent Claim Interpretation: The United States and China*, https://doi.org/10.1007/978-981-96-0836-2_3

3.1.2 Case Law

The Federal Circuit and Supreme Court have undertaken most of the responsibility to develop the rules for claim interpretation. Federal Circuit rules, established through court precedent, have undergone a number of changes in the past several years at a relatively rapid pace.[2]

The rules established through U.S. case law are merely a consensus reached by the twelve Federal Circuit judges. The majority consensus is sometimes reached through a sharply divided vote. Federal Circuit judges split in several important cases, like *Markman I*,[3] *Cybor*,[4] *Phillips*,[5] etc. For example, in *Cybor*, the Federal Circuit judges had different interpretations of the Supreme Court's decision in *Markman II* and reached different conclusions.[6] Also, the consensus can be merely temporary. Several judges expressed their willingness to reconsider *Cybor*.[7] This reflects an attempt to seek the best practice and also suggests that claim interpretation rules are unstable.

3.2 Structure of U.S. Claims

U.S. patents include a cover page, an abstract, specification and claims. A cover page is to present bibliographic information.[8] The specification, as provided by the statute, "shall contain a written description of the invention, and of the manner and process of making and using it… as to enable any person skilled in the art to which it pertains".[9] When necessary, drawings are also included as a part of specification.[10]

Manual of Patent Examination Procedure (MPEP) states that, in the specification, "specific operative embodiments or examples of the invention must be set forth".[11]

---

[2] See AMY L. LANDERS, UNDERSTANDING PATENT LAW 259 (2008).

[3] Judge Mayer in the concurring opinion and Judge Pauline Newman in the dissenting opinion claimed that the majority decision violates the seventh amendment. Markman v. Westview Instruments, Inc., 52 F.3d 967, 979, 34 USPQ2d 1321, 1329 (Fed.Cir.1995) (in banc) (Markman I).

[4] Judge Mayer, Judge Newman and judge Rader strongly disagreed with the majority's decision on de novo review. Judge Plager and Judge Bryson, although without objection to de novo review, suggested having at least some deference to trail decisions. Cybor Corp. v. FAS Technologies, Inc., 138 F.3d 1448 (Fed. Cir. 1998).

[5] Judge Lourie, Newman and Mayer dissented and disagreed with the majority's finding of claim interpretation. Phillips v. AWH Corp., 415 F.3d 1303 (Fed. Cir. 2005).

[6] Cybor, 138 F.3d at 1448.

[7] See discussion in part I procedure law C. Appellate Review Standard.

[8] MPEP § 601.

[9] 35 U. S. C. S § 112.

[10] 35 U. S. C. S § 112.

[11] MPEP 608.01 (p).

Although the words "embodiments" and "examples" are in the plural form, the number of embodiments can be one or more.[12]

Claims are the single-numbered sentences located at the end of specification. "The specification shall conclude with one or more claims particularly pointing out and distinctly claiming the subject matter which the applicant regards as his invention".[13] Claims are the most important part of a patent.

A brief abstract, no more than 150 words, is to enable the U.S. Patent and Trademark Office and the public to quickly learn about the invention.[14] An abstract is attached after the claims section, commencing on a separate sheet.[15]

3.3 Fundamental Rules

3.3.1 Claim Defines the Scope of Patent

It is a "bedrock principle" of patent law that "the claims of a patent define the invention to which the patentee is entitled the right to exclude".[16] Although not provided in the statute, it is a well-established rule in case law.

The words of a claim are generally given their ordinary and customary meaning.[17] The ordinary and customary meaning of a claim term is "the meaning that the term would have to a person of ordinary skill in the art in question at the time of the invention".[18] The skill level of an ordinary person is determined at the effective filing

[12] See, e.g., "Merely because the specification only describes one embodiment is not a sufficient reason to limit the claims to that embodiment." Altiris, Inc. v. Symantec Corp., 318 F.3d 1363, 1372 (Fed. Cir. 2003). See also Capon v. Eshhar, 418 F.3d 1349, 1357–58 (Fed. Cir. 2005) ("the level of detail required to satisfy the written description requirement varies depending on the nature and scope of the claims and on the complexity and predictability of the relevant technology").

[13] 35 U. S. C. S § 112.

[14] USPTO Law MPEP 608.01 (b) Abstract of the Disclosure.

[15] Ibid.

[16] Innova, 381 F.3d at 1115; see also Vitronics, 90 F.3d at 1582 ("we look to the words of the claims themselves ... to define the scope of the patented invention"); Markman, 52 F.3d at 980 ("The written description part of the specification itself does not delimit the right to exclude. That is the function and purpose of claims"). Phillips, 415 F.3d at 1312.

[17] Phillips, 415 F.3d at 1312–13. Vitronics, 90 F.3d at 1582; See also Toro Co. v. White Consol. Indus., Inc., 199 F.3d 1295, 1299 (Fed.Cir.1999); Renishaw PLC v. Marposs Societa' per Azioni, 158 F.3d 1243, 1249 (Fed.Cir.1998).

[18] Phillips, 415 F.3d at 1312–13. See Innova, 381 F.3d at 1116 ("A court construing a patent claim seeks to accord a claim the meaning it would have to a person of ordinary skill in the art at the time of the invention"); Home Diagnostics, Inc. v. Life Scan, Inc., 381 F.3d 1352, 1358 (Fed.Cir.2004) ("customary meaning" refers to the "customary meaning in [the] art field"); Ferguson Beauregard/Logic Controls v. Mega Sys., LLC, 350 F.3d 1327, 1338 (Fed.Cir.2003) (claim terms "are examined through the viewing glass of a person skilled in the art").

date of the patent application.[19] In order to determine the meaning of the claim, the courts always consult the specification as well as prosecution history.[20]

3.3.2 *All-Elements Rule*

a. All-Elements Rule in General

To establish infringement, every element of the claim must be present in the accused device or method, literally or by an equivalent.[21] In the all-elements rule, "element" may be used to mean a single limitation, but sometimes it also has been used to mean a series of limitations that, taken together, make up a component of the claimed invention.[22] Some judges think a more precise name for this rule would be the all limitations rule.[23] The different names have no bearing on the substance of this rule.[24]

Claims in patents usually contain a preamble, transition, and one or more elements.[25] No matter whether the element is present in the preamble or any other part of the patent claim, the all-elements rule applies without exception.

b. The Exception: Preamble Terms

Some cases involve issues concerning whether a part of the claim is an element or limitation. None of these cases phrase the issue as an exception to the all-elements rule. Nevertheless, those cases raised a question if a term in the claim does not limit the scope of patent.

---

[19] Phillips, 415 F.3d at 1312–13 (Fed. Cir. 2005). See also PC Connector Solutions LLC v. Smart Disk Corp., 406 F.3d 1359, 1363 (Fed.Cir.2005) (meaning of claim "must be interpreted as of [the] effective filing date" of the patent application); Schering Corp. v. Amgen Inc., 222 F.3d 1347, 1353 (Fed.Cir.200).

[20] Autogiro Co. of Am. v. United States, 384 F.2d 391, 397 (Ct. Cl. Oct. 13, 1967).

[21] Inpro II Licensing, S.A.R.L. v. T-Mobile USA, Inc., 450 F.3d 1350, 78 U.S.P.Q.2d 1786, 1791 (Fed. Cir. 2006).

[22] Corning Glass Works v. Sumitomo Elec. U.S.A., Inc., 868 F.2d 1251, 9 U.S.P.Q.2d 1962 (Fed. Cir. 1989).

[23] Johnston v. IVAC Corp., 885 F.2d 1574, 12 U.S.P.Q.2d 1382, 1384 (Fed. Cir. 1989).

[24] See CHISUM, supra Note 24 at 8.06[1][b]. 18.03. See e.g., Corning Glass Works v. Sumitomo Electric U.S.A., 868 F.2d 1251, 1259, 9 USPQ2d 1962, 1968 (Fed. Cir. 1989) (citing Treatise; "The premise [that where an element of a claim is entirely missing, there is no infringement] correctly states the law of this circuit adopted in banc in Pennwalt. … 'Element' may be used to mean a single limitation, but it has also been used to mean a series of limitations which, taken together make up a component of the claimed invention. In the All-Elements rule, 'element' is used in the sense of a limitation of a claim. … An equivalent must be found for every limitation of the claim somewhere in an accused device, but not necessarily in a corresponding component, although that is generally the case"). Some decisions state the rule as all limitation rules, see e.g., but there is no difference in substance between an all-elements rule and an all limitations rule. See Ethicon Endo-Surgery, Inc. v. United States Surgical Corp., 149 F.3d 1309, 1317. Some decisions state a preference for the word limitation over the word element, 1050 but there is no difference in substance between an all-elements rule and an all limitations rule. CHISUM, supra Note 24 at 8.06[1][b]. 18.03.

[25] Chisum, Supra Note 24 at 8.06[1][b].

In some infringement cases, the Federal Circuit has found that the preamble is "not a limitation" and thus does not limit the claim scope.[26] The Federal Circuit has set forth some general principles to determine when a preamble limits the claim scope.[27] Some cases stated that "the preamble does not limit the claims".[28] However, there is no simple test to determine when a preamble may limit the claim scope.[29] Whether a preamble term is a claim limitation is "determined on the facts of each case in light of the claim as a whole and the invention described in the patent".[30] Thus, the findings of limitation or non-limitation are based on a case-by-case basis according to the specific facts involved.

The Federal Circuit has found that the preamble should be interpreted as a claim limitation when a preamble is "necessary to give life, meaning, and vitality to the claim" or sets forth an "essential structure or steps" to the patented invention.[31] For example, in *Computer Docking Station v. Dell, Inc.*, the preamble language at issue described a microprocessor system as "portable". The court concluded that "portable" was a claim limitation, because the "portable" feature of the invention was "emphasized" in the written description and throughout the prosecution history but was not mentioned in the body of the claims.[32]

In some cases, preambles are not found as claim limitation, for reasons such as it is "merely duplicative of the limitations in the body of the claim",[33] "it was not added to overcome a prior art rejection"[34] or "the preamble merely gives a descriptive name to the set of limitations in the body of the claim that completely set forth the invention".[35] For example, in *American Medical*, the Federal Circuit held that the preamble language describing the function of the claim elements "photoselective vaporization of tissue" was not a claim limitation, because it did "not embody an essential component of the invention", but was "simply a descriptive name for the invention that was fully set forth in the bodies of the claims", and the claims described a "structurally complete device", so the court found that the preamble language "photoselective" was not a limitation.[36]

---

26 Syntex (U.S.A.) LLC v. Apotex, Inc., 407 F.3d 1371 (Fed. Cir. 2005); Altiris, Inc. v. Symantec Corp. 318 F.3d 1363 (2003); Storage Technology Corp. v. Cisco Systems, Inc. 329 F.3d 823 (2003); IMS Technology Inc. v. Haas Automation Inc. 206 F.3d 1422 (2000); Vaupel Textilmaschinen KG v. Meccanica Euro Italia S.P.A. 944 F.2d 870 (1991); Am. Med. Sys., Inc. v. Biolitec, Inc., 618 F.3d 1354, 1358 (Fed. Cir. 2010).

27 Am. Med. Sys., Inc., 618 F.3d at 1358.

28 Allen Eng'g Corp. v. Bartell Indus., Inc., 299 F.3d 1336, 1346 (Fed.Cir.2002).

29 Am. Med. Sys., Inc., 618 F.3d at 1358. See also Patrick J. Flinn, Claim Construction Trends in the Federal Circuit, 572 PLI/PAT 317, 335–36 (1999) (stating the preamble limitations test as "opaque").

30 Storage Tech. Corp. v. Cisco Sys., Inc., 329 F.3d 823, 831 (Fed.Cir.2003).

31 Catalina Mktg. Int'l, Inc. v. Coolsavings.com, Inc., 289 F.3d 801, 808 (Fed.Cir.2002).

32 Computer Docking Station v. Dell, Inc., 519 F.3d 1366 1375 (Fed.Cir.2008).

33 Symantec, 522 F.3d at 1288–89.

34 Ibid.

35 IMS Tech., Inc. v. Haas Automation, Inc., 206 F.3d 1422, 1434–35 (Fed.Cir.2000).

36 Am. Med. Sys. Inc., 618 F.3d at 1359.

Some judges have called for an *en banc* decision to set up a new rule that all preambles are limiting, since the current case law does not have an established framework to determine whether a preamble is limiting.[37] Judge DYK believes "there is, after all, little to be said in favor of allowing an applicant, in the claim drafting process, to include material in the claims that is not binding".[38] Also, patentees are urged to draft a patent that avoids confusion as to the scope of the claims by a uniform rule that all preambles are limiting.[39] Judge DYK quoted the Supreme Court's conclusion in *Merrill v. Yeomans* stating that "nothing can be more just and fair, both to the patentee and to the public, than that the former should understand, and correctly describe, just what he has invented, and for what he claims a patent".[40]

3.3.3 Specifications

Specification is the most frequently used reference in claim interpretation and also a place where the uncertainty of claim interpretation is frequently manifested. Specification is the single best reference in claim interpretation. Claim construction begins with, and remains focused on, the language of the claims.[41] Consulting the specification is always important and necessary.[42] Claims "must be read in view of the specification, of which they are a part".[43]

Specification may be used to narrow or clarify broad and general term in claims.[44] It has always been difficult to draw the line between impermissible "importing limitations into claims"[45] and permissible "reading claims in light of specification".[46] In a dissent opinion, Judge Moore noted that "nowhere is the conflict more apparent

---

[37] See e.g., Am. Med. Sys., Inc. v. Biolitec, Inc., at 1364 (dissent, Judge Dyk).

[38] Ibid.

[39] Ibid.

[40] Merrill v. Yeomans, 94 U.S. 568, 573–74, 24 L.Ed. 235 (1876).

[41] Innova/Pure Water, Inc., 381 F.3d at 1116 (reaffirmed in Phillips).

[42] "In deriving the meaning of a claim, we inspect all useful documents and reach what Justice Holmes called the 'felt meaning' of the claim. In seeking this goal, we make use of three parts of the patent: the specification, the drawings, and the file wrapper." Autogiro, 384 F.2d, at 397.

[43] Markman, 52 F.3d at 978.

[44] "As to the review of the intrinsic evidence, the specification is reviewed to determine whether the patentee used terms in a manner inconsistent with their ordinary meaning. Vitronics, 90 F.3d at 1582, 39 USPQ2d at 1577. The prosecution history is also mainly used to limit instead of expanding the interpretation. See DeMarini Sports, Inc. v. Worth, Inc., 239 F.3d 1314, 1323 (Fed. Cir. 2001); See also Vitronics, 90 F.3d at 1582, 39 USPQ2d at 1577, and Southwall Techs., Inc. v. Cardinal IG, Co., 54 F.3d 1570, 1576, 34 USPQ2d 1673, 1676 (Fed.Cir.1995) ("The prosecution history limits the interpretation of claim terms so as to exclude any interpretation that was disclaimed during prosecution").

[45] Superguide Corp. v. DirecTV Enterprises, Inc., 358 F.3d 870, 875, 69 USPQ2d 1865, 1868 (Fed. Cir. 2004).

[46] In re Fout, 675 F.2d 297, 300 (CCPA 1982) ("Claims must always be read in light of the specification. Here, the specification makes plain what the appellants did and did not invent ....").

than in our jurisprudence on the use of the specification in the interpretation of claim language".[47]

The *en banc* decision Phillips attempted to offer a solution to overcome the difficulty, but was not as successful.[48] The *en banc* court did not reach a consensus on claim interpretation of the disputed term "baffle" in *Phillips*.[49] Although *Phillips* established a framework of claim interpretation, it did not resolve the inconsistency problem.

Unifying the law to adhere to the contextualist approach does not necessarily produce consistent claim interpretation. Despite affirming the contextualist rationale which was applied by the panel majority, the *Phillips en banc* court disagreed with the panel majority's finding on the claim interpretation.[50] Instead, the *Phillips en banc* court adopted the broader interpretation, which is the same as the dissent judge's interpretation. This exemplifies how Federal Circuit judges reach different conclusions on claim interpretation by following the same contextualist approach. Similarly, Judge Lourie's dissenting opinion, while agreeing with the *en banc* majority on the interpretation approach, holds a different view on whether the specification discloses a restriction of the angle.[51] After affirming the contextualist approach and clarifying the hierarchy of the evidence, *Phillips* failed to reach a consensus framework for claim interpretation.

The majority opinion and dissent opinion of the panel decision in *Phillips* are considered as an example of "literalist" and "contextualist".[52] However, there is no substantial difference. Both the majority and dissent opinions considered the dictionary meaning as well as the information from the specification. Although the dissent judge finally adopted the ordinary meaning from the dictionary definition, he neither ignored the specification, nor asserted that the dictionary definition was superior to the specification itself.[53] Both the majority and the dissent attempted to interpret the term by consulting both dictionaries and the specification, and both groups inquired into whether the specification redefines the term or constitutes a disclaimer.[54] However, they had different views on what the specification provided and thus reached different conclusions.

---

[47] Retractable Technologies, Inc. v. Becton, Dickinson & Co., 659 F.3d 1369 (Fed. Cir. 2011).

[48] Phillips, 415 F.3d at1303.

[49] This is a proof of the difficulty in setting the line between improper importation of limitations and proper claim interpretation in light of specification and a proof that Federal Circuit has not resolved it. Toshiko Takenaka, Extent of patent protection in the United States, Germany, the United Kingdom and Japan: examination through the concept of 'person having ordinary skill in the art of the invention, in PATENT LAW AND THEORY: A HANDBOOK OF CONTEMPORARY RESEARCH 350. (TOSHIKO TAKENAKA ed, 2008).

[50] Phillips, 415 F.3d, at 1309.

[51] Ibid., at 1330. Judge Louries was the one who filed the opinion for the court on the previous panel decision. Phillips, 363 F.3d at 1209).

[52] Janice Muller, Federal Circuit 2004: Eight Significant Patent Law Developments Every IP Litigator Must Understand, 11 IP LITIGATOR 27–38 (2005).

[53] Phillips, 363 F.3d, at 1216. (DYK, dissent in part).

[54] Phillips, 363 F.3d, at 1217. Phillips, 415 F.3d, at 1310.

In *Phillips*, the accurate question to ask is not whether a specification should be superior to a dictionary. Instead, it is if the specification constitutes a disclaimer. The Federal Circuit repeatedly ruled that the narrower meaning should be adopted, if the patent specification reveals that an intentional is a claimer or a disavowal. However, the judges in Phillips failed to reach an agreement on this question.[55]

3.3.4 Prosecution History

In the United States, prosecution history can also be used to literally interpret claims to exclude some embodiments from the literal scope if the prosecution supports a surrender of such embodiments.[56] However, in some cases, the U.S. judges did not give much weight to prosecution history for interpreting claims because some statements in the prosecution record may not directly address whether a particular embodiment is excluded from the disputed claim term.[57]

3.3.5 PHOSITA—Philips

U.S. courts frequently use person having ordinary skills in the art (PHOSITA) as a conceptual tool in claim interpretation.[58] PHOSITA is used in both claim interpretation and determining infringement under doctrine of equivalents, but there is a difference. The knowledge level of PHOSITA in claim interpretation determined by the time of patent application date.[59] The knowledge level of PHOSITA in evaluation equivalents is determined by the time of infringement.[60]

---

[55] "Consistent with that general principle, our cases recognize that the specification may reveal a special definition given to a claim term by the patentee that differs from the meaning it would otherwise possess. In such cases, the inventor's lexicography governs. See CCS Fitness, Inc. v. Brunswick Corp., 288 F.3d 1359, 1366 (Fed.Cir.2002). In other cases, the specification may reveal an intentional disclaimer, or disavowal, of claim scope by the inventor. In that instance as well, the inventor has dictated the correct claim scope, and the inventor's intention, as expressed in the specification, is regarded as dispositive. See SciMed Life Sys., Inc. v. Advanced Cardiovascular Sys., Inc., 242 F.3d 1337, 1343–44 (Fed.Cir.2001). Phillips, 415 F.3d at 1316 (Fed. Cir. 2005).

[56] HARMON, Supra Note 56.

[57] AquaTex v. Techniche 419 F.3d 137,476 U.S.P.Q.2d 1213 (Fed. Cir. 2005). quoted Phillips for the conclusion that the prosecution history is an ongoing negotiation that "often lacks the clarity of the specification and thus is less useful for claim construction.".

[58] See Multiform Desiccants, Inc. v. Medzam, Ltd., 133 F.3d 1473, 1477, 45 USPQ2d 1429, 1432 (Fed.Cir.1998) ("It is the person of ordinary skill in the field of the invention through whose eyes the claims are construed"). Cybor Corp., 138 F.3d at 1475 The objective of claim interpretation is to discern the meaning of the claim terms to one of ordinary skill in the art at the time of invention.

[59] Phillips v. AWH Corp., 415 F.3d 1303, 1313 (Fed. Cir. 2005).

[60] Warner-Jenkinson Co. v. Hilton Davis Chem. Co., 520 U.S. 17(1997).

U.S. courts justified this approach by stating inventors are typically PHOSITAs and patents are addressed to and intended to be read by PHOSITAs.[61] But applying this standard is not always easy. In *LG Electronics, Inc. v. Bizcom Electronics, Inc.* (2006), the Federal Circuit held that an adopted industry standard, which is prior art, should be considered in construing the meaning of a disputed claim term to a person of ordinary skill in the relevant art. A district court "erred by failing to give proper weight to the incorporated industry standard; it failed to consider the standard as intrinsic evidence of the meaning to one of ordinary skill in the art as of the filing date".[62] *Phillips* warned that the extrinsic evidence does not necessarily reflect PHOSITA's understanding and discouraged the use of dictionaries and expert testimony. Instead, it emphasized the use of intrinsic evidence. However, the patent document itself cannot explain how a PHOSITA may read the patent document. Finding PHOSITA's understanding may be an impossible mission in practice.

This difficulty exists because "interpreting claims in PHOSITA's perspective" is merely idealistic. There might be many persons ordinarily skilled in the art holding the same understanding of a technical term. But there is no single understanding of a term which could be agreed upon by each and every person who is ordinarily skilled in the art. In other words, PHOSITA is merely hypothetical. Although this hypothetical concept can serve as a reminder that judges should attempt to understand how a patent is read in the industry and thus is helpful, it cannot be a singularly useful tool in practice.

In reality, an idealistic and intangible term like PHOSITA will not improve the certainty of decisions or the clearness of reasoning. Instead, it will become a vehicle to legitimate conclusion without persuasive analysis.[63]

3.4 Defining Literal Claim Scope

3.4.1 Canons

a. Canons in General

Claim interpretation precedents provide a number of canons of construction to assist in claim interpretation, including that a claim should be interpreted to maintain its

---

[61] Phillips, 415 F.3d a5 1303, at 1321. See also HARMON, supra note 56, at 444.

[62] LG Elecs., Inc. v. Bizcom Elecs., Inc., 453 F.3d 1364, 1375 (Fed. Cir. 2006). See also Chisum Supra note 28, at § 18.03 (D).

[63] "In tort negligence, US legal Scholars and courts identify the function of a reasonable person as a vehicle for making concealed choices among political preferences. The patent law PHOSITA also functions in the same way as the reasonable person as a vehicle to implement a political choice." Michael H. Davis, Patent Policies, 56 South Carolina Law Review, 337, 356 (2004).

validity[64]; a correct interpretation rarely excludes the preferred embodiment[65]; when two interpretations are equally valid, a narrow construction is preferred to a broad one[66]; that each claim within a patent should have a different scope[67]; and that limitations cannot be imported from the specification or prosecution history.[68] The utility of each of these canons is cabined by subsequent limitations thereof, but the case law does not provide much guidance on this topic.[69]

b. The Doctrine of Claim Differentiation

The doctrine of claim differentiation is a presumption that different claims have different meanings.[70] The underlining consideration is that if the different terms are interpreted as having the same meaning, one of them would be superfluous.[71] The assumption could be overcome, however, if there is "clear and persuasive evidence",[72] which shows that interpreting the terms differently will broaden the "correct scope" of patent rights.[73] In order to clarify the district courts' confusion, Curtiss suggested two considerations of claim differentiation.[74] However, since this is not an en banc

---

[64] See, e.g., Generation II Orthotics, Inc. v. Med. Tech., Inc., 263 F.3d 1356, 1365 (Fed. Cir. 2001) ("[C]laims can only be construed to preserve their validity where the proposed claim construction is 'practicable,' is based on sound claim construction principles, and does not revise or ignore the explicit language of the claims"); See also Phillips II, 415 F.3d at 1327; Modine Mfg. Co. v. U.S. Int'l Trade Comm'n, 75 F.3d 1545, 1557 (Fed. Cir. 1996).

[65] See, e.g., Playtex Prods., Inc. v. Procter & Gamble Co., 400 F.3d 901, 904 (Fed. Cir. 2005); Vitronics, 90 F.3d at 1583–84 (citing Hoechst Celanese Corp. v. BP Chems. Ltd., 78 F.3d 1575, 1581 (Fed. Cir. 1996)).

[66] See, e.g., Housey Pharms., Inc. v. Astrazeneca UK Ltd., 366 F.3d 1348, 1356 (Fed. Cir. 2004) (limiting this canon to the "unusual case" where the patentee made two contradictory representations of scope); Athletic Alternatives, Inc. v. Prince Mfg., Inc., 73 F.3d 1573, 1581 (Fed. Cir. 1996).

[67] See, e.g., Multiform Desiccants, Inc. v. Medzam, Ltd., 133 F.3d 1473, 1480 (Fed. Cir. 1998) (cautioning that "the doctrine of claim differentiation can not broaden claims beyond their correct scope, determined in light of the specification and the prosecution history and any relevant extrinsic evidence").72 See, e.g., Housey Pharms., 366 F.3d at 1355; Burke, Inc. v. Bruno Indep. Living Aids, Inc., 183 F.3d 1334, 1340 (Fed. Cir. 1999).

[68] See, e.g., Housey Pharms., 366 F.3d at 1355; Burke, Inc. v. Bruno Indep. Living Aids, Inc., 183 F.3d 1334, 1340 (Fed. Cir. 1999).

[69] Kristen Osenga, Linguistics and Patent Claim Construction, 38 Rutgers Law Journal 61, 75 (2006).

[70] Versa Corp. v. Ag-Bag Int'l Ltd., 392 F.3d 1325, 1330 (Fed.Cir.2004) (presumption that each claim in a patent has a different scope) (quoting Comark Commc'ns, Inc. v. Harris Corp., 156 F.3d 1182, 1187 (Fed.Cir.1998)).

[71] Tandon Corp. v. United States Int'l Trade Comm'n, 831 F.2d 1017, 1023, 4 USPQ2d 1283, 1288 (Fed.Cir.1987).

[72] Modine Mfg. Co. v. United States Int'l Trade Comm'n, 75 F.3d. 1545, 1551, 37 USPQ2d 1609, 1612 (Fed. Cir. 1996).

[73] Fantasy Sports Props. v. Sportsline.com, 287 F.3d 1108, 1115–16 (Fed.Cir.2002) (quoting Kraft Foods, Inc. v. International Trading Co., 203 F.3d 1362 (Fed.Cir.2000)).

[74] The district court's misapplication of that claim construction tool is understandable given the variability of explanations of claim differentiation. Curtiss-Wright Flow Control Corp. v. Velan, Inc., 438 F.3d 1374, 1380 (Fed. Cir. 2006). See supra, p. 67.

decision, it is still unclear whether other Federal Circuit Court judges would agree, and thus, its future impact is unknown.[75]

Claim differentiation can be applied regardless of the relationship among the claims,[76] but is more frequently used in the independent/dependent claim scenario.[77] Specifically, it is presumed that an independent claim should not be construed as requiring a limitation added by a dependent claim.[78] Reading an additional limitation from a dependent claim into an independent claim would not only make that additional limitation superfluous, it might render the dependent claim invalid.[79]

Phillips en banc case established a presumption that "the presence of a dependent claim that adds a particular limitation gives rise to a presumption that the limitation in question is not present in the independent claim".[80] The dependent claim 2 states that the baffles may be "disposed at angles for deflecting projectiles such as bullets".[81] The court concluded that since the dependent claim includes the limitation of angles for deflecting bullets, it is likely the independent claim 1 already contained that limitation.[82]

Curtiss-Wright Flow Control Corp. v. Velan (2006)[83] suggested two considerations regarding to whether the presumption can be rebutted. The two considerations are: (1) "claim differentiation takes on relevance in the context of a claim construction that would render additional, or different, language in another independent claim superfluous" and (2) "claim differentiation cannot broaden claims beyond their correct scope".[84]

---

[75] The district court's misapplication of that claim construction tool is understandable given the variability of explanations of claim differentiation. Curtiss-Wright Flow Control Corp., 438 F.3d, at 1380.

[76] Curtiss-Wright Flow Control Corp., 438 F.3d, at 1380–81.

[77] "Thus, the claim differentiation tool works best in the relationship between independent and dependent claims." Curtiss-Wright Flow Control Corp., 438 F.3d, at 1380–81 (quoting Versa Corp. v. Ag-Bag Int'l Ltd., 392 F.3d 1325, 1330 (Fed.Cir.2004)) See also Liebel-Flarsheim Co. v. Medrad, Inc., 358 F.3d 898, 910 (Fed.Cir.2004) (citing Sunrace Roots Enter. Co. v. SRAM Corp., 336 F.3d 1298, 1302–03 (Fed.Cir.2003)).

[78] Curtiss-Wright Flow Control Corp., 438 F.3d, at 1380–81 (Fed. Cir. 2006) (quoting Versa Corp. v. Ag-Bag Int'l Ltd., 392 F.3d 1325, 1330 (Fed.Cir.2004)). See also Nazomi Commc'ns, Inc. v. Arm Holdings, PLC., 403 F.3d 1364, 1370 (Fed.Cir.2005) ("[C]laim differentiation 'normally means that limitations stated in dependent claims are not to be read into the independent claim from which they depend'").

[79] Indeed, the statute stresses that a dependent claim must add a limitation to those recited in the independent claim. See 35 U.S.C. § 112, ¶ 4 (2000) ("[A] claim in dependent form shall contain a reference to a claim previously set forth and then specify a further limitation of the subject matter claimed").

[80] Phillips, 415 F.3d, at 1315.

[81] Ibid., at 1324.

[82] Ibid.

[83] Curtiss-Wright Flow Control Corp., 438 F.3d.at 1380.

[84] Ibid., at1380-81. (citing Fantasy Sports Props. v. Sportsline.com, 287 F.3d 1108, 1115–16 (Fed.Cir.2002) (quoting Kraft Foods, Inc. v. International Trading Co., 203 F.3d 1362 (Fed.Cir. 2000)).

The first consideration refers to when to apply the claim differentiation presumption. The second consideration explains how to overcome the presumption. It is easy to understand that "[c]laim differentiation is a guide, not a rigid rule"[85] and the presumption can be overcome. However, it is not an easy task to properly apply the rule in practice, since the "correct scope"[86] is a vague standard, which needs to be explained by more operational guidelines. Actually, the "correct scope" is just what the judges are struggling with. Merely telling a judge to avoid broadening the "correct scope" is perfectly proper but just not helpful at all. Similarly, a Federal Circuit precedent stressed that "clear and persuasive evidence"[87] must be provided to overcome the "correct scope" presumption, which suggests that the standard of review requires clear and persuasive evidence, but still does not provide an operational guideline. In Curtiss, Federal Circuit found that the district court broadened the correct scope of the claim, by using the specification as the evidence.[88]

In Curtiss, the district court broadly contused the term "adjustable" in the independent claim 14 of the '714 patent, specifically claims 1 and 18. All three claims recite an adjustment mechanism.[89] Both claims 1 and 18 describe an embodiment possessing an external seat adjustment mechanism, but claim 14 does not. The district court interpreted the term "adjustable" in claim 14 broadly, as it encompasses all devices that are simply "adjustable", regardless of the means or time in which this adjustment is made.[90] The district court interpreted "adjustable" very broadly, by eliminating any constraints on the adjustable limitation. Part of the legal analysis of the district court is based on that logic that claim 14 should have a different scope from claims 1 or 18.[91] Thus, it should not be interpreted as having a specific adjustment mechanism as specified in claim 1 and 18.[92] However, the Federal Circuit found that the district court's interpretation was too broad.[93] The Federal Circuit found that the district court may be right that there is no adjustable mechanism present in claim 14, but the term "adjustable" must have some constraints, like time and manner. Otherwise, all structures could be adjustable, thus rendering the term meaningless.[94]

The Federal Circuit based its analysis on the two considerations of claim differentiation: the redundancy and the consistency of the overall context of patents.[95] Construing "adjustable" in claim 14 with limitations does not necessarily result in

---

[85] Laitram Corp. v. Rexnord, Inc., 939 F.2d 1533, 1538 (Fed.Cir.1991).

[86] Fantasy Sports Props. v. Sportsline.com, 287 F.3d 1108, 1115–16 (Fed.Cir.2002) (quoting Kraft Foods, Inc. v. International Trading Co., 203 F.3d 1362 (Fed.Cir.2000)).

[87] Modine Mfg. Co. v. United States Int'l Trade Comm'n, 75 F.3d. 1545, 1551, 37 USPQ2d 1609, 1612 (Fed. Cir. 1996).

[88] Curtiss-Wright Flow Control Corp., 438 F.3d.

[89] Preliminary Injunction Order, slip op. at 11–13.

[90] Ibid.

[91] Curtiss-Wright Flow Control Corp., 438 F.3d, at 1381.

[92] Ibid.

[93] Ibid.

[94] Ibid.

[95] Ibid.

redundancy.[96] Also, the broad interpretation, contrary to the specification, emphasized a limitation on the time of adjustment: that the invention is "adjustable" during deheading.[97]

The Federal Circuit identified the doctrine of claim differentiation as an issue on appeal even though the district court did not mention this issue.[98] The court could apply this doctrine with or without explicitly using the term "differentiation".[99] For example, in Curtiss, although the district court neither mentioned differentiation in its judicial opinion, nor cited any precedent concerning the doctrine of differentiation, the Federal Circuit conducted its analysis on the two considerations of claim differentiation, citing precedent concerning the doctrine of differentiation in its legal analysis.

The doctrine of differentiation, as reviewed by the district and federal appeals courts exemplifies that the law in this area is still developing. It is important for the district courts and practitioners to pay close attention to the opinions issued by the appellate courts to stay informed of emerging legal developments in this area.

3.4.2 Special Types of Claims

a. Means plus Function

"Functional claiming refers to the general notion of claiming an invention by what it does, rather than what it is in terms of physical structure".[100] This kind of claim is more frequently used in mechanical or electronic inventions.[101]

35 U.S.C. 112(f) (formerly 35 U.S.C.112, Paragraph 6) is the governing statute for a means-plus-function claim. It states that "an element in a claim for a combination may be expressed as a means or step for performing a specified function without the recital of structure, material, or acts in support thereof, and such claim shall be construed to cover the corresponding structure, material, or acts described in the specification and equivalents thereof".[102]

35 U.S.C. 112(f) limits the scope of the means-plus-function claim to the disclosed embodiments and their equivalents. "Means plus function" claims express the element as a generic "means" that performs a recited function.[103] Without the limitations set forth in 35 U.S.C. 112 (f), the claim may be construed on its face to cover any possible structure that would perform the recited function.

---

[96] Ibid.

[97] Ibid.

[98] Ibid., at 1380.

[99] Phillips, 415 F.3d at 1314–15 (explaining the presumption without invoking the "claim differentiation" label).

[100] Janice M. Muller, An Introduction To Patent Law 87 (2006).

[101] Ibid.

[102] 35 U.S.C. 112 (f).

[103] Ergo Licensing, LLC v. CareFusion 303, Inc., 673 F.3d 1361, 1363 (Fed. Cir. 2012).

i. The Positive and Negative Presumptions

The means-plus-function claim interpretation rule applies only to purely functional limitations that do not provide the sufficient structure that performs the recited function.[104] The Federal Circuit has been working on finding a "solid test"[105] to determine whether a particular claim element is a means-plus-function element under 35 U.S.C. 112 (f). The determination of whether or not 35 U.S.C. 112 (f) applies is determined on an "element-by-element basis".[106] The test consists of two presumptions, and each of them can be rebutted. The use of the word "means" in patent claim creates a presumption that Section 112 (f) applies (positive presumption).[107] This presumption can be rebutted if the claim itself recites sufficient structure, material, or acts to perform the claimed function. The failure to use the word "means" creates a presumption that Section 112 (f) does not apply (negative presumption).[108] This presumption can be rebutted by showing that the claim element recited a function without reciting a sufficient structure to perform that function.[109]

In deciding whether either presumption has been rebutted, the legal threshold is the same: whether the claim recites a sufficiently definite structure to avoid the ambiguty forbidden by § 112 (f).[110]

ii. Evidence

In order to decide whether the claim recites a sufficiently definite structure, Federal Circuit has looked into the claim language, or other intrinsic evidence, or extrinsic evidence.[111] If the claim language itself specifies the structure that performs the functions in question, the recited structure is sufficient to avoid applying Section 112

[104] Phillips, 415 F.3d, at 1311, citing see Watts v. XL Sys., Inc., 232 F.3d 877, 880–81 (Fed. Cir. 2000).

[105] See HARMON, supra Note 56,, 410.

[106] Bausch & Lomb Inc. v. Moria S.A., 222 F. Supp. 2d 616, 631 (E.D. Pa. 2002).

[107] See e.g. York Prods., Inc. v. Central Tractor, 99 F.3d 1568, 1574, 40 U.S.P.Q.2D (BNA) 1619, 1623 (Fed. Cir. 1996) HN4 ("In determining whether to apply the statutory procedures of [§ 112, P 6], the use [**23] of the word 'means' triggers a presumption that the inventor used this term advisedly to invoke the statutory mandates for means-plus-function clauses.").

[108] See Mas-Hamilton, 156 F.3d at 1213, 48 U.S.P.Q.2D (BNA) at 1016.

[109] See Rodime PLC v. Seagate Tech., Inc., 174 F.3d 1294, 1302, 50 U.S.P.Q.2D (BNA) 1429, 1434 (Fed. Cir. 1999) (explaining the converse rules for rebutting a presumption that § 112, paragraph 6 does apply).

[110] See Sage Prods. v. Devon Indus., Inc., 126 F.3d 1420, 1427–28, 44 U.S.P.Q.2D (BNA) 1103, 1109 (Fed. Cir. 1997) ("Where a claim recites a function, but then goes on to elaborate sufficient structure, material, or acts within the claim itself to perform entirely the recited function, the claim is not in means-plus-function format" even if the claim uses the term "means"). See also Personalized Media Communs., L.L.C. v. ITC, 161 F.3d 696, 704 (Fed. Cir. 1998) ("the focus remains on whether the claim... recites sufficiently definite structure"). See supra subsection iii standard for determining "sufficient".

[111] See supra chapter I section C evidence for definition of intrinsic and extrinsic evidence.

(f),[112] and the relevant precedent does not dispute this issue. But the case law holds different views where the structures disclosed in a specification also account for a "sufficient structure" evaluation. Judges can use intrinsic evidence and extrinsic evidence to decide if the disclosed structure is sufficient. But there is evidence suggesting that the focus has shifted to intrinsic evidence since the *Phillips en banc* decision in 2005.

Claim itself as one kind of the extrinsic evidence is most important. Some precedent emphasizes that a sufficient structure is found only when the claim language specifies a structure.[113] For example, in *Altiris* the court considered a limitation of the "means of booting".[114] The claim itself disclosed "means of booting" to include two sets of commands. The court found that two sets of commands did not make the structure sufficient enough to overcome the means-plus-function presumption, because it is necessary to look at the specification to understand the structure in the commands. Although the patent disclosed further structures in the specification, the court did not find those additional disclosures to be a "sufficient structure" evaluation, because those were not disclosed in the claim itself.[115] However, at least some federal judges believe that as long as the precedent does not explicitly exclude other intrinsic evidence or extrinsic evidence, a sufficient structure can be found in other evidence besides the claim language itself.[116]

With respect to using extrinsic evidence or intrinsic evidence, it is notable to evaluate the differences between two opinions both drafted by Judge Louie. One of the opinions was issued in 1998, prior to Phillips, and the other one in 2011, after *Phillips*. Although in both opinions, Judge Louie states that the findings are based on both extrinsic and intrinsic evidence, the focus of analysis differs. The 1998 case merely

[112] See. E.g. TriMed, Inc. v. Stryker Corp., 514 F.3d 1256, 1259–60 (Fed. Cir. 2008) (Judge Moore) Altiris, Inc. v. Symantec Corp., 318 F.3d 1363, 1375–76 (Fed. Cir. 2003) (citing several precedent). Envirco Corp. v. Clestra Cleanroom, Inc., 209 F.3d 1360, 1365, 54 USPQ2d 1449, 1452–53 (Fed.Cir.2000) Rodime PLC v. Seagate Tech., Inc., 174 F.3d 1294, 1303–04, 50 USPQ2d 1429, 1435–36 (Fed.Cir.1999) Cole v. Kimberly-Clark Corp., 102 F.3d 524, 531–32, 41 USPQ2d 1001, 1006–07 (Fed.Cir.1996).

[113] See. e.g., "Sufficient structure exists when the claim language specifies the exact structure that performs the functions in question without need to resort to other portions of the specification or extrinsic evidence for an adequate understanding of the structure." TriMed, Inc. v. Stryker Corp., 514 F.3d 1256, 1259–60 (Fed. Cir. 2008) (Judge Moore) In the cases where we have found sufficient structure in the claims, the claim language specifies a specific physical structure that performs the function. Altiris, Inc. v. Symantec Corp., 318 F.3d 1363, 1375–76 (Fed. Cir. 2003) (citing several precedent).

[114] Altiris, Inc. 318 F.3d, at 1368.

[115] Ibid., at 1375–77.

[116] "TriMed does not preclude consideration of the written description, prosecution history, and extrinsic evidence to determine if a challenger has rebutted the presumption that a claim limitation that lacks the term "means" connotes sufficiently definite structure to those of skill in the art. " Inventio AG v. ThyssenKrupp Elevator Americas Corp., 2010–1525, 2011 WL 2,342,744 (Fed. Cir. June 15, 2011). See, e.g., Cole v. Kimberly-Clark Corp., 102 F.3d 524, 531, 41 U.S.P.Q.2D (BNA) 1001, 1006 (Fed. Cir. 1996) (noting that whether § 112, P 6 is invoked involves an analysis of the "patent and the prosecution history," and consulting a dictionary definition of "perforation" to understand if one of skill in the art would understand this term to connote structure.

cites extrinsic evidence, without discussing how the extrinsic evidence supports its conclusion. The 2011 case cites claim language and provides a written analysis to support its conclusion, without citing any extrinsic evidence. This difference can be an example of the impact of *Phillips en banc* (2005) on the means-plus-function issue.

In the 1998 case, *Personalized Media Communication*, the opinion only cites extrinsic evidence dictionary to reach the conclusion that "detector" recites a sufficiently definite structural term.[117] Although admitting that a "detector" is defined in terms of its function and does not specifically evoke a particular structure, the Federal Circuit believed that this term does convey to one knowledgeable in the art a variety of structures known as "detectors".[118] The Federal Circuit referred to the Webster dictionary definition of detector: "(1) a device for determining the presence of a signal; (2) a rectifier of high-frequency current (as a cat whisker and crystal or a vacuum tube); (3) a device for extracting the intelligence from a signal; (4) DEMODULATOR 1".[119] Based on the structure mentioned in the dictionary definition, namely demodulator and rectifier, the Federal Circuit found that one skilled in the art should understand that "detector" implies a structure, including a rectifier or demodulator.[120] Although *Personalized Media Communication* mentioned extrinsic evidence as a basis to conclude that a detector is a sufficiently definite structure, the opinion does not state that any part of the claim, specification, or prosecution history provides such information of the structure.

In contrast, in *Inventio AG* (2011),[121] the analysis toward a finding of sufficient structure only cites intrinsic claim language and specification, without citing any extrinsic evidence. The conclusion of the term "computing unit" is a sufficient structure, according to the opinion, based on the fact that the claim language specifies how this computing unit is connected to the other parts of the device, and the specification specifies that the computing unit is a computer.[122]

iii. Standard to Overcome the Presumptions

In several cases, the Federal Circuit has ruled that the limitations to the term "baffle" provide sufficient structure to overcome the positive presumption of the means-plus-function limitation.[123] In *Enviro Corp.* (2000), baffles in a compact air purification apparatus was a disputed term.[124] The court found "sufficient structure" on two

---

[117] Personalized Media Communications, LLC v. Int'l Trade Comm'n, 161 F.3d 696, 705 (Fed. Cir. 1998).

[118] Ibid.

[119] Ibid.

[120] Ibid.

[121] Inventio AG v. ThyssenKrupp Elevator Americas Corp., 2011 WL 2,342,744 (Fed. Cir. June 15, 2011).

[122] Ibid.

[123] Envirco Corp. v. Clestra Cleanroom, Inc., 209 F.3d 1360, 1365, 54 USPQ2d 1449, 1452–53 (Fed.Cir.2000).

[124] Ibid., at 1362–63.

grounds: (1) according to the dictionary meaning, "baffle" itself is a physical structure[125]; and (2) the claim itself describes the structure of a baffle ("having inner surfaces for directing airflow … radially outward … and thereafter … between said first baffle means and said air filter means").[126]

In *Phillips en banc* (2005), the Federal Circuit again found "sufficient structure" for a limitation "the steel baffles".[127] The court mainly relied on the structural description provided in the claim and specification to conclude that "the steel baffles" refer to a particular physical apparatus.[128] The claim describes the baffles as "extending inwardly" from the steel shell walls, and the court therefore implied that baffles are structures. Furthermore, the information in the specification[129] proves that "the steel baffles" refer to a "particular internal wall structures and not simply a general description of any structure that perform a particular function".[130]

In *Williamson en banc* (2015), the Federal Circuit overcame the negative presumption and ruled that the "distributed learning control module" element of Williamson's patent claim should be interpreted as a means-plus-function element, despite the lack of the word "means" in the element.[131] This *en banc* case overruled the strict standard on finding means-plus-function element in absence of the word "means" in the element established in *Lighting*.[132] In *Lighting*, the Federal Circuit established a standard to the negative presumption flowing from the absence of the word "means" and held that "the presumption flowing from the absence of the term 'means' is a strong one that is not readily overcome".[133] Since *Williamson*, the negative presumption is not so "strong" anymore. Overcoming the negative presumption does not require any heightened evidentiary showing or "a showing that the limitation essentially is devoid of anything that can be construed as structure".[134]

b. Product-by-Process Claim

In *Abbott* 2009, the Federal Circuit took the product-by-process issue en banc and clarified that "process terms in product-by-process claims serve as limitations in

[125] "The dictionary definition of the word "baffle" is "a device (as a plate, wall or screen) to deflect, check, or regulate flow". Webster's Ninth New Collegiate Dictionary 124 (1990). Envirco Corp. v. Clestra Cleanroom, Inc., 209 F.3d 1360, 1362–63 (Fed. Cir. 2000).

[126] Envirco Corp., 209 F.3d at 1362–63.

[127] Phillips, 415 F.3d, at 1311.

[128] Ibid.

[129] '798 patent, col. 4, ll. 25–26 ("the load bearing baffles 16 are optionally used with longer panels"); id., col. 4, ll. 49–50 (opposing panels are "compressed between the flange 35 and the baffle 26").

[130] Phillips, 415 F.3d, at 1311.

[131] Williamson v. Citrix Online, LLC, 792 F.3d 1339 (Fed. Cir. June 16, 2015) (en banc).

[132] Lighting World, Inc. v. Birchwood Lighting, Inc., 382 F.3d 1354 (Fed.Cir.2004).

[133] Lighting World, Inc. v. Birchwood Lighting, Inc., 382 F.3d 1354, 1358 (Fed.Cir.2004).

[134] Williamson v. Citrix Online, LLC, 792 F.3d 1339, 1349 (Fed. Cir. 2015).

determining infringement".[135] This resolved the conflict in Federal Circuit precedents in 1991 and 1992.[136]

In *Scripps Clinic* (1991), a panel of Federal Circuit judges ruled that "The correct reading of product-by-process claims is that they are not limited to product prepared by the process set forth in the claims"[137] and thus determined that the process terms do not comprise a limitation of the patent scope. One year later, another Federal Circuit panel nevertheless ruled that "process terms in product-by-process claims serve as limitations in determining infringement" in *Atlantic Thermoplastics*.[138] The conflicting panel decisions created confusion among the district courts. Some district court decisions chose to follow *Scripps Clinic* because it was earlier,[139] while other district courts believed that *Atlantic Thermoplastics* was binding because it cited Supreme Court precedent.[140]

The subject matter of the disputed patent in *Abbott* is a crystalline cefdinir, which can be used in medicine. It's competitor sought a declaratory judgment of non-infringement against the exclusive licensee and the owner of the patent U.S. Patent No. 4,935,507 (the '507 patent).[141] The district court construed the claims[142] and ultimately granted-in-part Lupin's motion for summary judgment of non-infringement, as to both literal and equivalent infringements for Claims 2–5 and as to equivalent infringement for claim 1.[143]

The district court found that claims 2–5 were product-by-process claims,[144] and the process terms of Claims 2–5, indicated by the phrase "obtainable by", limit the claims to the specified processes and process steps.[145] The narrow interpretation of "obtainable by" was challenged on appeal.[146]

Abbott Laboratories, the exclusive licensee, argued on appeal that according to Federal Circuit precedent in 1991, *Scripps Clinic*, the scope of a patent should not be limited to the products manufactured by the process in claim 2–5. The en banc court rejected it based on a "simple logic": if the process elements are not limitations on

---

135 Abbott Laboratories v. Sandoz, Inc., 566 F.3d 1282, 1293 (Fed. Cir. 2009).

136 Ibid., at 1291.

137 Scripps Clinic & Research Foundation v. Genentech, Inc., 927 F.2d 1565, 1583 (Fed.Cir.1991).

138 Atl. Thermoplastics Co., Inc. v. Faytex Corp., 970 F.2d 834, 846 (Fed. Cir. 1992).

139 See e.g., Aventis Pharmaceuticals, Inc. v. Barr Laboratories, Inc., 335 Federal Supplement. 2d 558, 581 (D.N.J. 2004).

140 See e.g., Lupin Ltd. v. Abbott Laboratories, 491 F. Supp. 2d 563, 567 (E.D. Va. 2007).

141 Abbott Laboratories v. Sandoz, Inc., 566 F.3d 1282 (Fed. Cir. 2009).

142 Lupin Ltd. v. Abbott Laboratories, 484 F.Supp.2d 448 (E.D.Va.2007) (Lupin CC Order).

143 Ibid., at 563.

144 Ibid., at 459, 466.

145 Ibid., at 459, 466.

146 Abbott Laboratories, 566 F.3d, at 1287–88 (Fed. Cir. 2009).

the scope of a patent, the court would have no method to define a scope of product-by-process claim.[147] There is no reason to construe the process by product element differently from the other limitations.[148]

Some cases questioned whether the USPTO should permit product-by-process claims.[149] Now the Patent Office permits product-by-process type claims to define a patentable product. Based on the fact that some courts have construed infringement claims as covering only the product made by the particular process set forth in the claim,[150] *Abbott en banc* argued that process elements as limitation are consistent with USPTO policy.[151]

c. The Combination of Chemistry Compounds

A frequently litigated issue in claims involving a combination of chemistry compounds is whether the scope of a patent is limited to the recited components. Federal Circuit precedent has identified that the phrase "consisting of" is a term of art in patent law signifying restriction and exclusion, while, in contrast, the term "comprising" indicates an open-ended construction.[152] As the Federal Circuit explained in *Vehicular*, a drafter uses the phrase "consisting of" to mean "I claim what follows and nothing else" and "comprising" to mean "I claim at least what follows and potentially more".[153] MPEP (Manual of Patent Examination Procedure also provides that the phrase "consisting of" signifies restriction and exclusion of unrecited steps or components.[154]

However, the restriction implied by "consisting of" has exceptions. The closed "consisting of" language does not exclude impurities. Impurities are the components which are irrelevant to the invention and have little or no impact on the effect of the invention.

In *Conoco* (2006), patentee Conoco asserted claims directed to a process for making drag-reducing agents ("DRA") that are injected into oil and gas pipelines to reduce friction inherent in pumping operations.[155] Federal Circuit ruled that the unrecited components in the accused infringing product are impurities and thus fell within the patent scope.

Claim 1 in the disputed patent says "[...]a suspending material selected from the group consisting of water and water-alcohol mixtures[...]"[156] The alleged infringer, EEI contended that the district court erred by allowing the scope of claim 1 to cover

---

[147] Ibid., at 1294–95.

[148] Ibid.

[149] Ex parte Painter, 1891 C.D. 200, 200–01 (Comm'r Pat. 1891. Abbott Laboratories., 566 F.3d at 1293.

[150] In re Bridgeford, 53 C.C.P.A. 1182, 357 F.2d 679, 683 n. 5 (1966).

[151] Abbott Laboratories, 566 F.3d, at 1293–94 (Fed. Cir. 2009).

[152] Vehicular Technologies Corp. v. Titan Wheel Int'l, Inc., 212 F.3d 1377, 1382 (Fed. Cir. 2000).

[153] Ibid., at 1383.

[154] MPEP § 2111.03.

[155] Conoco, Inc. v. Energy & Envtl. Int'l, L.C., 460 F.3d 1349, 1353 (Fed. Cir. 2006).

[156] Ibid.

the suspension medium used in the process to include MIBK, a non-alcohol.[157] EEI lost the bench trial and appealed on the basis of claim construction.

The Federal Circuit reviewed the cases of interpretation regarding the transitional phrase "comprising", including the district court cases.[158] For example, in *Norian Corp.*, the District Court for the Northern District of California found that a product containing an unrecited element did not infringe U.S. Patent No. 6,002,065 ("the '065 patent"), because the claim used the transitional phrase "consisting of" and thus excluded the additional element from the protection of the patent.[159]

However, the restriction signified by "consisting of" is not absolute. "Consisting of" does not exclude additional components or steps that are unrelated to the invention.[160] Containing the unrelated components, such as impurities, cannot exclude the accused infringing product from the scope of patent protection. The Patent Board of Appeals has also interpreted "consisting of" to "close the claim to the inclusion of materials other than those recited", but "except for impurities ordinarily associated therewith".[161]

The methyl isobutyl ketone ("MIBK") in the accused infringing product is found to be an "impurity" based on substantive evidence, such as testimony from EEI experts and experts.[162] The Federal Circuit rejected EEI's argument that MIBK is not an impurity because it was purposely added to the alcohol to denature it, as the intentional addition of a component does not change its status as an "impurity".[163] But the Federal Circuit did give a hypothetical example which could make the unrecited components not impurities. If "MIBK had been added to adjust the stability of the suspending medium or prevent agglomeration of polymer", it may not have been an impurity.[164]

d. Dependent Claim

It is expressly provided by statute that a dependent claim should be interpreted as including all the limitations of the independent claim to which it refers: "A claim in dependent form shall be construed to incorporate by reference all the limitations of the claim to which it refer[s]".[165] The narrow interpretation of dependent claims is not a frequently litigated issue but sometimes arises when the dependent claim is not written in the typical format.

The accused infringer, Syngenta, argued that claim 4 of the disputed patent depended on claim 1 and therefore included all the steps of claim 1. Thus, claim

---

157 Ibid., at 1360.

158 Ibid.

159 Norian Corp. v. Stryker Corp., 363 F.3d 1321, 1331 (Fed. Cir.2004).

160 Conoco, Inc. v. Energy & Envtl. Int'l, L.C., 460 F.3d 1349, 1360 (Fed. Cir. 2006). See Norian Corp. v. Stryker Corp., 363 F.3d 1321, 1331–32 (Fed. Cir.2004).

161 Ex Parte Davis & Tuukkanen, 1949 WL 3555 (Feb. 15, 1949).

162 Conoco, Inc., 460 F.3d, 1361 (Fed. Cir. 2006).

163 Ibid., at 1360 (Fed. Cir. 2006).

164 Ibid., 1360–61 (Fed. Cir. 2006).

165 35 U.S.C § 112, 4 (2000).

4 can only be infringed upon by the unauthorized performance of all the steps of claims 1 and 4.[166] Claim 1 recites a three-step process for generating an original RO fertile transgenic plant containing DNA that provides herbicide resistance.[167] Claim 4 is "A process comprising obtaining progeny from a fertile transgenic plant obtained by the process of claim 1 which comprise said DNA".[168] The district court construed claim 4 as including the three steps in claim 1 and the process in claim 4, as the fourth step, and the Federal Circuit agreed.[169]

The Federal Circuit affirmed the finding of claim 4 as a dependent claim, regardless of the fact that it was not written in the usual format of a dependent claim. "A claim's status as dependent or independent depends on the substance of the claim in light of the language of § 112, 4, and not the form alone".[170] Claim 4 expressly recites the process of claim 1 and includes the additional step of obtaining progeny. Claim 4 thus incorporates the format specified by the statute for dependent claims. Contrary to Monsanto's argument, claim 4 clearly referenced another claim, rather than simply a starting material.[171] Syngenta would still have to perform the steps of the process of claim 1 to infringe the product-by-process claim and thus claim 4 would contain the process steps of claim 1 to be meaningful.[172] The Federal Circuit concluded that the language requires reading the limitation of claim 1 into the new claim.[173]

3.5 Expanding the Literal Claim Scope: Doctrine of Equivalents

The purpose of the doctrine of equivalents is to remedy the "language's inability to capture the essence of innovation".[174] There are limitations to applying the doctrine of equivalents. The sequence of the analysis begins with a discussion of whether or not the limitations apply. If the limitations do not apply, the court may proceed to discuss the factors necessary to establish whether there is an infringement under the doctrine of equivalents.

In *Claude Neon Lights, Inc. v. E. Machlett & Sons* (1929), Judge Learned Hand noted: "Each case is inevitably a matter of degree, as so often happens, and other decisions have little or no value. The usual ritual, which is so often repeated and

---

[166] Monsanto Co. v. Syngenta Seeds, Inc., 503 F.3d 1352, 1357 (Fed. Cir. 2007).

[167] Ibid.

[168] Ibid., at 1355.

[169] Monsanto, 431Federal Supplement2d at 485.

[170] Monsanto Co. 503 F.3d at 1357. See also Manual of Patent Examining Procedure (MPEP) § 608.01 (m), (n) (August 2006); *1358 37 C.F.R. § 1.75 (2007) (setting forth proper drafts for independent and dependent claims).

[171] Monsanto Co., 503 F.3d, at 1358 (Fed. Cir. 2007).

[172] Ibid.

[173] Ibid.

[174] Festo Corp. 535 U.S. at 731, 62 USPQ2d at 1711. (2002).

which has so little meaning, that the same result must follow by substantially the same means, does not help much in application; it is no more than a way of stating the problem".[175]

3.5.1 Underlying Policy

Nowadays, the major justification for the doctrine of equivalents is to protect patented inventions which are after-arising technology.[176] Before 1997, Supreme Court cases used to rule that the equivalents have to exist at the time of filing a patent application. In *Warner-Jenkinson* (1997), the Supreme Court changed the law by establishing that equivalency is to be assessed "at the time of infringement".[177]

After-arising technology refers to the technology arising after the time of filing a patent application and no later than the infringement time. If a technology is available at the time of filing and could be foreseen as a replacement by a person skilled in the art, the patentee has an obligation to cover the technology in the claim.[178] If at the time of infringement, the technology was still not a foreseeable replacement to the ordinarily skilled person, it is not an "insubstantial difference" and thus not an infringement.

a. Existing Equivalents

Equivalents known at the time of invention constitute an infringement under the doctrine of equivalents. An inventor is not required to list all substitutes known when drafting the patent. The purpose of the doctrine of equivalents is to remedy the "language's inability to capture the essence of innovation".[179] As the Supreme Court noted in *Festo* "the nature of language makes it impossible to capture the essence of a thing in a patent application" and that "[t]he language in the patent claims may not capture every nuance of the invention or describe with complete precision the range of its novelty".[180]

Before *Warner-Jenkinson v. Hilton Davis*, some of the early Supreme Court decisions, case law was not clear whether an equivalent must have been known to be an equivalent at a patentee's invention date.[181] The holding of Supreme Court in *Gould v. Rees and Gill v. Wells* was summarized by a district court as "there can be no

---

[175] Ibid., at 787.

[176] Siemens Med. Solutions USA, Inc. v. Saint-Gobain Ceramics & Plastics, Inc., 647 F.3d 1373 (Fed. Cir. 2011).

[177] 520 U.S. at 19, 41 USPQ2d at 1867.

[178] Johnson & Johnston Assocs. Inc. v. R.E. Serv. Co., Inc., 285 F.3d 1046 (Fed.Cir.2002) (en banc) (per curiam).

[179] Festo Corp. v. Shoketsu Kinzoku Kogyo Kabushiki Co., Ltd. (2002) 535 U.S. at 731, 62 USPQ2d at 1711.

[180] Ibid.

[181] 5B-18 Chisum on Patents § 18.04. However, there was a split of authority and some other Supreme Court cases determine the equivalents by infringement time. See ibid.

infringement if the fact of equivalence of the two devices was not known at the date of the patent".[182]

For example, *Gould v. Rees* (1872)[183] states that "where the defendant in constructing his machine omits entirely one of the ingredients of the plaintiff's combination without substituting any other, he does not infringe and if he substitutes another in the place of the one omitted, which is new or which performs a substantially different function, or if it is old, but was not known at the date of the plaintiff's invention as a proper substitute for the omitted ingredient, then he does not infringe".[184]

b. After-Arising Technology

In *Warner-Jenkinson* (1997), the Supreme Court clarified that equivalency is to be assessed "at the time of infringement", which extends the patent scope to after-arising technology.[185] Prior to 1997, there was an inconsistency between the Federal Circuit the and the old Supreme Court precedent which stated that there could be no infringement if the fact of equivalence of the two devices was not known at the date of the patent.[186] In contrast, several Federal Circuit cases stated that equivalence is determined at the time the alleged infringement occurs.[187] Federal Circuit precedent found that equivalents enabled by new technology developed after invention time and before infringement time can infringe.

In *Waner-Jenkinson v. Hilton Davis*, the Federal Circuit stated in dictum that "limiting the range of potentially infringing substitutions to those known at the time of the patent's issuance would undermine the doctrine, denying patent owners protection of the substance of their inventions against new forms of infringement".[188] The Supreme Court, overruled the precious decisions, although without citing the case names, affirmed this "time of infringement" approach "insofar as the question under the doctrine of equivalents is whether an accused element is equivalent to a claimed element, the proper time for evaluating equivalency—and thus knowledge of interchangeability between elements—is at the time of infringement, not at the time the patent was issued".[189]

---

[182] Micro Motion, Inc. v. Exac Corp., 741 F. Supp. 1426 (1990).

[183] Gould v. Rees, 82 U.S. 187, 21 L. Ed. 39 (U.S. 1872).

[184] 82 U.S. (15 Wall.) at 194.

[185] 520 U.S. at 19, 41 USPQ2d at 1867.

[186] Gould, 82 U.S. at 194, 15 Wall. at 21 L. Ed. 39 (1872); Gill v. Wells, 89 U.S. 1, 28–29, 22 Wall. 1, 22 L. Ed. 699 (1874).

[187] Atlas Powder Co. v. E.I. duPont de Nemours & Co., 750 F.2d 1569, 1581, 224 U.S.P.Q. (BNA) 409 (Fed. Cir. 1984); Texas Instruments, 805 F.2d at 1563; Hughes Aircraft Co. v. United States, 717 F.2d 1351, 1365, 219 U.S.P.Q. (BNA) 473 Fed. Cir. 1983).

[188] Hilton Davis Chem. Co. v. Warner-Jenkinson Co., Inc., 62 F.3d 1512, 1528 (Fed. Cir. 1995) supplemented, 64 F.3d 675 (Federal Circuit. 1995) and rev'd, 520 U.S. 17, 117 S. Ct. 1040, 137 L. Ed. 2d 146 (1997) and adhered to, 114 F.3d 1161 (Fed. Cir. 1997).

[189] Warner-Jenkinson Co., Inc. v. Hilton Davis Chem. Co., 520 U.S. 17, 37, 117 S. Ct. 1040, 1053, 137 L. Ed. 2d 146 (1997).

After *Warner-Jenkinson*, protecting invention from infringement by after-arising technology became an important purpose of the doctrine of equivalents.[190] Some Federal Circuit judges strongly supported this position and explained the importance of preventing infringement from after-arising technology by including an example in *Festo* opinion.[191] A claim of tube technology before 1948 used anode and cathode.[192] Transistor technology emerged in 1948. Before that, vacuum tubes were used for amplifying and switching electronic signals in radio, etc.[193] Vacuum tubes rely on thermionic emission of electrons from a cathode, that then travel through a vacuum toward the anode, which is held at a positive voltage relative to the cathode.[194] The transistor technology emerged in 1948, which composes semiconductor materials to amplify and switch signals and thus became an alternative to vacuum tubes.[195] One of the two kinds of transistors is a bipolar transistor, which has terminals labeled base, collector and emitter.[196] In the example cited from *Festo*, an invention before 1948 used tube technology and recited "anode" and "cathode" in the claim.[197] A competitor after 1948 may be able to appropriate the invention by replacing the tube technology by using a transistor, which comprised of collectors and emitters.[198] Without the doctrine of equivalents, a claim drafted in current technological terms could be easily circumvented by using new technology to replace one of the elements.[199]

c. Non-obvious After-Arising Technology

In *Waner*, the Supreme Court did not directly address the issue of whether the patentability of an after-arising device or method is relevant to equivalency.[200] In *Siemen* (2011),[201] three Federal Circuit judges challenged this theory of after-arising technology. Judge Prost raised an important question in panel dissent: what if an after-arising technology is patented? Can it constitute patent infringement under the doctrine of equivalents? The majority of the Federal Circuit judges believed that a patent does not grant permission to infringe others' patents and refused to discuss Judge Post's question en banc. However, the two of the Federal Circuit Judges, Judge DYK and Gajarsa, are on the side of Judge Post and believe that a patented after-arising technology cannot be found to constitute infringement under

---

[190] SIemens Med. Solutions USA, Inc. v. Saint-Gobain Ceramics & Plastics, Inc., 647 F.3d 1373 (Fed. Cir. 2011) (Rader,J concurring).

[191] Siemens Med. Solutions USA, Inc., 647 F.3d at 1373 (Fed. Cir. 2011) (Rader, J., concurring).

[192] Ibid.

[193] Ibid.

[194] Ibid.

[195] Ibid.

[196] Ibid.

[197] Ibid.

[198] Ibid.

[199] Ibid.

[200] Donald S. Chisum, Chisum on Patent 18.04.

[201] Siemens Med. Solutions USA, Inc., 647 F.3d.

the doctrine of equivalents.[202] Judge Dyk filed a dissenting opinion on the rejection of en banc hearing, and Judge Gajarsa and Post joined. In dissent, Judge DYK argued that a product cannot be both "insubstantially different" from a disputed patent and "non-obvious" while the disputed patent is a part of the prior art.[203]

Judge DYK's argument implies an assumption: the standard of being "non-obvious" in patentability is the same, or at least not lower than the standard of being "substantially different" in infringement.[204] Precedent has not addressed this issue. Assuming Judge DYK's assumption is consistent with the current law, there is one flaw in Judge DYK's analysis. The time of being "insubstantially different" is different from the time of being "non-obvious". The time of the non-obviousness assessment is at the patent filing date of the after-arising technology. The time of the insubstantially different assessments is the date of infringement. Thus, a new patent could be non-obvious to an old patent at the filing date and insubstantially different according to a person skilled in the art at the time of infringing the old patent. For example, an inventor (Inventor B) filed a patent application on his own invention (Patent B), and which may be found non-obvious to a prior patent (Patent A). After Patent B is issued, inventor B used the technology in making products. If the owner of patent A (Inventor A) sued inventor B for infringement, inventor B could be found infringing under the doctrine of equivalents: at the time of infringement, it is foreseeable not only to inventor B, but also to persons skilled in the art, that invention B is a replacement to invention A, because inventor B's patent had disclosed it.

Although Judge DYK's analysis is flawed under the current law, his conclusion could be still valid. In the example discussed above, it is inventor B's own patent disclosure that resulted in his failing the insubstantially different test and rendered the finding of infringement. In this case, wouldn't it be a better option for inventor B to just keep his invention as a trade secret and not file a patent application? Thus, Judge DYK, Post and Gajarsa are right on the point that the current doctrine of equivalents blocks new invention. It is true that their theory is not current law, but it should be a proposed rule change for the other judges on the Federal Circuit to consider as a matter of public policy.

3.5.2 Elements to Establish the Doctrine of Equivalents

The Supreme Court and the Federal Circuit have developed three approaches to determine equivalents: function way result test (thereafter FWR test), insubstantial differences test and the known interchangeability test. The Supreme Court and the Federal Circuit hold different views regarding to the relationship among the

[202] Ibid.

[203] Ibid.

[204] Toshiko Takenaka, Doctrine of Equivalents After Hilton Davis: A Comparative Law Analysis, 22 Rutgers Computer & Technology Law Journal 479, 495 (1996) (the test for Infringement under the Doctrine of Equivalents is parallel with non-obviousness test).

three approaches. The Supreme Court considered the FWR test and the insubstantial difference test are alternatives, and each of them has its own advantage and disadvantage.[205] In *Graver Tank*, The Supreme Court referred to interchangeability as a "factor" which may influence the decision on equivalence.[206] It is unclear whether the Supreme Court meant to distinguish the role of interchangeability from those of the FWR test and insubstantial difference test. The Federal Circuit viewed substantiality is the definition of equivalents and the essential inquiry.[207] Both FWR test and interchangeability test are measurements to evaluate the substantiality.[208]

As Supreme Court of the United States clarified in Warner case, the proper time for evaluating equivalency—and thus knowledge of interchangeability between elements—is at the time of infringement, not at the time the patent was filed or issued.[209] As a result, the knowledge level of PHOSITA in claim interpretation is different from it is in the evaluation of equivalents.

a. Function Way Result Test

The U.S. court's most frequently used test for determining infringement under the doctrine of equivalents is the "function way result test": "if it performs substantially the same function in substantially the same way to obtain the same result", infringement will be found.[210] This test is referred to as the function/way/result (FWR) test, or triple identity test. In *Warner-Jenkinson*, both the Supreme Court and Federal Circuit agreed that thc FWR is not the exclusive test, but the Supreme Court did not provide any additional instructions concerning alternative tests for the doctrine of equivalents.[211]

The Federal Circuit in *Warner-Jenkinson* emphasized that the "substantiality of the differences" between the claimed and accused products or processes is the ultimate question.[212] In the 1950 landmark case *Graver Tank*, the Supreme Court did not use the term "substantial". Instead, it defined the issue as "the question which thus emerges is whether the substitution of the manganese which is not an alkaline earth metal for the magnesium which is".[213] In *Warner-Jenkinson*, the Federal Circuit citied

205 "While the triple identity test may be suitable for analyzing mechanical devices, it often provides a poor framework for analyzing other products or processes. On the other hand, the insubstantial differences test offers little additional guidance as to what might render any given difference "insubstantial." Warner-Jenkinson Co., Inc. 520 U.S. at 39–40, 117 S. Ct.at 1054, 137 L. Ed. 2d 146.

206 "An important factor is whether persons reasonably skilled in the art would have known of the interchangeability of an ingredient not contained in the patent with one that was." Graver Tank & Mfg. Co. v. Linde Air Products Co., 339 U.S. 605, 609, 70 S. Ct. 854, 857, 94 L. Ed. 1097 (1950).

207 The Court defined the doctrine of equivalents in terms of the substantiality of the differences between the claimed and accused products or processes. Hilton Davis Chem. Co.., 62 F.3d, at 1517.

208 Ibid., at 1518 (Fed. Cir. 1995). Interactive Pictures Corp. v. Infinite Pictures, Inc., 274 F.3d 1371 (Fed. Cir. 2001).

209 Warner-Jenkinson Co. v. Hilton Davis Chem. Co., 520 U.S. 17, 37 (1997).

210 Sanitary Refrringerator Co. v. Winters 280 US 30, 42 (1929).

211 Warner-Jenkinson, 520 U.S. 17 40 1997.

212 Hilton, 62 F.3d 1512.

213 Graver Tank, 339 U.S. at 610. 339 U.S. 605 (1950).

Graver Tank and summarized this definition as "the substantiality of the differences" test,[214] and explored various tests to evaluate it. The "substantiality of the differences" test is assessed according to an objective standard.[215] The most frequently used standard is the FWR test.

b. Insubstantial Difference Test

Neither the Supreme Court nor the Federal Circuit considered FWR as the exclusive test for the doctrine of equivalents.[216] The Federal Circuit cited the Supreme Court in *Graver Tank*, finding that the FWR test arose in an era characterized by relatively simple mechanical technology.[217] And when *Warner-Jenkinson* was appealed to Supreme Court, the Supreme Court also pointed out that the FWR test may not work well with technology other than mechanical devices.[218] In *Warner-Jenkinson*, both the Federal Circuit and the Supreme Court suggested that the FWR test may not be sufficient in some circumstances.[219] However, neither the Federal Circuit courts nor the Supreme Court offered an example to show when the FWR test would be insufficient.

The Federal Circuit's analysis in *Warner-Jenkinson* actually explained why it is difficult to have an example of the deficiency of the FWR test: "examination of function, way, and result often discloses the substantiality of the differences between the accused and claimed products or processes"[220] and "the similarity of function, way, and result leaves little room for doubt that only insubstantial differences distinguish the accused product or process from the claims".[221] If there is no case that shows when the FWR test is insufficient, is it appropriate to conclude that this test has not become out of date, even though the technology has become much more complex?

When *Warner-Jenkinson* was appealed to the Supreme Court, the Supreme Court's framework on the doctrine of equivalents test was different from the Federal Circuit. The Supreme Court did not observe the FWR test as a way to access "insubstantial differences". Instead, it views "insubstantial differences" as an alternative test to the "FWR test".[222]

Regardless of the discussion on the "linguistic framework", the Supreme Court concluded the essential inquiry: "does the accused product or process contain

[214] Hilton, 62 F.3d.

[215] Ibid.

[216] "It goes too far, however, to describe the function-way-result test as 'the' test for equivalency announced by Graver Tank." Hilton, 62 F.3d., at 1518.

[217] Hilton, 62 F.3d 1512, citing Graver Tank, 339 U.S. at 609.

[218] Warner-Jenkinson, 520 U.S., at 39–40.

[219] Hilton, 62 F.3d; Warner-Jenkinson Co., Inc., 520 U.S.

[220] Hilton, 62 F.3d, at 1518.

[221] Ibid.

[222] "While the triple identity test may be suitable for analyzing mechanical devices, it often provides a poor framework for analyzing other products or processes. On the other hand, the insubstantial differences test offers little additional guidance as to what might render any given difference 'insubstantial'." Warner-Jenkinson Co., Inc. 520 U.S., at 39–40.

elements identical or equivalent to each claimed element of the patented invention?"[223] It is less important which linguistic framework is used that if the framework is probative to this essential inquiry.[224] Nobody could dispute that "determination of an equivalent" is the essential question. However, as the Federal Circuit judges and the attorneys in *Warner-Jenkinson* debated, it is a question that how the determination should be made. The Supreme Court did not offer guidance on this question. Besides rejecting considering the factors including "evidence to copy or design around" and "evidence of independent experiment", the Supreme Court did not provide any further guidance for the test. Instead, the Supreme Court expected that the Federal Circuit will refine the formulation of the test for equivalence in the orderly course of case-by-case determination.[225]

So far, the FWR test remains the main test in the doctrine of equivalents. The substantiality is a critical component for the function, way and result evaluation. The substantiality is a highly abstract standard, which leaves space for judges' discretion and policy considerations.

c. Known Interchangeability Test

Supreme Court and Federal Circuit precedents inconsistently referred interchangeability as a "test", a "factor" or "evidence". While the Supreme Court referred to the FWR test and the insubstantial difference test as tests,[226] it refers to interchangeability as a factor which may influence the decision on equivalence in Graver Tank.[227] The Federal Circuit has stated that known interchangeability is evidence that one of ordinary skill in the relevant art would have considered the change insubstantial and has also referred to the known interchangeability as a "test".[228]

In *Graver Tank*, the Supreme Court held that "an important factor is whether persons reasonably skilled in the art would have known of the interchangeability of an ingredient not contained in the patent with one that was".[229]

The Federal Circuit has also stressed "the importance of evidence of known interchangeability".[230] For example, in *Waner*, the Federal Circuit held that "the known interchangeability of the accused and claimed elements is potent evidence that one of ordinary skill in the relevant art would have considered the change insubstantial. Without such evidence, the patentee will need other objective technological evidence

---

[223] Warner-Jenkinson Co., Inc.520 U.S., at 19.

[224] Ibid.

[225] Warner-Jenkinson Co., Inc. 520 U.S. 17, at 40.

[226] Ibid., at 39–40.

[227] Graver Tank, 339 U.S., at 609.

[228] Interactive Pictures Corp. v. Infinite Pictures, Inc., 274 F.3d 1371 (Fed. Cir. 2001).

[229] Graver Tank, 339 U.S., at 609.

[230] Hilton Davis Chem. Co. v. Warner-Jenkinson Co., Inc., 62 F.3d 1512, 1519 (Fed. Cir. 1995) supplemented, 64 F.3d 675 (Fed. Cir. 1995) and rev'd, 520 U.S. 17, 117 S. Ct. 1040, 137 L. Ed. 2d 146 (1997) and adhered to, 114 F.3d 1161 (Fed. Cir. 1997). See also Corning Glass Works v. Sumitomo Elec. U.S.A., Inc., 868 F.2d 1251, 1261, 9 USPQ2d 1962, 1969 (Fed.Cir.1989); Thomas & Betts Corp. v. Litton Sys., Inc., 720 F.2d 1572, 1579, 220 USPQ 1, 6 (Fed.Cir.1983), Interactive Pictures Corp. v. Infinite Pictures, Inc., 274 F.3d 1371 (Fed. Cir. 2001).

demonstrating that the substitute nevertheless represents a change that the ordinary artisan would have considered insubstantial at the time of infringement".[231]

In *Interactive Pictures Corp. v. Infinite Pictures, Inc.* (2001),[232] the Federal Circuit stated that interchangeability is a test: "[r]ather than focusing on physical or electronic compatibility, the known interchangeability test looks to the knowledge of a skilled artisan to see whether that artisan would contemplate the interchange as a design choice".[233]

The patent at issue concerned a computer system for correcting the distortion in a hemispherical image captured by a camera. The accused infringer argued that the claimed and accused image data forms are not compatible and, therefore, do not meet the "known interchangeability" test of the doctrine of equivalents. The court rejected this argument and held that "[W]e have upheld determinations of equivalence on the ground that hardware and software implementations of a component of an invention are interchangeable substitutes, even though such a substitution would require ancillary changes in affected circuitry and packaging".[234]

3.5.3 Limitation to the Doctrine of Equivalents

a. Dedication to the Public

Patentee cannot assert the doctrine of equivalents to cover a disclosed but unclaimed subject matter.[235] In *Maxwell v. J. Baker, Inc.* (1996), the Federal Circuit stated that "subject matter disclosed in the specification, but not claimed, is dedicated to the public".[236] *Maxwell* reiterated that a disclosed but unclaimed subject matter cannot be found to be a literal infringement as well as infringement under the doctrine of equivalents.[237] After two years, a panel of Federal Circuit judges ruled in *YBM Magnex* that the disclosure of an unclaimed subject matter does not necessarily prevent a finding of infringement.[238]

---

[231] Hilton Davis Chem. Co. v. Warner-Jenkinson Co., Inc., 62 F.3d 1512, 1519 (Fed. Cir. 1995) supplemented, 64 F.3d 675 (Fed. Cir. 1995) and rev'd, 520 U.S. 17, 117 S. Ct. 1040, 137 L. Ed. 2d 146 (1997) and adhered to, 114 F.3d 1161 (Fed. Cir. 1997).

[232] Interactive Pictures Corp. v. Infinite Pictures, Inc., 274 F.3d 1371 (Fed. Cir. 2001).

[233] Interactive Pictures Corp., 274 F.3d at 1371.

[234] Overhead Door Corp. v. Chamberlain Group, Inc., 194 F.3d 1261, 1269–70, 52 USPQ2d 1321, 1326 (Fed. Cir. 1999).

[235] See e.g., Johnson & Johnston Associates Inc. v. R.E. Serv. Co., Inc., 285 F.3d 1046, 1055 (Fed. Cir. 2002).

[236] Maxwell v. J. Baker, Inc., 86 F.3d 1098, 39 USPQ2d 1001 (Fed. Cir. 1996), cert. denied, 520 U.S. 1115 (1997). 86 F.3d at 1107, 39 USPQ2d at 1006.

[237] Maxwell v. J. Baker, Inc., 86 F.3d 1098, 1106–07 (Fed. Cir. 1996).

[238] YBM Magnex, Inc. v. Int'l Trade Comm'n, 145 F.3d 1317, 1320 (Fed. Cir. 1998) overruled by Johnson & Johnston Associates Inc. v. R.E. Serv. Co., Inc., 285 F.3d 1046 (Fed. Cir. 2002).

YBM Magnex was then overruled by *en banc* decision in *Johnson & Johnston Associates Inc. v. R.E. Service Co., Inc.* (2002).[239] The *en banc* decision confirmed the holding in *Maxwell* that "when a patent drafter discloses but declines to claim subject matter [...] this action dedicates that unclaimed subject matter to the public".[240]

The disputed patent '050 in *Johnson* relates to the manufacture of printed circuit boards. Printed circuit boards are composed of extremely thin sheets of conductive copper foil joined to sheets of a dielectric (nonconductive).[241] The patent claims specifically limit the dielectric sheets to "a sheet of aluminum" and "the aluminum sheet".[242] However, the specification states that "While aluminum is currently the preferred material for the substrate, other metals, such as stainless steel or nickel alloys may be used".[243] The Federal Circuit ruled that Johnson could not invoke the doctrine of equivalents to extend its aluminum limitations to encompass steel, because the patent was disclosed without claiming the steel substrates.[244]

The *en banc* court cited a series of precedents to emphasize that "application of the doctrine of equivalents to recapture subject matter deliberately left unclaimed" would conflict with the fundamental principle that claims define the limits of patents.[245] Another reason the *en banc* court gave to support its ruling is that a patentee should not be permitted to "narrowly claim an invention to avoid prosecution scrutiny by the USPTO, and then, after patent issuance, use the doctrine of equivalents to establish infringement because the specification discloses equivalents".[246]

In response to the concern that the rule of dedication to public will weaken the protection of patentee's interest, the *en banc* court particularly pointed out that patentee has two options to save the unclaimed subject matter: reissuance and continuation.[247] In *Johnson,* the patentee had filed two continuation applications which claimed the disputed subject matter.[248] Thus, dedication to the public rule does not reduce the incentive to promote innovation while it does preserve the legal certainty of claim scope.

b. Limitation on DOE: Prosecution History Estoppel

Prosecution history estoppel is the most important limitation to the doctrine of equivalents.[249] In short, prosecution history estoppel means that a patentee is estopped

---

239 Johnson & Johnston Associates Inc., 285 F.3d 1046, 62 USPQ2d 1046 (Fed. Cir. 2002) (en banc).

240 Ibid.

241 Ibid., at 1048 (Fed. Cir. 2002).

242 Ibid., at 1055 (Fed. Cir. 2002).

243 Ibid., at 1055 (Fed. Cir. 2002).

244 Johnson & Johnston Associates Inc., 285 F.3d at 1055.

245 Ibid., at 1054.

246 Ibid.

247 Ibid., at 1055.

248 Ibid.

249 Toshiko Takenaka, The Doctrine of Equivalents in Japan, 6 CASRIP Symposium Publication 125,129 (2001).

from recapturing the claim scope in an infringement suit if the patentee surrendered the claim scope by narrowing the claim through an amendment during prosecution.[250] The rules, which set conditions giving rise to estoppel and define the scope of surrender, comprise presumptions and exceptions and are not always explicit enough in practice.[251]

Any amendment which narrows a patent claim, regardless of the reason, would trigger estoppel. The Supreme Court in *Warner-Jenkinson Co. v. Hilton Davis Chem, Co.* established that if the patent owner narrowed a claim during prosecution without explaining the reason, a court should presume that the USPTO had a substantial reason related to patentability for making the amendment and thus estoppel is established.[252] The presumption can be rebutted only if the patent owner can provide evidence that the amendment was made for a non-patentability reason, which is extremely difficult.

With respect to the scope of surrender, the Supreme Court adopted a rebuttable presumption instead of the pervious Federal Circuit rule of a complete bar.[253] The equivalent, which is in the original claim scope but not in the narrowed claim scope, is presumed to be surrendered, unless the patent owner can overcome the presumption by proving the patentee could not reasonably be expected to have described the insubstantial substitute in question.[254] The examples listed by the Federal Circuit are "the equivalents may have been unforeseeable at the time of the amendment"[255] and "the rationale underlying the amendment may bear no more than a tangential relation to the equivalent question".[256]

c. Limitation on DOE: Prior Art (Hypothetical Claim Analysis)

U.S. courts have also developed a doctrine to limit the doctrine of equivalents in the context of the prior art. If an accused device is merely practicing the prior art and the technology used in the device has already been in the public domain, it cannot be found to be an infringement.[257] In order to determine whether the prior art operates as a limitation to the doctrine of equivalents, a hypothetical claim analysis

---

[250] Festo Corp., 535 U.S. at 723, 122 S. Ct. at 1833, 152 L. Ed. 2d 944.

[251] Takenka, supra note 249, 2001.

[252] 520 U.S. 17 (1997).

[253] Festo Corp. v. Shoketsu Kinzoku Kogyo Kabushiki Co., Ltd., 234 F.3d 558 (Fed. Cir. 2000) vacated, 122 S. Ct. 1831, 2d 944 (2002). Festo Corp., 535 U.S. at 722 (Fed. Cir. 2011).

[254] Festo Corp., 535 U.S. at 725 (Fed. Cir. 2011).

[255] Ibid.

[256] Ibid.

[257] Wilson, 904 F.2d. 677, 683.

is adopted.[258] To begin the analysis, the properly interpreted claim is expanded to the extent necessary for the literal scope of the claim to cover the accused device. Then the court will compare the hypothetically expanded claim to the prior art. If the hypothetically expanded claim cannot meet the novelty and non-obviousness requirement, the court will find non-infringement.[259]

---

[258] See e.g., Abbott, 287 F.3d 1097.

[259] 35 U.S.C. 102 103.

Chapter 4
Chinese Claim Interpretation: Substantive Law

Patent protection in China includes both the literal scope of patent claims and the expanded scope under the doctrine of equivalents.[1] In order to establish infringement, every technical feature in the patent claim must be found in the accused infringing product or process.[2] If the accused infringing product or process has all of the technical features in the patent claim, it is a literal infringement.[3] If at least one of the technical features is different, it could be non-infringement or infringement under the doctrine of equivalents.[4]

The basic framework of claim interpretation rules in China is similar to that in United States. The language in Chinese judicial opinions and judicial interpretations also demonstrate the similarity of claim interpretation rules between the United States and China. Despite the similarity in the overall framework, differences remain in some detailed rules, e.g., the conditions and consequences to apply a legal doctrine.

It is difficult to conclude that the scope of a claim is broader or narrower in China compared to that in United States, particularly because of the inconsistency of claim interpretation in the both countries. There are cases that exemplify both broad and narrow interpretation in China, especially in finding equivalents. For example, in litigation on the same invention involving a bicycle, one appellate court in China

[1] Zhuanli Fa (专利法) [Patent Law], (promulgated by the Standing Comm. Nat'l People's Cong., Mar.12, 1984, effective Apr. 1, 1985)1984 Standing Comm. Nat'l People's Cong. Gaz. (China). English version is available in lawinfochina.

[2] Guanyu Shenli Qinfan Zhuanliquan Jiufen Anjian Yingyong Falü Ruogan Wenti de Jieshi (关于审理侵犯专利权纠纷案件应用法律若干问题的解释) [Explanations of Issues regarding to Application of Law on Patent Infringement Trial] (Promulgated by Sup. People's Ct., Dec. 29, 2009, effective Jan.1, 2010), (Chinalawinfo) (China).

[3] Zhuanli Fa (专利法) [Patent Law], (promulgated by the Standing Comm. Nat'l People's Cong., Mar.12, 1984, effective Apr. 1, 1985)1984 Standing Comm. Nat'l People's Cong. Gaz. (China). English version is available in lawinfochina.

[4] Ibid.

© Intellectual Property Publishing House 2025

Z. Peng, *Comparative Study on Patent Claim Interpretation: The United States and China*, https://doi.org/10.1007/978-981-96-0836-2_4

found that one hole can be an equivalent to "a circle of holes", but another appellate court found one hole is not an equivalent to "a circle of holes".[5]

The Supreme People's Court (SPC) has noticed the inconsistency in patent litigation and the unclear guidance of claim interpretation.[6] The SPC believes that inconsistency hurts the public interest.[7] The SPC is particularly concerned that the lack of legal certainty also impacts judicial credibility.[8] In China, a proposal by the China National Intellectual Property Administration and practitioners to establish a specialized patent court, demonstrates widespread distrust of the current courts' capability to adjudicate patent cases.[9] The SPC is concerned about the criticism and deems the inconsistency in claim interpretation as one of the causes of this criticism.[10]

---

[5] Shanghai cases Yuanda v. Changzhou Heli (元大金属实业 (深圳) 有限公司与常州合力电器有限公司), Shanghai Hig. People's Ct., Feb.25, 2003.Yuanda v. Jiangsu Chunlan (元大金属实业 (深圳) 有限公司与江苏春兰进出口有限公司) Shanghai Hig. People's Ct., Feb.25, 2003. (Yuanda v. Ningbo Jixian)元大金属实业 (深圳) 有限公司与宁波市鄞县对外贸易有限责任公司)Shanghai Hig. People's Ct., Feb.25, 2003. Yuanda v. Shanghai Dongsong (元大金属实业 (深圳) 有限公司与上海东松国际贸易有限公司), Shanghai Hig. People's Ct., Feb.25, 2003. Yuanda v. Shanghai Wanju (元大金属实业 (深圳) 有限公司与上海玩具进出口有限公司). Shanghai Hig. People's Ct., Feb.25, 2003. Yuanda v. Shaoxing Jingmao (元大金属实业 (深圳) 有限公司与绍兴市瑞信经贸有限公司) Shanghai Hig. People's Ct., Feb.25, 2003. Yuanda v. Zhejiang Yongkang (元大金属实业 (深圳) 有限公司与浙江省永康市对外经济贸易公司), Shanghai Hig. People's Ct., Feb.25, 2003. (hearafter Yuanda (Shanghai))。

[6] Jianmin Cao (曹建民), Vice director, Supreme People's Court, Zai Quanguo Fayuan Zhishi Chanquan Shenpan Gongzuo Huiyi Shang de Jianghua (在全国法院知识产权审判工作会议上的讲话) [The Speech at National Intellectual Property Trial Conference] (2003), *in* Zhishi Chanquan Nianjian (CNIPA ed., 2004).

[7] E.g. see Cheng Yongshun (程永顺), Beijing High Court Judge's books Cheng Yongshun, China Patent Litigation (中国专利诉讼) [Cheng Yongshun, Chinese Patent Litigation] (Zhishi Chanquan Chubanshe.2005), Cheng Yongshun (程永顺) & Luo Lihua (罗李华), Zhuanli Qinquan Panding: Zhongmei Fatiao yu Anli Bijiao Yanjiu (专利侵权判定:中美法条与案例比较研究) [Cheng Yongshun, Luo Lihua, Deciding Patent Infringement: Comparative Study on Chinese and U.S. Law and Cases] (Zhishi Chanquan Chubanshe, 2002). See also Zhang Xiaodu (张晓都), Shanghai High Court judge's books Zhang Xiaodu, Zhuanli Qinquan Panding: Lilun Tantao Yu Shenpan Shijian (专利侵权判定:理论探讨与审判实践) [Deciding Patent Infringement: Theoretical Discussion and Practice in Trial] (2008). See also Shandong High Court Judges' books Yan Wenjun (闫文军), Zhuanliquan de Baohu Fanwei: Quanli Yaoqiu Jieshi he Dengtong Yuanze Shiyong (专利权的保护范围:权利要求解释和等同原则适用) [Yan Wenjun, Scope of Patent Protection: Interpretation of Claim and Application of Doctrine of Equivalents] (Falü Chubanshe 2007).

[8] Jianmin Cao (曹建民), Vice director, Supreme People's Court, Zai Quanguo Fayuan Zhishi Chanquan Shenpan Gongzuo Huiyi Shang de Jianghua (在全国法院知识产权审判工作会议上的讲话) [The Speech at National Intellectual Property Trial Conference] (2003), *in* Zhishi Chanquan Nianjian (CNIPA ed., 2004).

[9] See a collection of articles in STATE INTELLECTUAL PROPERTY OFFICE STATUTE SECTION, Research Report on The Third Amendment to The Patent Law and The Implementing Rule (Intellectual Property Press 2006).国家知识产权局条法司, 专利法及专利法实施细则第三次修改专题研究报告 (知识产权出版社, 2006).

[10] Jianmin Cao (曹建民), Vice director, Supreme People's Court, Zai Quanguo Fayuan Zhishi Chanquan Shenpan Gongzuo Huiyi Shang de Jianghua (在全国法院知识产权审判工作会议上的讲话) [The Speech at National Intellectual Property Trial Conference] (2003), *in* Zhishi Chanquan Nianjian (CNIPA ed., 2004).

4.1 Sources of Law

There are various sources of law, which provide the rules for claim interpretation. The SPC specified the kinds of resources which judges can cite in judicial opinions.[11] Those sources are officially provided by the Legislation Law[12] of China as the source of law. However, besides the official sources of law, there are other documents issued by courts that have a substantial impact on trials. This study refers to them as unofficial sources of law.

The official sources of law include statute, regulations, and Judicial Interpretations (including Interpretation and Response). As a statute, the patent law was promulgated by the People's Congress in 1984 and has been revised twice. The current effective version is the Patent Law (2020). To provide further instruction, a regulation named the Detailed Rule on Implementation of Patent Law (hereafter Detailed Rule 2001 and Detailed Rule 2010) was issued by the State Council in 2001 and 2010.[13] Both the statute and regulations were drafted by the China National Intellectual Property Administration (previously the State Intellectual Property Office). In addition, the Supreme People's Court issued three Judicial Interpretations in 2001, 2009 and 2016, which provide guidance on claim interpretation and doctrine of equivalents, named Rules on Patent Infringement (hereafter 2001 Judicial Interpretation, 2009 Judicial Interpretation, and 2016 Judicial Interpretation). Besides offering a systematic interpretation, the SPC also uses the Response as an opportunity to answer the specific questions submitted by the lower courts.

In addition to the official sources of law, the SPC also provides further instructions in other ways. For example, the SPC may further explain its Judicial Interpretation in either a document or an interview with the media right after issuing its Judicial Interpretation (hereafter Official Explanation).[14] Another way of providing further instruction is through judicial opinions. Both the SPC and appellate court's judicial opinions would impact a trial in a lower court, although they cannot be cited. Appellate courts sometimes also issue their own regulations to guide the trials within their

---

[11] Super People's Court, The Rules on Citing Normative Documents (关于裁判文书引用法律、法规等规范性法律文件的规定) (2009).

[12] Lifa Fa (立法法) [Law on Legislation] (promulgated by the Standing Comm. Nat'l People's Cong., Mar. 15, 2000, effective July 1, 2000) 2000 Standing Comm. Nat'l People's Cong. Gaz. (China).

[13] An amendment to the Detailed Rule 2010 drafted by the China National Intellectual Property Administration was proposed, but has not been officially approved yet.

[14] E.g., Zuigao Renmin Fayuan Zhishi Chanquanting Fuzeren Jiu ⟨Guanyu Shenli Qinfan Zhuanliquan Jiufen Anjian Yingyong Falü Ruogan Wenti de Jieshi⟩ Da Jizhe Wen (最高人民法院知识产权庭负责人就《关于审理侵犯专利权纠纷案件应用法律若干问题的解释》答记者问) [Public Interview with the Chief of the Intellectual Property Tribunal of Sup. People's Ct. Explanations of Issues regarding to Application of Law on Patent Infringement Trial, with Respect to ⟨Explanations of Issues regarding to Application of Law on Patent Infringement Trial⟩], Chinacourt (Sep.18, 2010, 19: 40 pm); http://rmfyb.chinacourt.org/public/detail.php?id=134762.

jurisdictions.[15] In the past, the academic studies of the law mainly focused on the official sources of law. In recent years, the recognition of the unofficial sources of law, especially in intellectual property law and administrative law, has increased.

The following section describes the types of rules Chinese judges establish through judicial interpretations and judicial decisions. This discussion mainly focuses on the SPC, which is the highest judicial institution in China, and the High People's Court (HPC). The judicial laws enacted by the HPCs have a significant impact within their jurisdictions. Most patent cases are litigated in selected intermediate courts in the first instance and high court in the second instance. Only a small number of cases reach the Supreme Court.[16]

Implementation of both official and unofficial sources of law in courts is an issue that merits attention. The Chinese court system, as a part of the bureaucratic system,[17] shares two defining characteristics of the Chinese bureaucracy: hierarchy[18] and variety.[19] Because of the hierarchical nature of the system, any documents issued by a higher court impact the practice of the lower court. Because of the variety of the legal practice across geographically scattered jurisdictions, one must always question how and to what extent the law is implemented in the various courts.

4.1.1 Statute

Chinese Patent Law provides in Article 59, Paragraph 1 that "the extent of protection of the patent right for invention or utility model shall be determined by the terms of the claims".[20] It further provides that "the description and the appended drawings

[15] E.g Zhuanli Qinquan Panding Ruogan Wenti de Yijian (专利侵权判定若干问题的意见) [The opinion on several issues of deciding patent infringement] (Promulgated by Beijing Hig. People's Ct., 2001), (Chinalawinfo) (China).

[16] Zhipei Jiang (蒋志培), *Patent Litigation in China*, 9 Federal Circuit Bar Journal 479, 482 (1999–2000).

[17] Kandishka Jayasuriya, *Corporatism and Judicial Independence within Statist Legal Institutions in East Asia, in* Law, Capitalism and Power in East Asia: The Rule of Law and Legal Institutions 195 (Kandishka Jayasuriya ed. 1999). See also BING LIANG, THE CHANGING CHINESE LEGAL SYSTEM, 1978-PRESENT: CENTRALIZATION OF POWER AND RATIONALIZATION OF THE LEGAL SYSTEM 45 (Routledg. 2008). See also Susan Trevaskes, *Courts on the Campaign Path in China: Criminal Court Work in the "Yanda 2001" Anti-Crime Campaign*, 42 Asian Survey 673,674 (2002).

[18] Ronald S. Fernando, *Understanding Judicial Patent Enforcement in China*, 2 China Patents and Trademarks 24 (2008).

[19] See Sida Liu, *Beyond Global* Convergence: Conflicts of Legitimacy in a Chinese Lower Court, 31 Law and Social Inquiry 75 (2006). Fernado, *Supra* note 18, at 29.

[20] Article 59 of Patent Law provided "The scope of protection of the patent right for an invention or utility model shall be determined by the terms of the claims." Zhuanli Fa (专利法) [Patent Law], art. 59 (promulgated by the Standing Comm. Nat'l People's Cong., Mar.12, 1984, effective Apr. 1, 1985)1984 Standing Comm. Nat'l People's Cong. Gaz. (China). English version is available in lawinfochina.

may be used to interpret the claims".[21] In U.S. law, the rules are the same but are established by case law rather than by statute.

4.1.2 The "Judge-Made Statute": Judicial Interpretation

Judges developed the law of claim interpretation in two formats: (1) Judicial Interpretations, which is promulgated in a format which is similar to statutes but are rather created by courts, and (2) Judicial Opinions, which are written by judges to explain their decision in a particular case.

This study refers to judicial interpretation as a "judge made statute," because it is in a format similar to a statute. Some scholars have observed that judicial interpretations are "abstract".[22] Unlike judicial opinions, judicial interpretations are not based on the factual pattern of one single case. Instead, they consist of a rule, or a set of rules, which apply to all cases, and aim to provide guidance to all cases of claim interpretation in general.

To illustrate the format of Chinese judicial interpretations, two provisions of the Supreme People's Court Judicial Interpretation 2009 are translated and quoted below:

> Article 2: The people's court shall determine the content of a claim as provided for in paragraph 1 of Article 59 of the Patent Law according to the description of the claim and in consideration of the understanding of the claim by regular technicians in the same field after reading the specification and drawings.[23]
>
> Article 3: The people's court may interpret a claim based on the description and drawings, relevant claim in the claims, and patent review files. If the description defines any particular wording of a claim, such particular definition shall apply. If the meaning of a claim cannot be clarified even by the approaches above, the claim may be interpreted according to reference books, textbooks and other public literature and the common understanding on the part of regular technicians in the same field.[24]

a. The Official "Judge Made Statute": Judicial Interpretation by Supreme People's Court

The Supreme People's Court issued three Judicial Interpretation in 2001, 2009 and 2016. They are named as "Several Provisions on Issues Concerning Applicable Laws to the Trial of Patent Controversies"(hereafter 2001 Judicial Interpreta-

---

21 Ibid.

22 He Weifang (贺卫方), Zhongguo Sifa Guanli Zhidu de Liangge Wenti (中国司法管理制度的两个问题) [China Two Issues of China's Judicial administration], Zhongguo Shehui Kexue (中国社会科学) [Social Sciences in China] (1997).

23 Guanyu Shenli Qinfan Zhuanliquan Jiufen Anjian Yingyong Falü Ruogan Wenti de Jieshi (关于审理侵犯专利权纠纷案件应用法律若干问题的解释) [Explanations of Issues regarding to Application of Law on Patent Infringement Trial] (Promulgated by Supreme People's Court., Dec. 29, 2009, effective Jan.1, 2010), (Chinalawinfo) (China), art. 2.

24 Ibid., art.3.

tion),[25] "Explanations of Issues regarding to Application of Law on Patent Infringement Trial" (hereafter 2009 Judicial Interpretation),[26] and "Explanations of Issues regarding to Application of Law on Patent Infringement Trial II" (hereafter 2016 Judicial Interpretation).[27] The 2001 Judicial Interpretation is mainly about procedure law, except one provision regarding to POHSITA and doctrine of equivalents. The 2009 and 2016 Judicial Interpretation include both procedure and substantive law. These judicial interpretations provided the hierarchy of evidence in claim interpretation, the all technical feature rule (similar to all-element rule in U.S. law), prosecution history estoppel, rules to interpret claims in special forms etc. However, the SPC Interpretations usually create nothing new. They mainly are confirmation of the rules which had already been created by the SPC Supreme People's Court judicial opinions and lower court's judicial opinions.

b. The Unofficial Judge Made Statute: Judicial Interpretation by High People's Court

Although no statute grants a HPC the authority to issue a judicial interpretation, some courts, like the Beijing High People's Court, promulgated a judicial interpretation in 2001 regarding regulations of the cannons of deciding patent infringement, including rules of claim interpretation (hereafter Beijing Interpretation 2001).[28] The format is similar to the SPC 2009 Judicial Interpretation.

4.1.3 Judicial Opinions

Judicial opinions, which are the court decision written by judges to explain the factual findings and legal reasoning, provide another important source to understand how judges to interpret patent claims. For example, the 2009 Judicial Interpretation was the first time SPC had ever addressed claim interpretation in a judicial interpretation provided prosecution history estoppel rule in article 6. But in the judicial opinions

[25] Guanyu Shenli Zhuanli Jiufen Anjian Shiyong Falü Wenti de Ruogan Guiding (关于审理专利纠纷案件适用法律问题的若干规定) [Several Provisions on Issues Concerning Applicable Laws to the Trial of Patent Controversies] (Promulgated by Sup. People's Ct., 2001, amended in 2013, 2015 & 2020), (Chinalawinfo) (China).

[26] Guanyu Shenli Qinfan Zhuanliquan Jiufen Anjian Yingyong Falü Ruogan Wenti de Jieshi (关于审理侵犯专利权纠纷案件应用法律若干问题的解释) [Explanations of Issues regarding to Application of Law on Patent Infringement Trial] (Promulgated by Sup. People's Ct., Dec. 29, 2009, effective Jan.1, 2010), (Chinalawinfo) (China).

[27] Guanyu Shenli Qinfan Zhuanliquan Jiufen Anjian Yingyong Falü Ruogan Wenti de Jieshi (Er) (关于审理侵犯专利权纠纷案件应用法律若干问题的解释(二)) [Explanations of Issues regarding to Application of Law on Patent Infringement Trial II] (Promulgated by Sup. People's Ct., Jan. 25, 2016, effective April.1, 2016, amended on Dec. 29, 2020), (Chinalawinfo) (China).

[28] Zhuanli Qinquan Panding Ruogan Wenti de Yijian (专利侵权判定若干问题的意见) [The opinion on several issues of deciding patent infringement] (Beijing People's high court, 2001).

before 2009, we can also see judges decide cases based on rationale of prosecution history estoppel.[29]

4.2 Fundamental Rules

The fundamental rules in U.S. claim interpretation, such as: the claim itself, defining the scope of the patent, the all-element rule, the understanding of a "PHOSITA", and regarding the specification as the most important aid in claim interpretation, all have nearly identical counterparts in Chinese law.

4.2.1 Central Role of Claims

The "claim defines the scope of patent" is a rule established since the first Chinese Patent Law was promulgated in 1984,[30] which is almost identical to the principle of patent protection in the United States. However, it took a long time for all of the courts to understand and implement this rule correctly. Mistakes such as using a patentee's product or the claims in a patent application document to determine the scope of patent used to occur from time to time.

Between the filing date and the issue date, a patentee may negotiate with a patent examiner and revise the drafting of claims. The claims—which are published when the China National Intellectual Property Administration grants the patent—are the final result of the negotiation.[31] Some judges mistakenly used earlier versions of claims (e.g., patent applications) when defining the scope of patent protection.[32]

---

[29] See landmark cases in Shanghai High People's Court in Judge Xiaodu Zhang's book: Xiaodu Zhang (张晓都), Zhuanli Qinquan Panding—Lilun Tantao yu Shenpan Shijian [专利侵权判定——理论探讨与审判实践, Determination of patent infringement—Theoretical discussion and judicial practice] (Falü Chubanshe 2008).

[30] Article 59 of Patent Law provided "The scope of protection of the patent right for an invention or utility model shall be determined by the terms of the claims". Zhuanli Fa (专利法) [Patent Law], art. 59 (promulgated by the Standing Comm. Nat'l People's Cong., Mar.12, 1984, effective Apr. 1, 1985)1984 Standing Comm. Nat'l People's Cong. Gaz. (China). English version is available in lawinfochina.

[31] Guanyu dui Henansheng Gaoji Renmin Fayuan Qingshi Zhengzhou Shi Zhenzhong Dianronggaoye Youxian Gongsi yu Zhengzhou Jiansong Naihuo Cailiao Youxian Gongsi Zhuanli Qinquan Jiufen Zaishen Yian Youguan Wenti De Dafu (关于对河南省高级人民法院请示郑州市振中电熔锆业有限公司与郑州建嵩耐火材料有限公司专利侵权纠纷再审一案有关问题的答复) [In re Henan Hig. People's Ct.'s request on Zhengzhou Zhengzhong Dianronggaoye LL.C v. Zhengzhou Jiansong Naihuo Cailiao LL.C.], ipr.chinacourt (Sup. People's Ct. Mar.7, 2006) (China).

[32] See examples in Cheng Yongshun (程永顺)& Luo Lihua (罗李华), Zhuanli Qinquan Panding: Zhongmei Fatiao yu Anli Bijiao Yanjiu (专利侵权判定:中美法条与案例比较研究) [Cheng Yongshun, Luo Lihua, Deciding Patent Infringement: Comparative Study on Chinese and U.S. Law and Cases] (2002).

Another mistake is to define the scope of patent rights by a patentee's product.[33] It happens that a patentee will present the patentee's own product and accused infringer's product as evidence of infringement.[34] Similarly, the defendant may also emphasize the difference between the accused infringing product and the patentee's product, in order to prove non-infringement.[35] Some judges consequently adopt this analysis and determine infringement based on a comparison of the patented product and the accused infringing product.[36] The risk inherent in this approach is that the scope of patent rights is consequently narrowed. The goal of a claims is to establish the broadest possible scope of a patent right. Usually, the patentee's product in question represents merely one of the possible applications of the patented technology. The scope defined by claims should be broader than that represented by one product. If the claim is so narrow that it only covers one product, the commercial value of the patent would be very low and perhaps even worthless.[37]

In order to correct the above incorrect approaches, the SPC issued a Response in 2005 to emphasize that the comparison should be made between the technical features of a claim and the accused infringing technology, and the claims should be the claims in the issued patents instead of patent application.[38]

4.2.2 The "All Feature" Rule

The current Chinese All Feature rule is the same as the United States all-element rule. The Chinese law has eliminated all exceptions in order to ensure legal certainty.

---

33 Ibid.

34 Qianrushi Zhengfaqi Yian (嵌入式蒸发器一案) [In Re Embedded evaporator], *in* Zhuanli Shangbiao Jishu Hetong Yinan Anli Pingxi (专利、商标、技术合同疑难案例评析) [Review of Patent, Trademark and Technology Transfer Contract] 111 (Yang Jinqi (杨金琪) eds., 1995). See comments in Cheng Yongshun (程永顺)& Luo Lihua (罗李华), Zhuanli Qinquan Panding: Zhongmei Fatiao yu Anli Bijiao Yanjiu (专利侵权判定:中美法条与案例比较研究) [Cheng Yongshun, Luo Lihua, Deciding Patent Infringement: Comparative Study on Chinese and U.S. Law and Cases] 107 (2002).

35 Ibid.

36 See examples in See, e.g., Li Guochang (李国昌), Panduan Qinquan Ying Yi Duli Quanli Yaoqiu Weizhun (判断侵权应以独立权利要求为准) [Determining Infringement Should Be Based on Independent Claim], Zhongguo Jishu Shichang Bao, Feb. 7th 1994. See also Cheng Yongshun (程永顺)& Luo Lihua (罗李华), Zhuanli Qinquan Panding: Zhongmei Fatiao yu Anli Bijiao Yanjiu (专利侵权判定:中美法条与案例比较研究) [Cheng Yongshun, Luo Lihua, Deciding Patent Infringement: Comparative Study on Chinese and U.S. Law and Cases] (2002).

37 Cheng Yongshun (程永顺)& Luo Lihua (罗李华), Zhuanli Qinquan Panding: Zhongmei Fatiao yu Anli Bijiao Yanjiu (专利侵权判定:中美法条与案例比较研究) [Cheng Yongshun, Luo Lihua, Deciding Patent Infringement: Comparative Study on Chinese and U.S. Law and Cases] 108 (2002).

38 Guanyu dui Henansheng Gaoji Renmin Fayuan Qingshi Zhengzhou Shi Zhenzhong Dianronggaoye Youxian Gongsi yu Zhengzhou Jiansong Naihuo Cailiao Youxian Gongsi Zhuanli Qinquan Jiufen Zaishen Yian Youguan Wenti De Dafu (关于对河南省高级人民法院请示郑州市振中电熔锆业有限公司与郑州建嵩耐火材料有限公司专利侵权纠纷再审一案有关问题的答复) [In re Henan Hig. People's Ct.'s request on Zhengzhou Zhengzhong Dianronggaoye LL.C v. Zhengzhou Jiansong Naihuo Cailiao LL.C.], ipr.chinacourt (Sup. People's Ct. Mar.7, 2006) (China).

The U.S. law still allows exceptions, e.g., some preamble terms are not limiting.[39] As stated above, several U.S. judges have proposed to change the United States all-element rule to make it a uniform rule in which all claim terms are limiting without exception.[40]

a. All Feature Rule in General

In claim interpretation, the court should split the claim into its distinct technical features in order to compare it to the accused infringing product.[41] In a 2009 Judicial Interpretation, the SPC provided that when determining patent infringement, all technical features found in the disputed claim (s) should be considered.[42] This officially established the "all feature" rule and denied any exceptions.[43]

Before 2009, most courts applied the all feature rule,[44] but there were two exceptions. One exception was that some courts would omit the technical features included in the preamble. Another one was the omission of technical features which were "unnecessary", when determining infringement under doctrine of equivalents. The latter is known as the "redundant feature rule".[45] The Beijing High Court strongly supported the redundant feature rule and opened a fierce debate in the patent law community.[46] Yet another exception was to omit the preamble portion. This approach has neither an official name nor explicit support from a court, but it did play a role

---

[39] *Allen Eng'g Corp. v. Bartell Indus., Inc.*, 299 F.3d 1336, 1346 (Fed.Cir.2002).

[40] See e.g. *Am. Med. Sys., Inc. v. Biolitec, Inc.*, 618 F.3d 1354, 1364 (Fed. Cir. 2010) (dissent, Judge Dyk).

[41] Guanyu dui Henansheng Gaoji Renmin Fayuan Qingshi Zhengzhou Shi Zhenzhong Dianronggaoye Youxian Gongsi yu Zhengzhou Jiansong Naihuo Cailiao Youxian Gongsi Zhuanli Qinquan Jiufen Zaishen Yian Youguan Wenti De Dafu (关于对河南省高级人民法院请示郑州市振中电熔锆业有限公司与郑州建嵩耐火材料有限公司专利侵权纠纷再审一案有关问题的答复) [In re Henan Hig. People's Ct.'s request on Zhengzhou Zhengzhong Dianronggaoye LL.C v. Zhengzhou Jiansong Naihuo Cailiao LL.C.], ipr.chinacourt (Sup. People's Ct. Mar.7, 2006) (China).

[42] Guanyu Shenli Qinfan Zhuanliquan Jiufen Anjian Yingyong Falü Ruogan Wenti de Jieshi (关于审理侵犯专利权纠纷案件应用法律若干问题的解释) [Explanations of Issues regarding to Application of Law on Patent Infringement Trial] art. 7, (Promulgated by Sup. People's Ct., Dec. 29, 2009, effective Jan.1, 2010), (Chinalawinfo) (China).

[43] Zuigao Renmin Fayuan Zhishi Chanquanting Fuzeren Jiu ⟨Guanyu Shenli Qinfan Zhuanliquan Jiufen Anjian Yingyong Falü Ruogan Wenti de Jieshi > Da Jizhe Wen (最高人民法院知识产权庭负责人就《关于审理侵犯专利权纠纷案件应用法律若干问题的解释》答记者问) [Public Interview with the Chief of the Intellectual Property Tribunal of Sup. People's Ct. Explanations of Issues regarding to Application of Law on Patent Infringement Trial, with Respect to ⟨Explanations of Issues regarding to Application of Law on Patent Infringement Trial⟩], Chinacourt (Sep.18, 2010, 19: 40 pm); http://rmfyb.chinacourt.org/public/detail.php?id=134762.

[44] Yan Wenjun (闫文军), Zhuanliquan de Baohu Fanwei: Quanli Yaoqiu Jieshi he Dengtong Yuanze Shiyong (专利权的保护范围:权利要求解释和等同原则适用) [Yan Wenjun, Scope of Patent Protection: Interpretation of Claim and Application of Doctrine of Equivalents] 367 (2007).

[45] Zhuanli Qinquan Panding Ruogan Wenti de Yijian (专利侵权判定若干问题的意见) [The opinion on several issues of deciding patent infringement] art. 10. (Promulgated by Beijing Hig. People's Ct., 2001), (Chinalawinfo) (China).

[46] E.g., Zhang Zewu (张泽吾), Duoyu Zhiding Yuanze zhi Quexian Fenxi ji Sifa Duice (多余指定原则之缺陷分析及司法对策) [The Analysis of The Problems of Redundant Element Rule and Judicial Solutions],2 Xingzheng yu Fa 124 (2004).

in some courts' judicial opinions. Omitting the technical features in the preamble was identified as a wrongful approach by appellate courts in the 1990s. Detailed Rule 2001 confirmed that decision. However, the debate surrounding the redundant feature rule lasted for many years, until 2009.

b. The Previous Exceptions

In the past, there were several cases in China which found that in some exceptional situations, some terms in a claim are not limiting. However, rule is now uniform and expressly eliminates the previous exceptions. In the current U.S. law, although the all-elements rule is the general principle, in some cases some claim terms, e.g., descriptive terms in the preamble, are not limiting.

i. Technical Features in Preamble

Although the limitations found in the preamble of a U.S. patent do not necessarily become a limitation to the patent scope, according to the current Chinese law, the technical features in a preamble are always relevant for claim interpretation. There used to be confusion concerning whether the preamble terms are also limiting, but now this issue has been clarified in both the Detailed Rule and cases that all terms in a claim are limiting. According to the Detailed Rule, the distinct technical features in combination with the technical features described in the preamble section constitute all of the essential technical features of the invention or utility model, and thereby define the scope of protection of the independent claim.[47]

In U.S. law, whether a preamble term is a claim limitation is "determined on the facts of each case in light of the claim as a whole and the invention described in the patent".[48] In some cases, preambles are found not to contain a claim limitation, for reasons such as it is "merely duplicative of the limitations in the body of the claim",[49] "it was not added to overcome a prior art rejection"[50] or "the preamble merely gives a descriptive name to the set of limitations in the body of the claim that completely set forth the invention"[51] etc.

In the past, some Chinese courts used an approach similar to the current U.S. law. *Dongnan* illustrates the trial court's omission of the technical features in the preamble. The trial court found infringement, but the appellate court overturned.[52]

---

[47] Zhuanli Fa Shishi Xize (专利法实施细则) [Detailed Rules for the Implementation of the Patent Law] arts.21, (promulgated by the St. Council., Jun.15, 2001, effective Jul. 1,2001, amended Jan.09., 2010) (Chinalawinfo) (China).

[48] *Storage Tech. Corp. v. Cisco Sys.*, Inc., 329 F.3d 823, 831 (Fed.Cir.2003).

[49] *Symantec Corp. v. Computer Assocs. Int'l, Inc.*, 522 F.3d 1279, 1288–89 (Fed. Cir. 2008).

[50] Ibid.

[51] *IMS Tech., Inc. v. Haas Automation, Inc.*, 206 F.3d 1422, 1434–35 (Fed.Cir.2000).

[52] Zhongguo Dongnan Jishu Maoyi Zonggongsi v. Beijing Shi Wangma Diannao Zonggongsi (中国东南技术贸易总公司与北京市王码电脑总公司) [China Dongnan Technology Trade Company v. Beijing Wangma Computer Company], ipr.chinacourt (Beijing Hig. People's Ct. Jul. 18, 1997) (China).

In *Dongnan*, the disputed patent involved a Five-Stroke input method, an encoding technology used to input Chinese characters into computers.[53] The patentee filed a patent application for a keyboard which employs a Modified Five-Stroke Chinese Input Encoding Method (Modified Five-Stroke) on April 1, 1985, and the patent was granted on February 26, 1992.[54] There are two kinds of Chinese character input methods.[55] One is the Pinyin method, which is based on pronunciation.[56] The second is the Five-Stroke method, which is based on the character pattern.[57] The latter breaks down the Chinese characters into five basic strokes, and as such is named the "Five-Stroke" method.[58] As determined at trial, the Modified Five-Stroke is not a brand new technology. Instead, it employs Version III Five-Stroke encoding technology.[59]

The accused infringer, Dongnan Company, employed Version IV Five-Stroke technology in its Chinese interface card.[60] On trial, the Beijing Intermediate Court, based on a comparison of the technical features in the characterization section of the independent claim and the accused infringing technology, concluded that the accused infringing technology was improved from the patented technology and thus the defendant should pay royalties to the patentee.[61]

On appeal, the Beijing High People's Court overturned that decision for erroneous factual findings and for using the wrong approach to determine infringement.[62] In its judicial opinion, the appellate court found that the lower court should consider the technical features in both the preamble section and the characterization section, and compare all technical features to the accused infringing device or method.[63] The intermediate court's analysis, which was only based on the characterization section, was wrong.[64] Also, the appellate court stated that the basic technology of the Five-Stroke encoding system was pre-existing technology, and the fact that those technical features were included in the preamble section was evidence that the patentee admitted that it was pre-existing technology. The appellate court compared all technical features in the independent claim and concluded that Version IV Five-Stroke technology represents a substantial improvement and is not an infringement under the doctrine of equivalents.

The Beijing High People's Court's ruling was later confirmed by a case decided by the Supreme People's Court in 2001, which pointed out that a case decided in 2001 found that the technical features in the preamble section of an independent claim

---

[53] Ibid.
[54] Ibid.
[55] Ibid.
[56] Ibid.
[57] Ibid.
[58] Ibid.
[59] Ibid.
[60] Ibid.
[61] Ibid.
[62] Ibid.
[63] Ibid.
[64] Ibid.

must be considered.[65] This rule was adopted in the 2016 Judicial Interpretation as article 5.[66]

ii. Redundant Feature Rule

Before 2005, some Chinese courts had a Redundant Feature Rule, which provided a scope of protection even broader than the protection under the doctrine of equivalents. Currently China applies the all feature rule, which is the same as the all-elements rule in United States.

The Redundant Feature Rule required that a technical feature could be removed from the claim if the court believed that it was an obvious mistake to include it. Thus, infringement could be found even when the accused infringing technology did not include all of the technical features or their equivalents. Although the number of cases applying this rule was small, the existence of this rule presented a significant challenge for the notice function of patent claims and the legal certainty of infringement determination.

This rule was established in China by some judges who strongly emphasized patentee interests. Some judges believe that the main function of the patent law system is to protect patent rights, and that the main function of the court is to support the patentee.[67] Consequently, if the patentee mistakenly includes unnecessary technical features, the judge should correct this mistake.[68] This view was fiercely criticized as a misunderstanding of the purpose of patent law, which should include both incentives for innovation and protect the public welfare.[69] This view had some practical value in the 1990s. At that time, the patent system was new in China. Most patentees and their agencies lacked experience.[70] Mistakes in patent drafting could be found in many patents.[71] Thus, some judges felt obligated to help patentees receive fair protection for their innovations.

---

[65] Zuigao Renmin Fayuan Minshi Shenpanting Guanyu Wangchuan yu Hefei Jichu Maoyi Youxian Zeren Gongsi deng Zhuanli Qinquan Jiufen An de Han (最高人民法院民事审判第三庭关于王川与合肥继初贸易有限责任公司等专利侵权纠纷案的函) [Wangchuan v. Hefei Jichu Trade LL.C], ipr. Chinacourt (Sup. People's Ct. Feb. 2, 2001).

[66] Guanyu Shenli Qinfan Zhuanliquan Jiufen Anjian Yingyong Falü Ruogan Wenti de Jieshi (Er) (关于审理侵犯专利权纠纷案件应用法律若干问题的解释(二)) [Explanations of Issues regarding to Application of Law on Patent Infringement Trial II] (Promulgated by Sup. People's Ct., Jan. 25, 2016, effective April.1, 2016, amended on Dec. 29, 2020), (Chinalawinfo) (China).

[67] Cheng Yongshun (程永顺), Zhuanli Qinquan Panding Shiwu (专利侵权判定实务) [The Practice of Patent Infringement Determination]2 (2001). See also Interview with Cheng Yongshun, Chief Justice, Intellectual Property Tribunal of Beijing Hig. People's Ct. (Dec. 20, 2006), (Sep. 18, 2010, 20:37 pm), http://www.sipo.gov.cn/sipo2008/mtjj/2006/200804/t20080401_362467.html

[68] Ibid.

[69] E.g., Zhang Zewu (张泽吾), Duoyu Zhiding Yuanze zhi Quexian Fenxi ji Sifa Duice (多余指定原则之缺陷分析及司法对策) [The Analysis of The Problems of Redundant Element Rule and Judicial Solutions],2 Xingzheng yu Fa 124 (2004).

[70] Zhang Xiaodu (张晓都), Zhuanli Qinquan Panding (专利侵权判定) [Determining Patent Infringement] 91 (2008), Yin Xingtian (尹新天), Zhuanliquan de Baohu (专利权的保护) [Protection of Patent Rights] 431 (2005).

[71] Ibid.

The practice of applying Redundant Feature Rule can be traced to a case in Beijing High People's Court in 1995,[72] but was questioned in a Supreme Court case in 2005,[73] and formally abandoned by Judicial Interpretation 2009.[74] The United States used to have a similar practice, which is applying the doctrine of equivalents to the claimed invention "as a whole".[75] The "as a whole" approach was eliminated in *Warner-Jenkinson* (1997) by holding that "the doctrine of equivalents must be applied to individual elements of the claim, not to the invention as a whole."[76]

During the period 1997–2009, China allows omitting an element entirely when applying doctrine of equivalents. The U.S. doctrine of equivalents does not allow such a broad application that eliminates an element in its entirety,[77] because such a broad scope is believed to be in conflict with the definitional and public-notice functions of the statutory claiming requirement.[78] During this period, a patent claim can obtain a broader scope of protection under Chinese doctrine of equivalents than that under the U.S. doctrine of equivalents. After 2009, Chinese courts changed the practice to be more in line with the U.S. courts.

(1) Origins of the Redundant Feature Rule

The Beijing High People's Court established the Redundant Feature Rule in *Zhou Lin Spectrum Analyzer* (1996).[79] Zhou Lin was a patentee who owned a patent describing "a device for the therapy of Spectrum Matching Human Body Effect Field of and the

[72] Zhoulin v. Beijing Aomei Guang Jidian Lianhe Kaifa Gongsi, Beijing Huaao Dianzi Yiliao Yiqi Youxian Gongsi (周林诉北京奥美光机电联合开发公司,北京华奥电子医疗仪器有限公司) [Zhoulin v. Beijing Aomei Guangjidian Lianhe Kaifa LL.C., Beijing Huaoa Electronic Medical Device LL.C.], ipr. Chinacourt (Beijing Hig. People's Ct., Mar. 22, 1996). A case note edited from judicial opinion and trial report by Judge Cheng Yongshun (程永顺), who trailed this case on appeal, is available in Zhishi Chanquan Shenpan Anli Yaolan (知识产权审判案例要览) [Review of the Key Cases of Intellectual Property] 151–159 (Cheng Yongshun (程永顺) eds.1999).

[73] Renda Jiancai Chang v. Xinyi Gongsi (仁达建材厂诉新益公司) [Renda Construction Material Factory v. Xinyi Company], ipr.Chinacourt (Sup. People's Ct. Aug. 22, 2005).

[74] Guanyu Shenli Qinfan Zhuanliquan Jiufen Anjian Yingyong Falü Ruogan Wenti de Jieshi (关于审理侵犯专利权纠纷案件应用法律若干问题的解释) [Explanations of Issues regarding to Application of Law on Patent Infringement Trial] (Promulgated by Sup. People's Ct., Dec. 29, 2009, effective Jan.1, 2010), (Chinalawinfo) (China).

[75] *Hughes Aircraft Co. v. United States*, 717 F.2d 1351, 219 USPQ 473 (Fed. Cir. 1983).

[76] *Warner-Jenkinson Co., Inc. v. Hilton Davis Chem. Co.*, 520 U.S. 17, 29 (1997).

[77] Ibid.

[78] "There can be no denying that the doctrine of equivalents, when applied broadly, conflicts with the definitional and public-notice functions of the statutory claiming requirement." *Warner-Jenkinson Co., Inc. v. Hilton Davis Chem. Co.*, 520 U.S. 17, 29, 117 S. Ct. 1040, 1049, 137 L. Ed. 2d 146 (1997).

[79] Zhoulin v. Beijing Aomei Guang Jidian Lianhe Kaifa Gongsi, Beijing Huaao Dianzi Yiliao Yiqi Youxian Gongsi (周林诉北京奥美光机电联合开发公司,北京华奥电子医疗仪器有限公司) [Zhoulin v. Beijing Aomei Guangjidian Lianhe Kaifa LL.C., Beijing Huaoa Electronic Medical Device LL.C.], ipr. Chinacourt (Beijing Hig. People's Ct., Mar. 22, 1996). A case note edited from judicial opinion and trial report by Judge Cheng Yongshun, who trailed this case on appeal, is available in Zhishi Chanquan Shenpan Anli Yaolan (知识产权审判案例要览) [Review of the Key Cases of Intellectual Property] 151–159 (Cheng Yongshun (程永顺) eds.1999).

Method of Manufacture" (patent No. 87103603). The patented device was named the Zhou Lin Spectrum Analyzer. Claim 7 included a Part A and a Part B. Part B stated that "a stereo system, an acupuncture point galvanism device and their control circuit are built in the machine".[80] All other technical features in Claim 7 were found in the accused infringing product, except for Part B. At trial, the Beijing Intermediate Court found infringement despite of omission of technical features in Part B, which was considered by the court as an unnecessary technical feature. The patent description provides that the device aims to achieve a therapeutic effect by a design of spectrum analyzer, and the built-in stereo system aims to provide additional effects to improve a patient's health.[81] The Beijing Intermediate Court decided that Part B (the stereo system) was not required to achieve the effect and that omitting Part B would not impact the technical solution[82]as a whole. Moreover, the Beijing Intermediate Court argued that the Zhou Lin Spectrum Analyzer is an important invention and had achieved a therapeutic effect as well as commercial success, thus the claim should be interpreted broadly.

The defendant appealed to the Beijing High People's Court, and the decision was affirmed. The appellate judges broke down the claim into seven technical features and found the accused infringing device had technical features No. 1 to 5, but did not have technical feature No. 7, which was the stereo system. In addition, the court found that the device had technical features that were different from technical feature No. 6. The appellate court found that the accused technical features of the accused infringing product were equivalent to technical feature No. 6, and that technical feature No. 7 was not necessary. With respect to technical feature No. 7, the appellate court stated that "[a]lthough technical feature No. 7 was written in an independent claim and found to have substantive uniqueness, it indeed does not produce any substantive effect or unnecessary function. It is obviously the patent applicant's misunderstanding and lack of experience".

(2) Conditions: Beijing High People's Court 2001 Judicial Document

The redundant element rule is considered as an exception to the all feature rule and should be applied only after careful consideration.[83] The Beijing High People's Court, which established this rule, determined the necessary conditions to limit the application of the redundant element rule in 2001.[84]

In general, the redundant element rule should be applied only when the technical feature is obviously added into the claim by mistake.[85] This conclusion must be

---

[80] Ibid.

[81] Ibid.

[82] Ibid.

[83] ZHISHI CHANQUAN SHENPAN ANLI YAOLAN (知识产权审判案例要览) [REVIEW OF THE KEY CASES OF INTELLECTUAL PROPERTY] 151 (CHENG YONGSHUN (程永顺) eds.1999).

[84] Zhuanli Qinquan Panding Ruogan Wenti de Yijian (专利侵权判定若干问题的意见) [The opinion on several issues of deciding patent infringement] (Promulgated by Beijing Hig. People's Ct., 2001), (Chinalawinfo) (China).

[85] Ibid.

made by a comprehensive analysis of the purpose, effect, and the technical solution of the patent.[86]

In order to apply the redundant element rule, two conditions must be fulfilled, where the technical future is removed: (1) the patent still meets the novelty and creativity requirement where the technical feature is omitted; and (2) the technical solution of the patent can still achieve its purpose and effect.[87]

The redundant element rule cannot be applied if: (1) the technical feature is included in the claim but description does not explain its function or effect[88]; (2) applying the rule would be controversial or against prosecution history[89]; and (3) the accused infringing product works better than the prior art.[90]

(3) Criticism against the Redundant Feature Rule

The redundant feature rule mainly emphasized a patentee's interest. Ironically, the redundant feature rule is not only criticized by those who are concerned about the public interest, but also by individuals who wish to protect a patentee's interests.

Some judges, scholars, and attorneys criticized the redundant feature rule as detrimental for both legal certainty and the public interest.[91] For example, one judge argued that the public' right to use unpatented technology must be protected.[92] He argued that the effort to find an alternative technical solution to a patent is not an illegal attempt to take advantage of the loopholes in the law.[93] Instead, it is a normal competitive action and necessary for the public to make use of the technology in the public domain.[94] Thus, it should be encouraged instead of prohibited.[95] If the public hesitates to use the technology in the public domain because of the potential risk of infringement, it is an institutional failure.[96] The law should not remedy the patentee's mistake at the expense of the public interest.[97]

Although the redundant feature rule favors the patentee's interests, some international practitioners do not think highly of it. Since the rule is not common in other patent jurisdictions,[98] their attitude toward it is doubtful and defensive. Although there is no supporting evidence, international practitioners strongly suspect that the

---

[86] Ibid.

[87] Ibid.

[88] Ibid.

[89] Ibid.

[90] Ibid.

[91] E.g. Zhang Zewu (张泽吾), Duoyu Zhiding Yuanze zhi Quexian Fenxi ji Sifa Duice (多余指定原则之缺陷分析及司法对策) [The Analysis of The Problems of Redundant Element Rule and Judicial Solutions],2 Xingzheng yu Fa 124 (2004).

[92] Ibid.

[93] Ibid.

[94] Ibid.

[95] Ibid.

[96] Ibid.

[97] Ibid.

[98] Yalei Sun, *A Comparative Study of the Chinese Patent Law Practice Part II: Patent Litigation and Case Studies*, 7 Perspective 5, 13 (2006).

courts would only apply this rule to a Chinese patent, thus disadvantaging foreign patents.[99]

(4) Abolishment of Redundant Feature Rule

The Supreme People's Court started to express its discomfort with the redundant feature rule since 2005. By stating that "this Court does not support the hasty application of the redundant feature rule" in two cases, the Court expressed its negative view of the rule but did not explicitly abandon it.[100] In the 2009 Judicial Interpretation, the Supreme People's Court finally clarified that the all feature rule should be applied and the redundant feature rule should no longer be applied.[101]

In a judicial supervision case in 2005,[102] the Court for the first time addressed the redundant feature rule. The Court stated, "considering the function of claims, all technical features in claims are necessary technical features and should not be omitted in comparison.[103] This Court does not support the hasty application of redundant feature rule".[104] The Court further emphasized the importance of the notice function of claims and of promoting legal certainty.[105] The purpose of a claim is to tell the public all of the technical features of a patented technology, in order to make the public understand what kind of action would infringe on a patent.[106] This will provide reasonable and effective protection to patentees while safeguarding the public's freedom to use technology.[107] Only when all technical features in claims are fully and thoroughly recognized, the Court stated, will the public cease to be confused about the unpredictability of the content of claims.[108] In order to disseminate its opinion and get the attention of the lower courts, the SPC repeated its ruling using similar language in another case in 2006.[109]

---

99 Ibid.

100 Guanyu Shenli Qinfan Zhuanliquan Jiufen Anjian Yingyong Falü Ruogan Wenti de Jieshi (关于审理侵犯专利权纠纷案件应用法律若干问题的解释) [Explanations of Issues regarding to Application of Law on Patent Infringement Trial] (Promulgated by Sup. People's Ct., Dec. 29, 2009, effective Jan.1, 2010), (Chinalawinfo) (China).

101 Zuigao Renmin Fayuan Zhishi Chanquanting Fuzeren Jiu 〈Guanyu Shenli Qinfan Zhuanliquan Jiufen Anjian Yingyong Falü Ruogan Wenti de Jieshi > Da Jizhe Wen (最高人民法院知识产权庭负责人就《关于审理侵犯专利权纠纷案件应用法律若干问题的解释》答记者问) [Public Interview with the Chief of the Intellectual Property Tribunal of Sup. People's Ct. Explanations of Issues regarding to Application of Law on Patent Infringement Trial, with Respect to 〈Explanations of Issues regarding to Application of Law on Patent Infringement Tria〉], Chinacourt (Sep.18, 2010, 19: 40 pm); http://rmfyb.chinacourt.org/public/detail.php?id=134762.

102 Renda Jiancai Chang v. Xinyi Gongsi (仁达建材厂诉新益公司) [Renda Construction Material Factory v. Xinyi Company], ipr.Chinacourt (Sup. People's Ct. Aug. 22, 2005).

103 Ibid.

104 Ibid.

105 Ibid.

106 Ibid.

107 Ibid.

108 Ibid.

109 Guanyu dui Henansheng Gaoji Renmin Fayuan Qingshi Zhengzhou Shi Zhenzhong Dianronggaoye Youxian Gongsi yu Zhengzhou Jiansong Naihuo Cailiao Youxian Gongsi Zhuanli Qinquan

By the end of 2009, the SPC's reservation about the redundant feature rule finally became an explicit prohibition. Although the text of the 2009 Judicial Interpretation emphasizes the all feature rule without addressing the redundant feature rule,[110] the official explanation published afterward made it clear that the redundant element rule shall be abolished at the time that this judicial interpretation takes effect.[111]

4.2.3 Description and Drawings

i. Judicial Interpretation 2009

The 2009 Judicial Interpretation clarified that courts should first review a description in claim interpretation.[112] This clarification legitimized the widespread practice in which the description was the most frequently used reference. Also, the judicial interpretation adopted PHOSITA in interpreting the literal meaning of claims. These clarifications have made Chinese law nearly identical to the U.S. law in this area.

Article 3 of the 2009 Judicial Interpretation states that the description shall be the first reference to be consulted in claim interpretation.[113] In the official explanation, the SPC further explained that if the meaning of claim terms can be clarified by the description, then the courts do not need to consult any other documents. Also, for the first time, the 2009 Judicial Interpretation adopted the PHOSITA standard to understand the description.[114]

Jiufen Zaishen Yian Youguan Wenti De Dafu (关于对河南省高级人民法院请示郑州市振中电熔锆业有限公司与郑州建嵩耐火材料有限公司专利侵权纠纷再审一案有关问题的答复) [In re Henan Hig. People's Ct.'s request on Zhengzhou Zhengzhong Dianronggaoye LL.C v. Zhengzhou Jiansong Naihuo Cailiao LL.C.], ipr.chinacourt (Sup. People's Ct. Mar.7, 2006) (China).

[110] Guanyu Shenli Qinfan Zhuanliquan Jiufen Anjian Yingyong Falü Ruogan Wenti de Jieshi (关于审理侵犯专利权纠纷案件应用法律若干问题的解释) [Explanations of Issues regarding to Application of Law on Patent Infringement Trial] (Promulgated by Sup. People's Ct., Dec. 29, 2009, effective Jan.1, 2010), (Chinalawinfo) (China).

[111] Zuigao Renmin Fayuan Zhishi Chanquanting Fuzeren Jiu ⟨Guanyu Shenli Qinfan Zhuanliquan Jiufen Anjian Yingyong Falü Ruogan Wenti de Jieshi > Da Jizhe Wen (最高人民法院知识产权庭负责人就《关于审理侵犯专利权纠纷案件应用法律若干问题的解释》答记者问) [Public Interview with the Chief of the Intellectual Property Tribunal of Sup. People's Ct. Explanations of Issues regarding to Application of Law on Patent Infringement Trial, with Respect to ⟨Explanations of Issues regarding to Application of Law on Patent Infringement Tria⟩], Chinacourt (Sep.18, 2010, 19: 40 pm); http://rmfyb.chinacourt.org/public/detail.php?id=134762.

[112] Guanyu Shenli Qinfan Zhuanliquan Jiufen Anjian Yingyong Falü Ruogan Wenti de Jieshi (关于审理侵犯专利权纠纷案件应用法律若干问题的解释) [Explanations of Issues regarding to Application of Law on Patent Infringement Trial] (Promulgated by Sup. People's Ct., Dec. 29, 2009, effective Jan.1, 2010), (Chinalawinfo) (China).

[113] Ibid.

[114] Ibid.

Some judges question whether the description should be consulted only when the claim terms are unclear.[115] The SPC examined this issue in two judicial opinions. In both opinions, the SPC emphasized that the description can only be referenced when the meaning of the claim is unclear.[116] Some critics argued that the description should always be consulted to ensure that the correct understanding of the claims is ascertained, and thus have argued that the SPC's approach is not ideal.[117] However, if a claim is under dispute, there must be some confusion as to its meaning. A claim term with a clear meaning rarely is brought to trial. Thus, the description is consulted in almost all patent infringement cases. What the SPC emphasized in its two judicial opinions is that the claim is superior to the description.[118]

ii. Practice in Courts before Judicial Interpretation 2009

Before the 2009 Judicial Interpretation, the courts have frequently used the description as the most important reference to understand the meaning of patent claims. The description is usually used to clarify the meaning of claim terms. In some cases, it is also used to broaden or narrow the literal meaning of claim terms. If an accused infringing technology is identical to the embodiment in the description, literal infringement is established. However, if the embodiment does not fall into the scope of a patent claim, there is no literal infringement.

(a) Description Clarifies the Meaning of a Claim Term

Sometimes a claim term can be understood in different ways and has more than one meaning. Under these circumstances, the description can be used to choose the correct meaning of the claim term.

---

[115] Yan Wenjun (闫文军), Zhuanliquan de Baohu Fanwei: Quanli Yaoqiu Jieshi he Dengtong Yuanze Shiyong (专利权的保护范围:权利要求解释和等同原则适用) [Yan Wenjun, Scope of Patent Protection: Interpretation of Claim and Application of Doctrine of Equivalents] (2007).

[116] Zuigao Renmin Fayuan Minshi Shenpanting Guanyu Wangchuan yu Hefei Jichu Maoyi Youxian Zeren Gongsi deng Zhuanli Qinquan Jiufen An de Han (最高人民法院民事审判第三庭关于王川与合肥继初贸易有限责任公司等专利侵权纠纷案的函) [Wangchuan v. Hefei Jichu Trade LL.C], ipr. Chinacourt (Sup. People's Ct. Feb. 2, 2001), Ningbo Shi Dongfang Jixin Zongchang v. Jiangyin Jinling Wujin Zhipin Youxian Gongsi (宁波市东方机芯总厂与江阴金铃五金制品有限公司) [Ningbo Dongfang Jixin Zongchang v. Jiangyin Jinling Wujin Zhipin Youxian LL.C],ipr. Chinacourt (Sup. People's Ct. Mar. 6, 2002).

[117] Yan Wenjun (闫文军), Zhuanliquan de Baohu Fanwei: Quanli Yaoqiu Jieshi he Dengtong Yuanze Shiyong (专利权的保护范围:权利要求解释和等同原则适用) [Yan Wenjun, Scope of Patent Protection: Interpretation of Claim and Application of Doctrine of Equivalents] (2007), Tang Zhongshun.

[118] Description and drawing cannot be used to limit the meaning which is already clear. Ningbo Shi Dongfang Jixin Zongchang v. Jiangyin Jinling Wujin Zhipin Youxian Gongsi (宁波市东方机芯总厂与江阴金铃五金制品有限公司) [Ningbo Dongfang Jixin Zongchang v. Jiangyin Jinling Wujin Zhipin Youxian LL.C],ipr. Chinacourt (Sup. People's Ct. Mar. 6, 2002).

In one case, a claim stated "one pipe is added". The plaintiff and defendant disputed whether the patented device should have more than one pipe.[119] The defendant argued that "one pipe is added" indicates that another pipe already exists. The plaintiff argued that the pipe is added to the structure, which did not have an existing pipe.[120] The court discussed the description and found that the function of the pipe was to carry water and to control oxygen content.[121] One pipe was sufficient to achieve this function.[122] Also, the technical solutions in the prior art did not show a pipe. Thus, the court concluded "one pipe is added" means there is one rather than two pipes.[123]

(b) Description Broadens or Narrows the Literal Meaning of a Claim Term

Chinese judges generally begin their analysis by ascertaining the "literal meaning" of a claim term. The literal meaning is usually the definition commonly adopted by a dictionary. Sometimes, a claim term's literal meaning is clear, but a court will then use the description to broaden or narrow the meaning of the term.[124]

a. Broader than the dictionary meaning

In an early case decided in the 1980s, a court used the description to interpret a claim term broadly. The disputed word was overlapped.[125] The claims stated that after a particular manufacturing step edge No. 1 and edge No. 3 should be overlapped to close the product.[126] In the accused infringing technical solution after undergoing a similar manufacturing step, edge No. 1 and edge No. 3 failed to connect together. Instead,

---

[119] Qinghua Daxue v. Jixie Dianzi Gongye Shejiyuan, Beijing Weiken Jixie Dianzi Shebei Youxian Gongsi (清华大学诉机械电子工业设计院,北京威肯机械电子设备有限公司) [Qinghua University v. Mechenical & Electornic Industry Design Institute, Beijing Weiken Mechincl & Electronical Device LL.C.], *in* Zhishi Chanquan Mingan Pingxi (知识产权名案评析) [Review of Famous Intellectual Property Cases] 413–420 (Sun Jian (孙建), Luo Dongchuan (罗东川) ed., 1998). See discussion in Yan Wenjun (闫文军), Zhuanliquan de Baohu Fanwei: Quanli Yaoqiu Jieshi he Dengtong Yuanze Shiyong (专利权的保护范围:权利要求解释和等同原则适用) [Yan Wenjun, Scope of Patent Protection: Interpretation of Claim and Application of Doctrine of Equivalents]329 (2007).

[120] Ibid.

[121] Ibid.

[122] Ibid.

[123] Ibid.

[124] Yan Wenjun (闫文军), Zhuanliquan de Baohu Fanwei: Quanli Yaoqiu Jieshi he Dengtong Yuanze Shiyong (专利权的保护范围:权利要求解释和等同原则适用) [Yan Wenjun, Scope of Patent Protection: Interpretation of Claim and Application of Doctrine of Equivalents] 326 327 (2007).

[125] Zhang Yuejin (张跃进), Shuoming Shu Zai Zhuanli Qinquan Panduan zhong de Zuoyong (说明书在专利侵权判断中的作用) [The function of Claims in Patent Infringement Determination], Zhongguo Zhuanli Bao, Jan.19, 1990. See discussion in Yan Wenjun (闫文军), Zhuanliquan de Baohu Fanwei: Quanli Yaoqiu Jieshi he Dengtong Yuanze Shiyong (专利权的保护范围:权利要求解释和等同原则适用) [Yan Wenjun, Scope of Patent Protection: Interpretation of Claim and Application of Doctrine of Equivalents] 326 327 (2007). Cheng Yongshun (程永顺), Zhuanli Qinquan Panding Shiwu (专利侵权判定实务) [The Practice of Patent Infringement Determination] 28,29 (2001).

[126] Ibid.

there was a gap of 4 mm.[127] Literally, the meaning of "overlapping" is reclosing or matching together. Two dictionaries explain "overlapping" as "two geometric figures occupying the same space."[128] Since there was a gap between edges No. 1 and No. 3, they neither matched together nor occupied the same space.[129] They did not literally overlap.[130] However, the court still found infringement based on the description. The court examined the description, and analyzed the purpose of invention and the overall technical solution. The court concluded that the key in this patented technical solution was that the two edges needed to have the same shape and size. Thus, the two edges can be connected when the manufacture was completed. According to the court's understanding, it was not important whether the two edges were connected together in one particular step, as long as they could be connected later. Consequently, the court interpreted "overlapped" as "having the same shape and length," and found infringement.[131]

This approach provides a very broad protection for patents while reducing legal certainty. However, once can question whether broad protection is fair protection. If the accused infringing technology does not fall within the literal meaning of the patent claim, it should be evaluated under the doctrine of equivalents. This case did not distinguish literal infringement and infringement under the doctrine of equivalents. Although it compared the function and effect of the two technical solutions, it did not discuss whether the accused infringing technology was obvious enough for a PHOSITA to find infringement. Neither did it consider the limitations on the doctrine of equivalents. The court's approach, which mixed the patent protection scope under the doctrine of equivalents and the literal meaning of claim interpretation, makes any variation of technology which can achieve a similar effect an infringement and exceeds the usual protection scope under the doctrine of equivalents. As the doctrine of equivalents and its limitations are better recognized by Chinese courts, this broad interpretation rarely happens.

b. Narrower than dictionary meaning

The courts sometimes use the description to narrow the literal meaning of claim terms. This usually happens when the term is generic and does not disclose the specific structure. Sometimes, courts will identify them as functional technical features and limit the literal scope to the embodiments disclosed in the description.[132]Because Chinese patent law does provide a clear definition of a functional technical feature, some courts limit the scope of the claim to the embodiments without discussing whether

---

[127] Ibid.

[128] Ibid.

[129] Ibid.

[130] Ibid.

[131] Ibid.

[132] Zhanchi v. Zhenyu Gongsi (展翅诉珍誉公司) [Zhanchi v. Zhenyu Company], ipr. Chinacourt, (Beijing Hig. People's Ct., Jun. 13, 2006) http://www.panjueshu.com/beijing/gaoyuan/m20060613 2006367.html. Liang Jinshui v. Li Changzhong etc. (梁锦水与李昌众等) [Liang Jinshui v. Li Changzhong ect] ipr. Chinacourt. (Shanghai Hig. People's Ct. July 10th, 2006) ipr. Chincout. (July10,2006).

it is a functional technical feature. In one Shandong High People's Court case,[133] the disputed term was "flue". Although the accused infringing product also had a flue, the Shandong High People's Court found it non-infringing. The reason was that the accused infringer's flue was different in shape and position from the embodiments disclosed in the description.[134] The court interpreted the flue to only include the structure with the shape and position disclosed in the description. Similarly, in a Xiamen Intermediate Court case, the court decided that the claim term "tightly locked" could not include "connected by the thread of a screw", because the description only disclosed a structure "locked by the connection of convex grains and holes of rectangle shape".[135] There are many cases that take this same approach.[136] This approach limits the scope of patent protection to what the description provides.

(c) Exception: Excluding an Embodiment in Description

If an accused infringing product is identical to an embodiment disclosed in the description, the court can usually find literal infringement. Although Chinese law

133 Shuitao Qunuan Lu (水套取暖炉) [In Re Residential heating furnace], (Shandong High People's Court), see summary and comments in Yan Wenjun (闫文军), Zhuanliquan de Baohu Fanwei: Quanli Yaoqiu Jieshi he Dengtong Yuanze Shiyong (专利权的保护范围:权利要求解释和等同原则适用) [Yan Wenjun, Scope of Patent Protection: Interpretation of Claim and Application of Doctrine of Equivalents] 327 (2007).

134 Yan Wenjun (闫文军), Zhuanliquan de Baohu Fanwei: Quanli Yaoqiu Jieshi he Dengtong Yuanze Shiyong (专利权的保护范围:权利要求解释和等同原则适用) [Yan Wenjun, Scope of Patent Protection: Interpretation of Claim and Application of Doctrine of Equivalents] 328 (2007).

135 Xiamen Weidiya Jiancai Youxian Gongsi yu Xiamen Ruierte Weiyu Gongye Youxian Gongsi (厦门威迪亚建材工业有限公司与厦门瑞尔特卫浴工业有限公司) [Xiamen Weidiya Jiancai Youxian LL.C. v. Xiamen Ruierte Weiyu Youxian LL.C], (Xiamen Interm. People's Ct., 2000), see summary and comments in Zheng Wei (郑伟), Zhishi Chanquan Jingan Pingxi (知识产权精案评析) [Review of Classic Intllectual Property Cases], (2004). See summary and comments in Yan Wenjun (闫文军), Zhuanliquan de Baohu Fanwei: Quanli Yaoqiu Jieshi he Dengtong Yuanze Shiyong (专利权的保护范围:权利要求解释和等同原则适用) [Yan Wenjun, Scope of Patent Protection: Interpretation of Claim and Application of Doctrine of Equivalents] 328 (2007).Qinghua Daxue v. Jixie Dianzi Gongye Shejiyuan, Beijing Weiken Jixie Dianzi Shebei Youxian Gongsi (清华大学诉机械电子工业设计院,北京威肯机械电子设备有限公司) [Qinghua University v. Mechenical & Electornic Industry Design Institute, Beijing Weiken Mechincl & Electronical Device LL.C.], *in* Zhishi Chanquan Mingan Pingxi (知识产权名案评析) [Review of Famous Intellectual Property Cases] 413–420 (Sun Jian (孙建), Luo Dongchuan (罗东川) ed., 1998).

136 Qinghua Daxue v. Jixie Dianzi Gongcheng Sheji Yuan, Beijing Weiken Jixie Dianzi Shebei Youxian Gongsi (清华大学诉机械电子工业设计院,北京威肯机械电子设备有限公司) [Qinghua University v. Mechenical & Electornic Industry Design Institute, Beijing Weiken Mechincl & Electronical Device LL.C.], *in* Zhishi Chanquan Mingan Pingxi (知识产权名案评析) [Review of Famous Intellectual Property Cases] 413–420 (Sun Jian (孙建), Luo Dongchuan (罗东川) ed., 1998). See summary and comments in Yan Wenjun (闫文军), Zhuanliquan de Baohu Fanwei: Quanli Yaoqiu Jieshi he Dengtong Yuanze Shiyong (专利权的保护范围:权利要求解释和等同原则适用) [Yan Wenjun, Scope of Patent Protection: Interpretation of Claim and Application of Doctrine of Equivalents] 328 (2007). See other examples in summary and comments in Yan Wenjun (闫文军), Zhuanliquan de Baohu Fanwei: Quanli Yaoqiu Jieshi he Dengtong Yuanze Shiyong (专利权的保护范围:权利要求解释和等同原则适用) [Yan Wenjun, Scope of Patent Protection: Interpretation of Claim and Application of Doctrine of Equivalents] 329–330 (2007).

does not require a claim to be interpreted to cover all embodiments, it is a rare case that a claim is interpreted to exclude any embodiments. However, under exceptional conditions, an embodiment may be excluded from the patent scope.

In *Zuhe Yichu Shiyong Zhuanli*, a case decided by the Shanghai High People's Court, the accused infringing product was identical with two of the embodiments, but the court found non-infringement.[137]

The claim stated that the product was constructed by pipes and boards. The accused infringing product used pipes and a kind of material called support bars. The description stated that one example of prior art was made of pipes, and in the attached drawings parts of the example were marked as support bars. The court concluded that the support bar in this patent should be understood as a pipe. The embodiments, including the support bars, were not within the scope of patent, which required both pipes and boards, and thus should be excluded from the patent protection scope. The accused infringing product, which was the same as the two embodiments, was different from the patented product and therefore not an infringement.[138]

The ruling in this case is similar to the U.S. dedication to the public rule, e.g., *Unique Concepts, Inc. v. Brown.*[139] In this case, support bars were disclosed in the embodiments but not claimed in the claim. Thus, the accused infringing products using support bars were not infringing. This U.S. case preceded the Dedication to the Public rule in China, promulgated in the 2009 Judicial Interpretation. Therefore, the rule was not identified as Dedication to the Public, but the rational was the same.

In *Unique Concepts, Inc. v. Brown*, the patent was directed to an "assembly of border pieces" used to attach a fabric wall covering to a wall.[140] Like *Zuhe* in which a patent claim claims "pipes and boards", the patent claim in *Unique Concepts* states that the assembly is made up of a number of "right angle corner border pieces" and "linear border pieces" which are arranged so as to form a frame. The Federal Circuit found no infringement, because "right angle corner pieces" are absent from the accused infringing product.[141] The accused infringing product did not have a "right angle corner piece".[142] Instead, it had two mitered linear pieces.[143]

The mitered linear pieces used in accused products were described in the specification.[144] The specification referred to "improvise[d] corner pieces", which are mitered, as an alternative to the preformed pieces:

> Instead of using preformed right-angle corner pieces of the type previously disclosed, one may improvise corner pieces by miter-cutting the ends of a pair of short linear border pieces at

---

137 Zuhe Yichu Shiyong Zhuanli (组合衣橱实用新型专利) [In Re Zhuhe Yichu Utility Patent] Xiaodu Zhang 17–34.

138 Ibid.

139 For example, Unique Concepts, Inc. v. Brown, 939 F.2d 1558, 19 USPQ2d 1500 (Fed. Cir. 1991).

140 *Unique Concepts, Inc. v. Brown,* 939 F.2d 1558, 1559 (Fed. Cir. 1991).

141 Ibid., 1561.

142 Ibid.

143 Ibid.

144 Ibid.

right angles to each other and providing a space between the cut ends to define the necessary storage slot.[145]

However, the Federal Circuit did not find that this reference can negate the fact that the claim language clearly recited right angle corner pieces.[146] The Federal Circuit cited the well-established Dedication to the Public Rule that "subject matter disclosed but not claimed in a patent application is dedicated to the public,"[147] and asserted that if *Unique Concepts* intended to claim the mitered linear border pieces as an alternative to its right angle corner border pieces, it had to draft the claim to cover that alternative.[148]

iii. Impact of 2009 Judicial Interpretation

The 2009 Judicial Interpretation affirmed the important role of the description in claim interpretation. It also provides for a PHOSITA's understanding of the description, to expand the use of PHOSITA from infringement under the doctrine of equivalents to literal infringement as a new tool. Many courts heavily relied on technical experts to use PHOSITA in determining infringement under the doctrine of equivalents. It is very likely that the courts will apply the same approach when using PHOSITA in determining literal infringement.

4.2.4 Prosecution History: The Estoppel Principle

Article 6 of the 2009 Judicial Interpretation defines the Principle of Estoppel,[149] which provides that prosecution history can be used to limit both the literal scope of a patent and its expanded scope under the doctrine of equivalents. Article 6 provides that in patent infringement litigation, the scope of a patent cannot include "the technology solution which was abandoned by patentee or applicant during patent prosecution or invalidation procedure, by amending claims or description or making a statement."[150] Although the text of the Judicial Interpretation does not use the wording of the Estoppel Principle, the official interpretation by the Third Tribunal of the SPC affirmed that Article 6 shall be construed as the definition of the Estoppel Principle, and clarified that this principle applies to both literal claim interpretation and to the doctrine of equivalents. The evolution of this principle is discussed infra "Estoppel Principle" in "the Doctrine of Equivalents."

---

145 Ibid., Col. 8, lines 28–41.

146 *Unique Concepts*, Inc., at 1562.

147 Ibid., at 1562–63.

148 Ibid.

149 Guanyu Shenli Qinfan Zhuanliquan Jiufen Anjian Yingyong Falü Ruogan Wenti de Jieshi (关于审理侵犯专利权纠纷案件应用法律若干问题的解释) [Explanations of Issues regarding to Application of Law on Patent Infringement Trial] Art 6 (Promulgated by Sup. People's Ct., Dec. 29, 2009, effective Jan.1, 2010), (Chinalawinfo) (China).

150 Ibid.

4.2.5 PHOSITA—2009 and 2016 Judicial Interpretation

For the first time, the 2009 Judicial Interpretation adopted PHOSITA.[151] In the 1990s, PHOSITA had only been used by the courts to determine infringement under the doctrine of equivalents.[152] The 2009 Judicial Interpretation adopted PHOSITA in claim interpretation in general, which also includes literal infringement. The 2016 Judicial Interpretation further emphasized that if there are more than one proposed interpretation of a claim term but PHOSITA would have only one interpretation after reading the claim and description, the court should adopt this one interpretation according to PHOSITA.[153]

The U.S. case law clarifies that the knowledge level of PHOSITA claim interpretation is determined by invent date, and the knowledge level of PHOISTA in doctrine of equivalents is determined by infringement date.

4.3 Structure of a Chinese Patent

A patent includes three parts: a description, an abstract of description, and the claims.[154] In contrast to the practice in the United States, where claims are included at the end of the specification,[155] claims in Chinese patents appear in a separate section. Descriptions of Chinese patents serve similar functions as the specification in U.S. patents.[156] Drawings can be attached and are a part of the description.[157] Descriptions aim to provide clear and complete instructions that are sufficient for a person skilled in the relevant technology field to carry them out.[158] Descriptions, including

---

151 Ibid.

152 E.g. Zhoulin v. Beijing Aomei Guang Jidian Lianhe Kaifa Gongsi, Beijing Huaao Dianzi Yiliao Yiqi Youxian Gongsi (周林诉北京奥美光机电联合开发公司,北京华奥电子医疗仪器有限公司) [Zhoulin v. Beijing Aomei Guangjidian Lianhe Kaifa LL.C., Beijing Huaoa Electronic Medical Device LL.C.], ipr. Chinacourt (Beijing Hig. People's Ct., Mar. 22, 1996).

153 Guanyu Shenli Qinfan Zhuanliquan Jiufen Anjian Yingyong Falü Ruogan Wenti de Jieshi (Er) (关于审理侵犯专利权纠纷案件应用法律若干问题的解释(二)) [Explanations of Issues regarding to Application of Law on Patent Infringement Trial II] (Promulgated by Sup. People's Ct., Jan. 25, 2016, effective April.1, 2016, amended on Dec. 29, 2020), (Chinalawinfo) (China).

154 Zhuanli Fa (专利法) [Patent Law], art.26, (promulgated by the Standing Comm. Nat'l People's Cong., Mar.12, 1984, effective Apr. 1, 1985)1984 Standing Comm. Nat'l People's Cong. Gaz. (China). English version is available in lawinfochina. The official English version of Chinese Patent Law translates "说明书" as description, although some secondary resource translates the "说明书" as specification.

155 Patent Act, 35 U.S.C. § 111.

156 Ibid.

157 Zhuanli Fa (专利法) [Patent Law], art.26, (promulgated by the Standing Comm. Nat'l People's Cong., Mar.12, 1984, effective Apr. 1, 1985)1984 Standing Comm. Nat'l People's Cong. Gaz. (China). English version is available in lawinfochina.

158 Ibid.

attached drawings, are most frequently considered in claim interpretation.[159] Some courts explicitly provide that the abstract of the description cannot be used as a reference in claim interpretation.[160]

"Technical feature" is a concept similar to the "element" in U.S. patent claims. Detailed Rules for the Implementation of the Patent Law (hereafter Detailed Rules) provide that "the patent claim shall state the technical features of the invention or utility model, and define clearly and concisely the scope of the requested protection".[161]

There are two kinds of claims: independent claims and dependent claims.[162] Chinese Patent Law generally requires that independent claims should be drafted in two sections—a preamble section and a characterization section—unless this two-section format is inappropriate or ineffective to define the patented technology.[163] The purpose is to make it easier for the public to distinguish the unique technical features of the patented technology and the common technical features shared by the patented technology and the prior art.[164]

The preamble section includes two kinds of information: (1) subject matter of the patented technology, and (2) prior art.[165] If the patented technology included some technical features available in the prior art, those technical features should be written in the preamble.[166] For instance, the invention point of a photographic camera is

---

159 Guanyu Shenli Qinfan Zhuanliquan Jiufen Anjian Yingyong Falü Ruogan Wenti de Jieshi (关于审理侵犯专利权纠纷案件应用法律若干问题的解释) [Explanations of Issues regarding to Application of Law on Patent Infringement Trial] art 3, (Promulgated by Sup. People's Ct., Dec. 29, 2009, effective Jan.1, 2010), (Chinalawinfo) (China).

160 E.g. Zhuanli Qinquan Panding Ruogan Wenti de Yijian (专利侵权判定若干问题的意见) [The opinion on several issues of deciding patent infringement] art. 10. (Promulgated by Beijing Hig. People's Ct., 2001), (Chinalawinfo) (China). Beijing High People's Court ruled that abstract cannot be used to interpret patent claims.

161 Zhuanli Fa Shishi Xize (专利法实施细则) [Detailed Rules for the Implementation of the Patent Law] arts.19, (promulgated by the St. Council., Jun.15, 2001, effective Jul. 1,2001, amended Jan.09., 2010) (Chinalawinfo) (China). Some scholar translated as elements. But the official version in infolawchina database is technical feature.

162 "The patent claim shall have an independent claim, and may also contain dependent claims. An independent claim shall outline the technical solution of an invention or utility model and record the technical features necessary for solving technical problems Dependent claims shall further define the quoted claim with additional technical features." Zhuanli Fa Shishi Xize (专利法实施细则) [Detailed Rules for the Implementation of the Patent Law] arts.20, (promulgated by the St. Council., Jun.15, 2001, effective Jul. 1,2001, amended Jan.09., 2010) (Chinalawinfo) (China).

163 Zhuanli Fa Shishi Xize (专利法实施细则) [Detailed Rules for the Implementation of the Patent Law] arts.21, (promulgated by the St. Council., Jun.15, 2001, effective Jul. 1,2001, amended Jan.09., 2010) (Chinalawinfo) (China).

164 Zhuanli Shencha Zhinan (专利审查指南) [Patent Examination Guideline] part II Chapter 2. (promulgated by the St. Intellectual Property Office, Jan.1, 2010, effective Feb. 1, 2010) (CNIPA) (China).

165 Zhuanli Fa Shishi Xize (专利法实施细则) [Detailed Rules for the Implementation of the Patent Law] arts.21, (promulgated by the St. Council., Jun.15, 2001, effective Jul. 1,2001, amended Jan.09., 2010) (Chinalawinfo) (China).

166 Ibid.

"an improvement to the cloth shutter of the camera."[167] The preamble section of the independent claim can simply describe "a photographic camera, including a cloth shutter".[168] However, it is not necessary to state other common features shared by the prior art and the invention, such as lens, viewfinder or other parts of a camera.[169]

The purpose of the characterization section of the independent claim is to describe the new or improved technical features[170] that are created by the patented invention. The characterization section begins with phrase: "characterized in that," or other similar wording.[171]

4.4 Defining the Literal Claim Scope

4.4.1 Canons of Claim Interpretation

a. Claim Interpretation Canons in General

The canons of claim interpretation found in U.S. law have been explicitly addressed in either Chinese statutes or cases. Although Chinese claim interpretation rules have not been developed to the same level of detail as the corresponding U.S. laws, U.S. canons of claim interpretation have been recognized by Chinese patent law scholars and discussed in patent law literature. Also, some Chinese cases addressed similar issues to those found in U.S. claim interpretation canons.[172]

b. Claim Differentiation Principle

The Claim Differentiation Principle is understood as an assumption that the two patent claims should be interpreted to have different scopes and no claim is unnec-

---

[167] Zhuanli Shencha Zhinan (专利审查指南) [Patent Examination Guideline] part II Chapter 2. (promulgated by the St. Intellectual Property Office, Jan.1, 2010, effective Feb. 1, 2010) (CNIPA) (China).

[168] Ibid.

[169] Ibid.

[170] Zhuanli Fa Shishi Xize (专利法实施细则) [Detailed Rules for the Implementation of the Patent Law] arts.21, (promulgated by the St. Council., Jun.15, 2001, effective Jul. 1,2001, amended Jan.09., 2010) (Chinalawinfo) (China).

[171] Zhuanli Shencha Zhinan (专利审查指南) [Patent Examination Guideline] part II Chapter 2 3.31 (promulgated by the St. Intellectual Property Office, Jan.1, 2010, effective Feb. 1, 2010) (CNIPA) (China).

[172] *E.g.* application of claim differentiation principle Zuhe Yichu Shiyong Zhuanli (组合衣橱实用新型专利) [In Re Zhuhe Yichu Utility Patent] in Zhang Xiaodu (张晓都), Zhuanli Qinquan Panding: Lilun Tantao Yu Shenpan Shijian [张晓都,专利侵权判定:理论探讨与审判实践,2008.Zhang Xiaodu, Deciding Patent Infringement: Theoretical Discussion and Practice in Trial] (2008), and Haodeng Jituan Gongsi v. Shanghai Kesheng (豪登集团公司诉上海科盛) [Howden Group Limited v. Shanghai Kesheng], ipr.Chinacourt. (2005).

essary.[173] Although it is not named as a principle in patent law provisions and is only mentioned in literature, it is actually applied in practice. *Howden*, decided by the Shanghai High People's Court, is a typical example.[174] Although the judicial opinion does not use the term "differentiation principle," the judge, Xiaodu Zhang, who handled the case used this term in his book in order to explain his own reasoning in this case.[175] Judge Zhang reported in his book that he heavily relied on U.S. case law as a reference in his own practice. Therefore, it is not surprising that the analysis in his case is very similar to the U.S. claim differentiation principle.

The issue in *Howden* was whether a dependent claim should be a limitation to an independent claim.[176] The Shanghai High People's Court's answered in the negative.[177] In *Howden*, claim 1 stated that "the first and the second fanshaped boards, and at least the second fanshaped board is made of a board which is almost flat."[178] Claim 2 stated that "the fanshaped board, which is closer to the rotor, is convex in surface."[179] The trial court interpreted "the fanshaped boards" in claim 1 as a fanshaped board which is convex in surface.[180] The appellate court overturned and held that the "fanshaped board" should have a broader meaning than "a fanshaped board which is convex in surface."[181] "The fanshaped boards", the appellate court held, should cover other technical solutions in description besides a "fanshaped board which is convex in surface, because otherwise claim 1 and claim 2 has the same scope and one of them is unnecessary".[182] Judge Xiaodu Zhang, who presided over Howden, argued that the differentiation principle should be an assumption, which can be rebutted if evidence (prosecution or invalidation history) shows that the two claims define the same technical solution.[183]

The SPC addressed the relationship between claims in 2007 in its official Responses to lower courts' questions. The SPC clarified that the technical features should not be limitations to other dependent claims, and that the technical features

[173] Zuhe Yichu Shiyong Zhuanli (组合衣橱实用新型专利) [In Re Zhuhe Yichu Utility Patent], in Zhang Xiaodu, Zhuanli Qinquan Panding: Lilun Tantao Yu Shenpan Shijian [张晓都,专利侵权判定:理论探讨与审判实践,2008.Zhang Xiaodu, Deciding Patent Infringement: Theoretical Discussion and Practice in Trial] 17–34 (2008).

[174] Haodeng Jituan Gongsi v. Shanghai Kesheng (豪登集团公司诉上海科盛) [Howden Group Limited v. Shanghai Kesheng], ipr.Chinacourt. (2005). See comments in Zhang Xiaodu, Zhuanli Qinquan Panding: Lilun Tantao Yu Shenpan Shijian [张晓都,专利侵权判定:理论探讨与审判实践,2008. Zhang Xiaodu, Deciding Patent Infringement: Theoretical Discussion and Practice in Trial] (2008).

[175] Ibid.

[176] Ibid.

[177] Ibid.

[178] Ibid.

[179] Ibid.

[180] Ibid.

[181] Ibid.

[182] Ibid.

[183] Ibid.

also should not be limitations to other dependent claims.[184] However, when interpreting a dependent claim, the scope of a patent should include technical features in both the disputed dependent claim and the independent claim cited by the disputed dependent claims.[185] The document did not address the issue in *Howden*, which questions whether a dependent claim can be a limitation to an independent claim. Thus, there is still a question of whether the ruling in *Howden* would be applied in jurisdictions other than Shanghai.

4.4.2 Special Types of Claims

a. Functional Technical Features

Paragraph 6 of 35 U.S.C. 112 limits the scope of the means plus function claim to the disclosed embodiments and their equivalents. The Federal Circuit has been working on finding a "solid test"[186] to determine whether a particular claim element is a means-plus-function element. In China, a means-plus-function element is referred to as a functional technical feature,[187] Similar to the U.S. law, determining a functional technical feature in China is made on an "element-by-element basis."

Before 2016, the Chinese law is not clear on the issue of whether a judge has to narrowly interpret a functional technical feature. The ambiguity of the law reflects

---

[184] Kunming Zhiyao Jituan Gufen Youxian Gongsi yu Kunming Longjin Yaoye Youxian Gongsi Zhuanli Qinquan Jiufen Yian de Dafu (关于昆明制药集团股份有限公司与昆明龙津药业有限公司专利侵权纠纷一案的答复) [In Re Kunming Zhiyao LL.C. v. Kunming Longjin LL.C], ipr.chinacourt. (Sup. People's Ct. 2005) 2005.

Guanyu dui Dangshiren Nengfou Xuanze Congshu Quanli Yaoqiu Queding Zhuanliquan Baohu Fanwei de Qingshi de Dafu (关于对当事人能否选择从属权利要求确定专利权保护范围的请示的答复) [In Re the dependent claims], ipr. Chinacourt. (Sup. People's Ct. 2007).

[185] Guanyu dui Dangshiren Nengfou Xuanze Congshu Quanli Yaoqiu Queding Zhuanliquan Baohu Fanwei de Qingshi de Dafu (关于对当事人能否选择从属权利要求确定专利权保护范围的请示的答复) [In Re the dependent claims], ipr. Guanyu Shenli Qinfan Zhuanliquan Jiufen Anjian Yingyong Falü Ruogan Wenti de Jieshi (关于审理侵犯专利权纠纷案件应用法律若干问题的解释) [Explanations of Issues regarding to Application of Law on Patent Infringement Trial] (Promulgated by Sup. People's Ct., Dec. 29, 2009, effective Jan.1, 2010), Chinalawinfo (China). Chinacourt. (Sup. People's Ct. 2007).

[186] Robert L. Harmon, Cynthia A. Homan, and Charles M. McMahon, Patents and the Federal Circuit 410 (2011).

[187] Art.8 Guanyu Shenli Qinfan Zhuanliquan Jiufen Anjian Yingyong Falü Ruogan Wenti de Jieshi (Er) (关于审理侵犯专利权纠纷案件应用法律若干问题的解释(二)) [Explanations of Issues regarding to Application of Law on Patent Infringement Trial II] (Promulgated by Sup. People's Ct., Jan. 25, 2016, effective April.1, 2016, amended on Dec. 29, 2020), (Chinalawinfo) (China).

a hesitation to adopt the same approach of 35 U.S.C. 112 (f). The Patent Examination Guidelines discourage using functional technical features to define an invention.[188] It instructs applicants to do their best to avoid the usage of a functional technical feature.[189] Xintian Yin, the former director of the Legal Department of CNIPA (China National Intellectual Property Administration),[190] criticized using functional technical features in claims in his book.[191] According to Xintian Yin, permitting functional technical features is unnecessary and increases the uncertainty of claim interpretation. Although CNIPA holds a negative attitude toward functional technical features, many applicants, especially applicants from the United States, have insisted on drafting claims by function instead of by structure.[192] This practice means that the judiciary must determine how to interpret functional technical features.

The 2016 Judicial interpretation established a presumption that if a technical feature is defined by its function or effect, it is a functional feature and its interpretation should be limited to its embodiments.[193] The 2019 Judicial Interpretation clarified that if "only by reading the claims, a PHOSITA can directly and explicitly determine the specific means for achieving the aforesaid functions or effects", this presumption can be rebutted.[194] This is similar to the U.S. "positive presumption" but with a higher standard to rebut. So far there is nothing in Chinese law similar to the U.S. "rebutting negative presumption". This is good news for the right holders of Chinese patents, because as long as your claim is not defined by function or effect, you can be sure that a Chinese court won't find functional technical feature.

---

[188] Zhuanli Shencha Zhinan (专利审查指南) [Patent Examination Guideline] Part2 Chapter 2, 3.2.1 (promulgated by the St. Intellectual Property Office, Jan.1, 2010, effective Feb. 1, 2010) (SIPO) (China).

[189] Ibid.

[190] The Legal Department of SIPO's responsibility includes provide the draft of patent law proposal and thus plays an important role in patent legislation.

[191] Yin Xingtian (尹新天), Zhuanliquan de Baohu (专利权的保护) [Protection of Patent Rights] 339 (2005).

[192] Yan Wenjun (闫文军), Zhuanliquan de Baohu Fanwei: Quanli Yaoqiu Jieshi he Dengtong Yuanze Shiyong (专利权的保护范围:权利要求解释和等同原则适用) [Yan Wenjun, Scope of Patent Protection: Interpretation of Claim and Application of Doctrine of Equivalents] (2007). Yin Xingtian (尹新天), Zhuanliquan de Baohu (专利权的保护) [Protection of Patent Rights] 339 (2005).

[193] Article 4, Guanyu Shenli Qinfan Zhuanliquan Jiufen Anjian Yingyong Falü Ruogan Wenti de Jieshi (关于审理侵犯专利权纠纷案件应用法律若干问题的解释) [Explanations of Issues regarding to Application of Law on Patent Infringement Trial] (Promulgated by Sup. People's Ct., Dec. 29, 2009, effective Jan.1, 2010), (Chinalawinfo)art.4 (China), art 4.

[194] Article 8, Guanyu Shenli Qinfan Zhuanliquan Jiufen Anjian Yingyong Falü Ruogan Wenti de Jieshi (Er) (关于审理侵犯专利权纠纷案件应用法律若干问题的解释(二)) [Explanations of Issues regarding to Application of Law on Patent Infringement Trial II] (Promulgated by Sup. People's Ct., Jan. 25, 2016, effective April.1, 2016, amended on Dec. 29, 2020), (Chinalawinfo) (China).

i. Cases in Beijing and Shanghai Jurisdiction before 2006

Both Beijing and Shanghai People's High Courts' decided cases regarding to functional technical features in 2006. In both cases, the functional technical feature is identified as the technical feature that only contains a function. Similarly, the two courts limited the scope of functional technical features by the embodiments and their equivalents.

(1) Identifying Functional Technical Features

In cases tried in the Shanghai and the Beijing High People's Courts, the judges identified the technical features as "functional" because they were only defined by their functions without specific structures.

The disputed claim in *Zhan Chi*, decided by the Beijing High People's Court, involved an invention of insoles which can keep shoes stink-free.[195] The claim disclosed the components of the insole, but all components were described by their functions instead of by the structures.[196] The disputed technical feature was one of the components, which is a layer allowing liquid to infiltrate unidirectionally.[197] The claim merely defined the layer by its function: "allows liquid to unidirectionally infiltrate."[198]

Similarly, the disputed claim in *Liang Jinshui*, decided by the Shanghai High People's Court, listed the components of the patented device but only defined the components by their functions.[199] For example, one of the components was "a device which can brush the glue on the side".[200]

(2) Interpreting Functional Technical Features

In both cases, the Beijing and the Shanghai High People's Court interpreted the functional technical features using the same approach: the functional technical feature should not be literally interpreted as it includes all the methods which have the claimed function. Instead, the meaning of the technical feature should be limited to the method (s) disclosed in the description and the equivalents (s).

As a result, in *Zhan Chi*, the functional technical feature was interpreted as limited to the structure disclosed in the description, which was a kind of fabric with funnel-form holes.[201] The accused infringing product used a non-weaving cloth to allow liquid to unidirectionally infiltrate.[202] The Beijing High People's Court compared

---

[195] Zhanchi v. Zhenyu Gongsi (展翅诉珍誉公司) [Zhanchi v. Zhenyu Company], ipr. Chinacourt, (Beijing Hig. People's Ct., Jun. 13, 2006)) http://www.panjueshu.com/beijing/gaoyuan/m20060613 2006367.html.

[196] Ibid.

[197] Ibid.

[198] Ibid.

[199] Liang Jinshui v. Li Changzhong etc. (梁锦水与李昌众等) [Liang Jinshui v. Li Changzhong ect] ipr. Chinacourt. (Shanghai Hig. People's Ct. July 10th, 2006) ipr. Chincout. (July10,2006).

[200] Ibid.

[201] Zhanchi v. Zhenyu Gongsi (展翅诉珍誉公司) [Zhanchi v. Zhenyu Company], ipr. Chinacourt, (Beijing Hig. People's Ct., Jun. 13, 2006)).

[202] Ibid.

non-weaving cloth and fabric with funnel-form, and decided they are not the same or equivalent.[203]

On the other hand, the Shanghai High People's Court interpreted "the device which can brush the glue on the side" as a device that has the structure disclosed on the description, which has driving wheels, a wheel which brushes the glue, and a sensor.[204] Because the accused infringing device had a manual glue brushing procedure and did not have the wheel which brushes the glue or any equivalents, the court found non-infringement.[205]

ii. Different Approach: A case in Zhejiang High People's Court 2008

Notably, Beijing and Shanghai High People's Courts' approach to interpreting functional claims has not been adopted in all other jurisdictions. For example, in *Liang Jinshui* (Zhejiang), the Zhejiang High People's Court did not think it was necessary to treat the functional technical feature in different ways. And this case was later affirmed by Supreme People's Court.

The factual patterns between Liang Jinshui (Shanghai) and Liang Jinshui (Zhejianng) were similar. The plaintiff in the Shanghai case, which was decided by the Shanghai People's Court, litigated the same patent claim in the Zhejiang High People's Court. Although one of defendants to the Zhejiang litigation was not a defendant in the Shanghai litigation, the accused infringing device was basically the same.

However, the Zhejiang High People's Court did not adopt a particular approach to interpret the functional technical claim. It found non-infringement without considering the limitations from the description to the claim.[206]Without discussing the structure of the claimed device, the Zhejiang High People's Court simply held that "manually brushing glue" is not a device.[207] Consequently, that court found that it was substantially different from the claimed device.[208] The Zhejiang High People's Court thus concluded there is no literal infringement or infringement under the doctrine of equivalents.[209]

In comparison, the Shanghai High People's Court identified the devices used in the procedure for the manual brushing of glue.[210] It admitted that the accused infringer did use devices to brush the glue, but held that the devices were different from the patented structure. Thus, the Shanghai and the Zhejiang High People's Courts reached conclusions of non-infringement using very different approaches.

---

203 Ibid.

204 Liang Jinshui v. Li Changzhong etc. (梁锦水诉李昌众等) [Liang Jinshui v. Li Changzhong ect] ipr. Chinacourt. (Shanghai Hig. People's Ct. July 10th, 2006) ipr. Chincout. (July10, 2006).

205 Ibid.

206 Ibid.

207 Ibid.

208 Ibid.

209 Ibid.

210 Ibid.

iii. 2009 Judicial Interpretation

According to the new provision in the 2009 Judicial Interpretation, if a technical feature is expressed by its function or effect, courts should limit the scope of the technical feature to the embodiments in description and in the attached drawings.[211] Thus, the 2009 Judicial Interpretation created an presumption that if the expression of a claim defines a technical feature by its function or effect, then it is a functional technical feature. This provision clarifies that a functional technical feature is limited by its embodiments. However, it does not clarify that in what kind of situation this presumption can be rebutted.

iv. 2016 Judicial Interpretation

The 2016 Judicial Interpretation continued on what the 2009 Judicial Interpretation did not finish, by providing the presumption of functional technical feature can be rebutted if "only by reading the claims, a PHOSITA can directly and explicitly determine the specific means for achieving the aforesaid functions or effects".[212] This is similar to the rebuttable "positive presumption" in the U.S. case law. But comparing to the U.S. rule to rebut the presumption with "sufficient structure", the Chinese standard to rebut is higher.

In *Phillips en banc*, the Federal Circuit found "sufficient structure" and rebut the positive presumption, based on a PHOSITA'S understanding on claim and specification.[213] However, in order overcome the presumption in China, a PHOSITA has to figure out the structure by merely reading the claim. For example, in a Supreme People's Court case decided in 2020, the court found the technical feature is not functional, because there is a common sense in the industry about what "device for transmission" is in a hoverboard product and a PHOSITA can directly and explicitly determine the specific means for device for transmission" by merely reading the clam itself.[214]

---

[211] Article 4, Guanyu Shenli Qinfan Zhuanliquan Jiufen Anjian Yingyong Falü Ruogan Wenti de Jieshi (关于审理侵犯专利权纠纷案件应用法律若干问题的解释) [Explanations of Issues regarding to Application of Law on Patent Infringement Trial] (Promulgated by Sup. People's Ct., Dec. 29, 2009, effective Jan.1, 2010), (Chinalawinfo)art.4 (China), art 4.

[212] Article 8, Guanyu Shenli Qinfan Zhuanliquan Jiufen Anjian Yingyong Falü Ruogan Wenti de Jieshi (Er) (关于审理侵犯专利权纠纷案件应用法律若干问题的解释(二)) [Explanations of Issues regarding to Application of Law on Patent Infringement Trial II] (Promulgated by Sup. People's Ct., Jan. 25, 2016, effective April.1, 2016, amended on Dec. 29, 2020), (Chinalawinfo) (China).

[213] *Phillips*, 415 F.3d, at 1311.

[214] Zhejiang Bosuer Yundong Qixie Youxian Gongsi v. Hangzhou Qike Zhineng Keji Youxian Gongsi (浙江波速尔运动器械有限公司与杭州骑客智能科技有限公司), (2018)Zui Gao Fa Min Shen 2345 Hao (Sup. People's Ct. 2020) (China).

b. Product-by-Process Claim

A product-by-process claim is a claim that defines a product by its manufacturing process.[215] There are two kinds of product-by-process claims.[216] One holds that the subject matter of a patent claim is a product, but at least part of the technical feature is technology involved in the manufacturing process.[217] Another kind of product-by-process claim is one of two independent claims: one independent claim defines the manufacturing process of the product and another defines the other technical features of the product.[218] There are very few cases which have treated the product-by-process claim in a different way from other claims. In one Shanghai High People's Court case, *Pan Luli*,[219] the court held that in either kind of product-by-process claim the process is a necessary technical feature. Therefore, the claim cannot be interpreted so broadly as to allow the scope to include a product with the same characteristics but manufactured by a different process.

In *Pan Luli*,[220] the dependent claim disclosed the structure and the manufacturing process of a frame. The frame, as the claim disclosed, was made of osier which had been soaked by liquid medicine. The accused infringing product was a frame made of osier which was not soaked by liquid medicine. The court found non-infringement, since the scope of the patent only included the product made by the same process. Missing "soaked by liquid medicine" resulted in a product that was beyond the patent's scope.

In 2016 Judicial Interpretation, the SPC made it clear that process terms in product-by-process claims serve as limitations in determining infringement, which is consistent with the *Panluli* case. Article 10 of the 2016 judicial interpretation defines the process claim as "the technical features of a product are defined through manufacture process in the claims".[221]

c. Combination of Chemistry Components

As required by the CNIPA Examination Guideline, the claim for a chemical composition shall be characterized by the features of the composition, such as the components

---

[215] Zhang Xiaodu (张晓都), Shanghai High Court judge's books Zhang Xiaodu, Zhuanli Qinquan Panding: Lilun Tantao Yu Shenpan Shijian (专利侵权判定:理论探讨与审判实践) [Deciding Patent Infringement: Theoretical Discussion and Practice in Trial] (Falü Chubanshe 2008).

[216] Yin Xingtian (尹新天), Zhuanliquan de Baohu (专利权的保护) [Protection of Patent Rights] 280 (2005).

[217] Ibid.

[218] Ibid.

[219] Pan Luli v. Shanghai Gaoyu Yiliao Qixie Chang (潘璐莉与上海高宇医疗器材厂) [Pan Luli v. Shanghai Gaoyu Medical Device Factory], ipr. Chinacourt (Shanghai High People's Ct., 2004).

[220] Ibid.

[221] Guanyu Shenli Qinfan Zhuanliquan Jiufen Anjian Yingyong Falü Ruogan Wenti de Jieshi (Er) (关于审理侵犯专利权纠纷案件应用法律若干问题的解释(二)) [Explanations of Issues regarding to Application of Law on Patent Infringement Trial II] (Promulgated by Sup. People's Ct., Jan. 25, 2016, effective April.1, 2016, amended on Dec. 29, 2020), (Chinalawinfo) (China).

or the contents.[222] There are two ways to present a claim of a composition: open-ended or close-ended.[223] The open-ended claim should be interpreted more broadly than the components listed in the claim, while the close-ended approach should be limited to the components listed in the claim.[224]

Open-ended claims are identified by their wording as well as descriptions.[225] The commonly used wording for the open-ended approach is as follows: "comprising" "including" "containing" "essentially comprising" "substantially comprising" "mainly consisting of" "be mainly composed of" "substantially consist of" "be substantially composed of," etc.[226] To be identified as an open-ended claim, the use of open-ended language is not sufficient.[227] The claim has to be supported by a description.[228] If the description does not explain other components, the claim is deemed a close-ended claim and therefore interpreted narrowly.[229]

In close-ended claims, the commonly used wording must include: "consisting of" "be composed of" "be balanced with," etc.[230] All of these phrases indicate that the composition claim is composed of the indicated components only, without any other components to be included therein.[231] Even if the description disclosed other components, as held by some courts, the scope of the patent should still be limited to the components listed in the patent.[232] Therefore, if the accused infringing product contains another component, it should be deemed non-infringement. The exception is that impurities in the content are not considered to be components, as long as the percentage of impurities in the content is "normal."[233]

In infringement litigation, judges would interpret a claim of chemistry components by reference to the CNIPA Examination Guideline. Once a claim is identified as a closed-ended claim based on its wording, the frequently disputed issue is whether "other" components in a defendant's product are merely "impurities."[234]

---

[222] Zhuanli Shencha Zhinan (专利审查指南) [Patent Examination Guideline]part 2, chapter10, 4.2.1, art. 26.4 (promulgated by the St. Intellectual Property Office, Jan.1, 2010, effective Feb. 1, 2010) (CNIPA) (China).

[223] Ibid.

[224] Ibid.

[225] Ibid.

[226] Ibid.

[227] Ibid.

[228] Ibid.

[229] Ibid.

[230] Ibid.

[231] Ibid.

[232] Beijing Nanchen Touzi Youxian Gongsi, Beijing Weihao Lüye Youxian Gongsi v. Wujiang Feile Dianzi Youxian Gongsi (北京南辰投资有限公司 北京伟豪铝业有限公司诉吴江飞乐电子有限公司), (Shanghai Hig. People's Ct., 2004).

[233] Zhuanli Shencha Zhinan (专利审查指南) [Patent Examination Guideline]part 2, chapter10, 4.2.1, art. 26.4 (promulgated by the St. Intellectual Property Office, Jan.1, 2010, effective Feb. 1, 2010) (CNIPA) (China).

[234] Ibid.

In *Nanchen* decided by Shanghai High People's Court, the claim used the phrase "balanced with" in front of a list of chemical components.[235] The accused product contained titanium, magnesium and zinc, which were not listed in the claim.[236] The forensic report supported a finding of infringement, since it stated that titanium, magnesium and zinc are considered as unavoidable impurities.[237] Despite the forensic report, the trial court found non-infringement.[238] The patentee appealed and the appellate court affirmed, and further explained the reasoning concerning the close-ended claim.[239] The appellate court agreed with the forensic report that magnesium and zinc are unavoidable impurities, but pointed out that titanium is an additional component.[240] Although the component aluminum in the claim usually contains a small portion of titanium as an impurity, the description suggested it should be no more than 0.01%.[241] The accused product had titanium—as much as 0.013%—which exceeded the amount of the normal level of impurity.[242] Accordingly, the appellate court found non-infringement because of the additional component in the accused infringing product.[243]

The patentee argued that the description disclosed that a grain refinement was added during the manufacturing process, and this increased the amount of titanium. Therefore, the product, despite having 0.013% titanium, should still be within the scope of the patent. The appellate court rejected this argument by stating the technical solution in the description could not be imported into the claim.

The 2016 Judicial Interpretation confirmed that "impurities" is an exception. Article 7 provides that "where any alleged infringing technical solution is supplemented with other technical features on the basis of including all technical features of the claims for any enclosed composition, the people's court shall determine the alleged infringing technical solution does not fall within the scope of protection of the patent right, except when the added technical features do fall within the scope of the conventional quantity of inevitable impurities."[244]

---

[235] Beijing Nanchen Touzi Youxian Gongsi, Beijing Weihao Lüye Youxian Gongsi v. Wujiang Feile Dianzi Youxian Gongsi (北京南辰投资有限公司 北京伟豪铝业有限公司诉吴江飞乐电子有限公司), (Shanghai Hig. People's Ct., 2004).

[236] Ibid.

[237] Ibid.

[238] Ibid.

[239] Ibid.

[240] Ibid.

[241] Ibid.

[242] Ibid.

[243] Ibid.

[244] Guanyu Shenli Qinfan Zhuanliquan Jiufen Anjian Yingyong Falü Ruogan Wenti de Jieshi (Er) (关于审理侵犯专利权纠纷案件应用法律若干问题的解释(二)) [Explanations of Issues regarding to Application of Law on Patent Infringement Trial II] (Promulgated by Sup. People's Ct., Jan. 25, 2016, effective April.1, 2016, amended on Dec. 29, 2020), (Chinalawinfo) (China).

d. Dependent Claims

It used to be unclear among practitioners in China whether a patentee could enforce patent rights solely based on a dependent claim. It was forbidden by some courts but finally permitted by the SPC. As an exception to the Claim Differentiation Principle, the limitations of independent claims should be read into dependent claims.[245]

In the past, courts emphasized the importance of independent claims, since these should be broader than dependent claims.[246] Some courts forbade patentees from solely litigating a dependent claim, unless the independent claim was invalidated and the dependent claim replaced the independent claim.[247] If the infringement could be established by a dependent claim, forcing the patentee to litigate the broadest claim, was a waste of time and money. Some courts changed this rigid rule to allow patentees to choose between claims,[248] but the issue remained unresolved until 2007.

In 2007, in an official Response to a lower court's question, the SPC clarified that if the patentee gave up the independent claim and only asserted infringement based on a dependent claim, the court should permit it. Further, the SPC clarified the rule concerning interpretation of a dependent claim. Both the technical features in the disputed dependent claim and in the independent claim, which is cited by the disputed dependent claim, should establish the limitations of the patent scope. It is wrongful to omit the technical features in independent claims or to include limitations of other irrelevant claims.[249] These rules are confirmed by the SPC's Interpretation at the end of 2009.[250]

---

[245] Guanyu dui Dangshiren Nengfou Xuanze Congshu Quanli Yaoqiu Queding Zhuanliquan Baohu Fanwei de Qingshi de Dafu (关于对当事人能否选择从属权利要求确定专利权保护范围的请示的答复) [In Re the dependent claims], ipr. Chinacourt. (Sup. People's Ct. 2007) Guanyu Shenli Qinfan Zhuanliquan Jiufen Anjian Yingyong Falü Ruogan Wenti de Jieshi (关于审理侵犯专利权纠纷案件应用法律若干问题的解释) [Explanations of Issues regarding to Application of Law on Patent Infringement Trial] (Promulgated by Sup. People's Ct., Dec. 29, 2009, effective Jan.1, 2010), (Chinalawinfo) (China).

[246] E.g. Zhuanli Qinquan Panding Ruogan Wenti de Yijian (专利侵权判定若干问题的意见) [The opinion on several issues of deciding patent infringement] (Beijing People's high court, 2001).

[247] Cheng Yongshun (程永顺) & Luo Lihua (罗李华), Zhuanli Qinquan Panding: Zhongmei Fatiao yu Anli Bijiao Yanjiu (专利侵权判定:中美法条与案例比较研究) [Cheng Yongshun, Luo Lihua, Deciding Patent Infringement: Comparative Study on Chinese and U.S. Law and Cases] 107 (Zhishi Chanquan Chubanshe, 2002).

[248] Zhuanli Qinquan Panding Ruogan Wenti de Yijian (专利侵权判定若干问题的意见) [The opinion on several issues of deciding patent infringement] (Beijing People's high court, 2001).

[249] Guanyu dui Dangshiren Nengfou Xuanze Congshu Quanli Yaoqiu Queding Zhuanliquan Baohu Fanwei de Qingshi de Dafu (关于对当事人能否选择从属权利要求确定专利权保护范围的请示的答复) [In Re the dependent claims], ipr. Chinacourt. (Sup. People's Ct. 2007).

[250] Guanyu Shenli Qinfan Zhuanliquan Jiufen Anjian Yingyong Falü Ruogan Wenti de Jieshi (关于审理侵犯专利权纠纷案件应用法律若干问题的解释) [Explanations of Issues regarding to Application of Law on Patent Infringement Trial] art.1 (Promulgated by Sup. People's Ct., Dec. 29, 2009, effective Jan.1, 2010), (Chinalawinfo) (China).

4.5 The Doctrine of Equivalents

In order to determine whether the doctrine of equivalents applies, Chinese courts discuss if any legal limitations exist before examining the evidence to the elements of the doctrine of equivalents.[251] This practice is similar to that established by U.S. case law. There are two major limitations on the doctrine equivalents in China: the dedication principle and the estoppel principle. The Chinese dedication principle is almost identical to that in the United States. The Chinese Estoppel principle is similar to prosecution history estoppel in the United States but has some key differences.

If the Estoppel principle or Dedication principle applies, there is no need to conduct further analysis and there is no infringement.[252] If the legal limitations do not apply, the court will evaluate the differences between the accused technical solution and claims. In order to establish infringement under the doctrine of equivalents, the technical feature in the accused infringing product or process should perform essentially the same function, by essentially the same technical means, and achieve the same general effect.[253] In addition, a PHOSITA should be able to come up with the accused infringing technical feature without any creativity.[254] In practice, determining the level of a PHOSITA relies heavily on the technical experts.

In the early 1990s, some courts found infringement under the doctrine of equivalents without addressing the differences in the technical means.[255] Although this

---

[251] Cheng Yongshun (程永顺)& Luo Lihua (罗李华), Zhuanli Qinquan Panding: Zhongmei Fatiao yu Anli Bijiao Yanjiu (专利侵权判定:中美法条与案例比较研究) [Cheng Yongshun, Luo Lihua, Deciding Patent Infringement: Comparative Study on Chinese and U.S. Law and Cases] (2002).

Yan Wenjun (闫文军), Zhuanliquan de Baohu Fanwei: Quanli Yaoqiu Jieshi he Dengtong Yuanze Shiyong (专利权的保护范围:权利要求解释和等同原则适用) [Yan Wenjun, Scope of Patent Protection: Interpretation of Claim and Application of Doctrine of Equivalents] (2007).

[252] Cheng Yongshun (程永顺)& Luo Lihua (罗李华), Zhuanli Qinquan Panding: Zhongmei Fatiao yu Anli Bijiao Yanjiu (专利侵权判定:中美法条与案例比较研究) [Cheng Yongshun, Luo Lihua, Deciding Patent Infringement: Comparative Study on Chinese and U.S. Law and Cases] (2002).

Yan Wenjun (闫文军), Zhuanliquan de Baohu Fanwei: Quanli Yaoqiu Jieshi he Dengtong Yuanze Shiyong (专利权的保护范围:权利要求解释和等同原则适用) [Yan Wenjun, Scope of Patent Protection: Interpretation of Claim and Application of Doctrine of Equivalents] (2007).

[253] Guanyu Shenli Qinfan Zhuanliquan Jiufen Anjian Yingyong Falü Ruogan Wenti de Jieshi (关于审理侵犯专利权纠纷案件应用法律若干问题的解释) [Explanations of Issues regarding to Application of Law on Patent Infringement Trial] (Promulgated by Sup. People's Ct., 2001), (Chinalawinfo) (China).

[254] Ibid.

[255] E.g. Zhang Yuejin (张跃进), Shuoming Shu Zai Zhuanli Qinquan Panduan zhong de Zuoyong (说明书在专利侵权判断中的作用) [The function of Claims in Patent Infringement Determination], Zhongguo Zhuanli Bao, Jan.19, 1990. Yan Wenjun (闫文军), Zhuanliquan de Baohu Fanwei: Quanli Yaoqiu Jieshi he Dengtong Yuanze Shiyong (专利权的保护范围:权利要求解释和等同原则适用) [Yan Wenjun, Scope of Patent Protection: Interpretation of Claim and Application of Doctrine of Equivalents] 326 327 (2007);Cheng Yongshun (程永顺), Zhuanli Qinquan Panding Shiwu (专利侵权判定实务) [The Practice of Patent Infringement Determination] 28,291 (2001). Jiguang Tance Yi case (激光探测仪案), in Zhishi Chanquan Anli Pingxi (知识产权案例评析) 175 (Chengsi Zheng ed., 1994).

wrongful approach was corrected by some appellate courts' judicial opinions[256] and the Detailed Rule (2001),[257] some judicial opinions still found infringement under the doctrine of equivalents without discussing whether the technical means were basically the same or could be found by a PHOSITA without creativity.[258]

In contrast to the old redundant feature rule, which determined the equivalents as a whole, the doctrine of equivalents requires finding the same or equivalent for every element in the accused infringing technology.

4.5.1 Elements to Establish the Doctrine of Equivalents

According to 2001 Judicial Interpretation, the technical features of accused infringing technology are equivalent to the technical features in a patent if: (a) they perform basically the same function, (b) they achieve basically the same effect, (c) through basically the same technical means, and (d) the technical feature in the accused infringing technology can be found by a person with ordinary skills in the art without any creative effort.[259] The first three elements are similar to a U.S. court's classic test: the function way result test: "if it performs substantially the same function in substantially the same way to obtain the same result", infringement will be found.[260] Also, the last element is similar to the U.S. interchangeability standard.

The evolution of the doctrine of equivalents in Chinese cases has shown that the standard to establish the doctrine of equivalents has become more rigorous. In the early 1990s, one could prove that the doctrine of equivalents applied merely by showing the same function and effect. The difference in technical means was not considered. Before recognizing that the 'obviousness' of the replacement should be evaluated by a PHOSITA, courts used to evaluate it by the opinions of technical experts, whose skill level was higher than average.

The 2001 Judicial Interpretation listed all of the elements to be considered when establishing the doctrine of equivalents. However, judicial opinions show that some courts did not strictly follow the standard provided in that document. Thus, besides

---

[256] Ibid.

[257] Guanyu Shenli Qinfan Zhuanliquan Jiufen Anjian Yingyong Falü Ruogan Wenti de Jieshi (关于审理侵犯专利权纠纷案件应用法律若干问题的解释) [Explanations of Issues regarding to Application of Law on Patent Infringement Trial] (Promulgated by Sup. People's Ct., 2001), (Chinalawinfo) (China).

[258] E.g Chong Yang Dongtai Fajiaoji [充氧动态发酵机], Beijign High People's Court (1992) (离经终字第16号), *in* Cheng Yongshun (程永顺)& Luo Lihua (罗李华), Zhuanli Qinquan Panding: Zhongmei Fatiao yu Anli Bijiao Yanjiu (专利侵权判定:中美法条与案例比较研究) [Cheng Yongshun, Luo Lihua, Deciding Patent Infringement: Comparative Study on Chinese and U.S. Law and Cases] 163 (2002).

[259] Guanyu Shenli Qinfan Zhuanliquan Jiufen Anjian Yingyong Falü Ruogan Wenti de Jieshi (关于审理侵犯专利权纠纷案件适用法律若干问题的解释) [Explanations of Issues regarding to Application of Law on Patent Infringement Trial] art.17 (Promulgated by Sup. People's Ct., 2001), (Chinalawinfo) (China).

[260] *Sanitary Refrigerator Co. v. Winters*, 280 U.S. 30 (1929).

the legal clarity of the standard, the implementation of the standard is also a factor that impacts the legal certainty of patent infringement litigation.

a. Cases before the 1990s

There are few records of patent infringement cases between 1985, when the Patent Law became effective, to 1990. One case indicated that some judges, without adopting the view of the doctrine of equivalents, found infringement in a product which was beyond the literal meaning of the patent claim.

As previously discussed, a court interpreted overlapped edges to mean any edges which have the same shape and size, even if they are separated.[261] By analyzing the purpose of the invention and the overall technical solution, the court concluded that the critical factor in this patented technical solution was that the two edges needed to have the same shape and size. Thus, the two edges did not have to be connected when the manufacturing process was complete. According to the court's understanding, as long as two edges had the same shape and size, and could be connected later, they could achieve the same goal as that of the patent. Consequently, the court found infringement. Without considering the obviousness of the variation or legal limitations, this approach made it much easier to establish the doctrine of equivalents.

b. Cases in the Early 1990s

In the early 1990s, only some cases considered the differences in technical means. Many cases merely discussed an effect and function, without examining the differences in technical means. The PHOSITA standard was not used. Some courts used the concept of "person skilled in the art".[262] The analysis in judicial opinions was usually very brief.[263] In some cases, it is unclear how courts measured the differences to determine if the accused infringement technology was equivalent.[264] Omitting the differences in technical means and the concept of "person skilled in the art" likely resulted in broad patent protection.

The PHOSITA standard was not well recognized by judges in the early 1990s in China. Some cases adopted a concept similar to "a person skilled in the art" to determine whether the replacement of a technical feature in a patent was obvious

---

261 Zhang Yuejin (张跃进), Shuoming Shu Zai Zhuanli Qinquan Panduan zhong de Zuoyong (说明书在专利侵权判断中的作用) [The function of Claims in Patent Infringement Determination], Zhongguo Zhuanli Bao, Jan.19, 1990. Yan Wenjun (闫文军), Zhuanliquan de Baohu Fanwei: Quanli Yaoqiu Jieshi he Dengtong Yuanze Shiyong (专利权的保护范围:权利要求解释和等同原则适用) [Yan Wenjun, Scope of Patent Protection: Interpretation of Claim and Application of Doctrine of Equivalents] 326 327 (2007); Cheng Yongshun (程永顺), Zhuanli Qinquan Panding Shiwu (专利侵权判定实务) [The Practice of Patent Infringement Determination] 28 29 (2001).

262 Jiguang Tance Yi case *(激光探测仪案)*, in Zhishi Chanquan Anli Pingxi (知识产权案例评析) 175 (Chengsi Zheng es., 1994).

263 Cheng Yongshun (程永顺), Zhuanli Qinquan Panding Shiwu (专利侵权判定实务) [The Practice of Patent Infringement Determination] 165 (2001).

264 Ibid.

enough to be equivalent.[265] The earlier analysis did not specify whether the level of knowledge should be "ordinary." Although some scholars suggested that the level of knowledge of a college graduate in the relevant field should be the standard to measure the obviousness of the replacement, this suggestion was not adopted by courts.[266] According to one judge's memoir, the judicial practice during that period was to invite professionals from the forensic center or other expert witnesses to comment on the obviousness of the replacement.[267] In the early 1990s, most forensic centers were administrated by the courts or government agencies (e.g., the China National Intellectual Property Administration). Most professionals holding an appointment in a forensic center were experts with a high level of achievement in their fields. Similarly, most expert witnesses that were invited by the courts to testify were professors or highly successful engineers.[268] As a result, most experts who commented on the obviousness of the replacement actually had higher levels of knowledge than the PHOSITA standard.[269] If a replacement was obvious to these experts, it was not necessarily evident to a PHOSTA. Without their own understanding of what would constitute an ordinary level of knowledge, some judges used to ask these experts to evaluate the replacement, without specifying that their opinion should be based on the PHOSITA standard rather than their higher level of knowledge. Given the courts' practices, the "persons skilled in the art" standard sometimes made it easier to establish infringement under the doctrine of equivalents than "an ordinary person skilled in the art."[270]

In some early 1990s cases, the key issue in determining equivalents was whether the invention and the accused infringing technology differed in function and effect. The technical means was ignored.[271]

---

[265] Jiguang Tance Yi case (激光探测仪案), in Zhishi Chanquan Anli Pingxi (知识产权案例评析) 175 (Chengsi Zheng es., 1994).

[266] Cheng Yongshun (程永顺)& Luo Lihua (罗李华), Zhuanli Qinquan Panding: Zhongmei Fatiao yu Anli Bijiao Yanjiu (专利侵权判定:中美法条与案例比较研究) [Cheng Yongshun, Luo Lihua, Deciding Patent Infringement: Comparative Study on Chinese and U.S. Law and Cases] (2002).

[267] Ibid.

[268] Ibid.

[269] Ibid.

[270] Ibid.

[271] E.g. Qianrushi Zhengfaqi Yian (嵌入式蒸发器一案) [In Re Embedded evaporator], *in* Zhuanli Shangbiao Jishu Hetong Yinan Anli Pingxi (专利、商标、技术合同疑难案例评析) [Review of Patent, Trademark and Technology Transfer Contract] 111 (Yang Jinqi (杨金琪) ed., 1995), and Cheng Yongshun (程永顺)& Luo Lihua (罗李华), Zhuanli Qinquan Panding: Zhongmei Fatiao yu Anli Bijiao Yanjiu (专利侵权判定:中美法条与案例比较研究) [Cheng Yongshun, Luo Lihua, Deciding Patent Infringement: Comparative Study on Chinese and U.S. Law and Cases] 164 (2002). Motuo Che Wuji Biansu Pidai Lun Shiyong Xinxing Zhuanli Qinquan An (摩托车无级变速皮带轮实用新型专利侵权案), *in* Zhuanli Shangbiao Jishu Hetong Yinan Anli Pingxi (专利、商标、技术合同疑难案例评析) [Review of Patent, Trademark and Technology Transfer Contract] 111 (Yang Jinqi (杨金琪) ed., 1995).

In order to change this approach, some appellate courts reversed cases which found equivalents without analyzing the technical means.[272] The SPC also paid attention to this issue and addressed it in a Response in 1995.[273] The lower court had requested the Response in a case involving a device which controlled the amount of liquid in containers. The SPC instructed the lower court to examine whether the accused infringing device and the patented device had the same structure and controlled the amount of liquid in the same way. If the two devices had different structures or controlled the amount of liquid in different ways, the SPC said, infringement under the doctrine of equivalents should not be found. Since then, the technical means became a part of the equivalents test.

Some judges pointed out that the early 1990s approach to determining equivalents may have inappropriately broadened the scope of patent protection.[274] The same effect could be achieved by multiple technical solutions.[275] The patentee was only entitled to the technical solution he/she invented and wrote in claims. If the scope of the patent expanded to all technology which had the same function and effect, it would discourage new and better solutions to resolve the technical problem.

However, some cases in the 1990s were also later criticized for their narrow scope of patent protection. These cases were vague as to what extent the difference in function or effect may make a replacement not in compliance with equivalents. A typical example was a case about steamers.[276] The utility patent claim stated that the steamer had folded edges to connect the pieces. The accused infringing product used a plastic strip to connect the pieces. The trial court found that this difference did not result in different functions or effects, and found infringement under the doctrine of equivalents. The appellate court overturned and found non-infringement because the plastic strip made the installation easier and therefore produced a different effect. The appellate court did not provide further analysis to explain why this different effect was significant enough to make the plastic strip not equivalent to the folded edge. Thus, some judges later criticized this case, because in their view, the replacement

---

[272] Chong Yang Dongtai Fajiaoji (充氧动态发酵机), Beijing High People's Court (北京市高级人民法院))离经终字第16号), *in* Cheng Yongshun (程永顺)& Luo Lihua (罗李华), Zhuanli Qinquan Panding: Zhongmei Fatiao yu Anli Bijiao Yanjiu (专利侵权判定:中美法条与案例比较研究) [Cheng Yongshun, Luo Lihua, Deciding Patent Infringement: Comparative Study on Chinese and U.S. Law and Cases] 163 (2002). Motuo Che Wuji Biansu Pidai Lun Shiyong Xinxing Zhuanli Qinquan An (摩托车无级变速皮带轮实用新型专利侵权案), *in* Zhuanli Shangbiao Jishu Hetong Yinan Anli Pingxi (专利、商标、技术合同疑难案例评析) [Review of Patent, Trademark and Technology Transfer Contract] 111 (Yang Jinqi (杨金琪) ed., 1995).

[273] Yan Wenjun (闫文军), Zhuanliquan de Baohu Fanwei: Quanli Yaoqiu Jieshi he Dengtong Yuanze Shiyong (专利权的保护范围:权利要求解释和等同原则适用) [Yan Wenjun, Scope of Patent Protection: Interpretation of Claim and Application of Doctrine of Equivalents] (2007).

[274] E.g. Motuo Che Wuji Biansu Pidai Lun Shiyong Xinxing Zhuanli Qinquan An (摩托车无级变速皮带轮实用新型专利侵权案), *in* Zhuanli Shangbiao Jishu Hetong Yinan Anli Pingxi (专利、商标、技术合同疑难案例评析) [Review of Patent, Trademark and Technology Transfer Contract] 111 (Yang Jinqi (杨金琪) ed., 1995).

[275] Ibid.

[276] Ibid.

was very easy for an ordinary technician and the effect was not significant.[277] Without more evidence, it is actually difficult to determine which judge's understanding of this factual issue is correct. However, the vague standard and the brief analysis leave the judicial opinion in this case open to attack.

c. Cases in the Late 1990s

After the SPC 1995 Response, more courts considered technical means in addition to function and effect when determining equivalents. There were two concepts adopted by courts which appeared in judicial opinions during this period: (1) "a person with ordinary skills in the art" and (2) "substantial difference." The concept of "a person with ordinary skills in the art" was confirmed in the 2001 Judicial Interpretation. The expression of "substantial difference" was not adopted in the 2001 Judicial Interpretation and was rarely used in later judicial opinions.[278] The courts' conservative attitude toward the doctrine of equivalents also appeared during this period. As recalled by a judge, *Dongnan*,[279] decided in 1997, reflected of the consensus on "cautious use of the doctrine of equivalents" reached within the court system. In Dongnan, although the court pointed out the differences between the patented invention and the accused infringing technology, it did not explain its approach to distinguishing substantial and non-substantial differences. Thus, the judicial opinion was not sufficient to understand how the court implemented the "cautious attitude" in finding infringement under the doctrine of equivalents. But the cautious attitude toward the doctrine of equivalents as a policy was confirmed later in various official documents by the SPC.[280]

---

[277] Motuo Che Wuji Biansu Pidai Lun Shiyong Xinxing Zhuanli Qinquan An (摩托车无级变速皮带轮实用新型专利侵权案), *in* Zhuanli Shangbiao Jishu Hetong Yinan Anli Pingxi (专利、商标、技术合同疑难案例评析) [Review of Patent, Trademark and Technology Transfer Contract] 111 (Yang Jinqi (杨金琪) ed., 1995).

Cheng Yongshun (程永顺)& Luo Lihua (罗李华), Zhuanli Qinquan Panding: Zhongmei Fatiao yu Anli Bijiao Yanjiu (专利侵权判定:中美法条与案例比较研究) [Cheng Yongshun, Luo Lihua, Deciding Patent Infringement: Comparative Study on Chinese and U.S. Law and Cases] 62 (2002).

[278] The 2001 Judicial Interpretation adopted a term "basically the same", which is hard to tell if it is different from "substantial difference".

[279] Zhongguo Dongnan Jishu Maoyi Zonggongsi v. Beijing Shi Wangma Diannao Zonggongsi (中国东南技术贸易总公司与北京市王码电脑总公司) [China Dongnan Technology Trade Company v. Beijing Wangma Computer Company], ipr.chinacourt (Beijing Hig. People's Ct. Jul. 18, 1997) (China).

[280] Supreme Court Conference Document: Zuigao Renmin Fayuan Guanyu Dangqian Jingji Xingshi Xia Zhishi Chanquan Shenpan Daju Ruogan Wenti de Yijian (最高人民法院关于当前经济形势下知识产权审判大局若干问题的意见), April. 4, 2009. (strict application of DOE). Guangdong High People's Court Conference. Documents, Guangdong Sheng Gaoji Renmin Fayuan Quansheng Zhishi Chanquan Shenpan Gongzuo Huiyi (广东省高级人民法院全省知识产权审判工作会议), May 2004. (strict application of DOE. Factors including pioneer invention should be considered. The application of DOE in untitlity patent should be limited. DOE does not apply to design patent). Tan Xiaoqing (谭筱清), Dui Dengtong Yuanze Shiyong Xianzhi Tiaojian de Tantao (对等同原则适用限制条件的探讨), 2 Intellectual Property (知识产权) (2004).

i. Substantial Difference

In the late 1990s, the phrase "substantial difference" began to appear in judicial opinions. Courts found infringement under the doctrine of equivalents because "the difference is not substantial,"[281] or found non-infringement because "the difference is substantial."[282] Usually, judges used "substantial difference" to evaluate the difference between technical means (structure of the devices, the way they work, combination of the chemical components), but rarely used it to evaluate the differences in function or effect.[283]

Some judicial opinions did not make it clear how judges drew the line between substantial and non-substantial differences. In *Dongnan*, although the court explained the difference between the coding system of the patented invention and that of the infringing product, it was unclear why the court found the difference to be non-substantial.[284] Some judicial opinions used the PHOSITA standard to determine whether the difference was substantial.

ii. PHOSITA

The PHOSITA standard was adopted and used by some (but not all) courts in the 1990s. For example, the Beijing High People's Court, in determining that the replacement in the infringing devices was not substantially different from that in the patented

---

[281] *E.g.* Zhoulin v. Beijing Aomei Guang Jidian Lianhe Kaifa Gongsi, Beijing Huaao Dianzi Yiliao Yiqi Youxian Gongsi (周林诉北京奥美光机电联合开发公司,北京华奥电子医疗仪器有限公司) [Zhoulin v. Beijing Aomei Guangjidian Lianhe Kaifa LL.C., Beijing Huaoa Electronic Medical Device LL.C.], ipr. Chinacourt (Beijing Hig. People's Ct., Mar. 22, 1996) See summary and comments in Zhishi Chanquan Shenpan Anli Yaolan (知识产权审判案例要览) [Review of the Key Cases of Intellectual Property] (Cheng Yongshun (程永顺) eds.1999). 151–159.

[282] Zhongguo Dongnan Jishu Maoyi Zonggongsi v. Beijing Shi Wangma Diannao Zonggongsi (中国东南技术贸易总公司与北京市王码电脑总公司) [China Dongnan Technology Trade Company v. Beijing Wangma Computer Company], ipr.chinacourt (Beijing Hig. People's Ct. Jul. 18, 1997) (China).

[283] Zhoulin v. Beijing Aomei Guang Jidian Lianhe Kaifa Gongsi, Beijing Huaao Dianzi Yiliao Yiqi Youxian Gongsi (周林诉北京奥美光机电联合开发公司,北京华奥电子医疗仪器有限公司) [Zhoulin v. Beijing Aomei Guangjidian Lianhe Kaifa LL.C., Beijing Huaoa Electronic Medical Device LL.C.], ipr. Chinacourt (Beijing Hig. People's Ct., Mar. 22, 1996) See summary and comments in Zhishi Chanquan Shenpan Anli Yaolan (知识产权审判案例要览) [Review of the Key Cases of Intellectual Property] (Cheng Yongshun (程永顺) eds.1999). 151–159. See the report of the trail *in* Cheng Yongshun (程永顺).

Zhongguo Dongnan Jishu Maoyi Zonggongsi v. Beijing Shi Wangma Diannao Zonggongsi (中国东南技术贸易总公司与北京市王码电脑总公司) [China Dongnan Technology Trade Company v. Beijing Wangma Computer Company], ipr. chinacourt (Beijing Hig. People's Ct. Jul. 18, 1997) (China).

[284] Zhongguo Dongnan Jishu Maoyi Zonggongsi v. Beijing Shi Wangma Diannao Zonggongsi (中国东南技术贸易总公司与北京市王码电脑总公司) [China Dongnan Technology Trade Company v. Beijing Wangma Computer Company], ipr.chinacourt (Beijing Hig. People's Ct. Jul. 18, 1997) (China).

Table 4.1 Amount of chemical compounds (Zhou Lin Case 1996)

	Patented invention	Infringing product 1	Infringing product 2	Infringing product 3	Infringing product 4	Average amount in infringing products
Chromic oxide	25–85%	*6.88%*	*44.04%*	49.74%	58.77%	39.9%
Ferric oxide	7–30%	*0.3%*	*4.48%*	*6.7%*	7.95%	*4.9%*
Magnesium oxide	0.5–8%	*0.043%*	*0.067%*	*0.093%*	*0.16%*	*0.1%*
Molybdenum oxide	0.6–5%	*Much less*				
Zinc oxide	1–17%	*Much less*				
Cupric oxide	1–7%	*Much less*				
Chromium	0.5–4%	*Much less*				

The trial court examined four of defendant's products, and each had different amounts of chemical components
The numbers which exceeded the ranges in patent claims are in italic

inventions, said that "a person with ordinary skill in the art is able to find this replacement without any creative effort".[285] This standard has been used by many courts since the 1990s to the present.

The Beijing High People's Court case, which adopted the PHOSITA standard, was decided in 1996. The trial court, Beijing Intermediate People's Court, found infringement under the doctrine of equivalents; the appellate court, Beijing High People's Court, affirmed. The patented invention was a medical device that used a combination of chemical compounds to produce rays. The accused infringing device was a medical device that had a combination of chemical compounds; the amount of some compounds in the infringing device was different from that of those found in the patented invention. The trial court found that there was no difference in function and effect. The defendant and plaintiff did not dispute this issue on appeal. The main issue disputed on appeal was whether the difference in amounts made the two combinations of chemical compounds substantially different.

The patent claims specified the range of the amounts. Some of the compounds in the infringing device exceeded the range (see Table 4.1.) The difference in the amounts of compounds did not result in much difference in function and effect. However, is the difference in amount a creative innovation, or merely a replacement known by the average person? It is a scientific question. Thus, PHOSITA should be an appropriate standard to make this assessment.

[285] Zhoulin v. Beijing Aomei Guang Jidian Lianhe Kaifa Gongsi, Beijing Huaao Dianzi Yiliao Yiqi Youxian Gongsi (周林诉北京奥美光机电联合开发公司,北京华奥电子医疗仪器有限公司) [Zhoulin v. Beijing Aomei Guangjidian Lianhe Kaifa LL.C., Beijing Huaoa Electronic Medical Device LL.C.], ipr. Chinacourt (Beijing Hig. People's Ct., Mar. 22, 1996) See summary and comments in Zhishi Chanquan Shenpan Anli Yaolan (知识产权审判案例要览) [Review of the Key Cases of Intellectual Property] (Cheng Yongshun (程永顺) eds.1999). 151–159.

However, the court simplistically stated that "a person with ordinary skill in the art is able to find this replacement without any creative effort," without any analysis or evidence.[286] Many courts at that time used to ask experts from forensic centers or expert witnesses to help with scientific questions.[287] The judicial opinion in this case explained that the trial court invited a forensic center to examine the device and report on the amount of the chemical compounds. But it did not explain if there were any forensic reports, expert testimony, or any other evidence showing whether the replacement was obvious to a PHOSITA. Although PHOSITA is an objective standard, the determination of PHOSITA without any evidence weakened the credibility of the finding and therefore increased legal uncertainty regarding this issue.

d. 2001 Judicial Interpretation and Its Implementation

Article 17 of the 2001 Judicial Interpretation provided that "equivalent is a technical feature, which performs basically the same function and achieves basically the same effect, in basically the same way as the patented technical feature, and it can be found by a person with ordinary skills in the art without any creative effort."[288] In the official explanation, the SPC further emphasized that the level of knowledge of a PHOSITA should be the average level of a technician in the field instead of that expected of an expert. If the court requests a forensic center or expert witness to make an assessment, the court must make it clear to such experts that they must explain whether the replacement would be obvious to an ordinary technician rather than to an expert.[289] In the 2015 amendment, a few words were added to article 17, to clarify that the knowledge level of PHOSITA in evaluation of equivalents is determined by the time of infringement.[290]

The 2001 Judicial Interpretation is largely a confirmation of previous judicial practice and improves the clarity of the rule by providing a cohesive summary. It does not make any changes or establish any new rules. Although the 2001 Judicial Interpretation used the phrase "basically the same," and some cases in the late

---

286 Zhoulin v. Beijing Aomei Guang Jidian Lianhe Kaifa Gongsi, Beijing Huaao Dianzi Yiliao Yiqi Youxian Gongsi (周林诉北京奥美光机电联合开发公司,北京华奥电子医疗仪器有限公司) [Zhoulin v. Beijing Aomei Guangjidian Lianhe Kaifa LL.C., Beijing Huaoa Electronic Medical Device LL.C.], ipr. Chinacourt (Beijing Hig. People's Ct., Mar. 22, 1996) See summary and comments in Zhishi Chanquan Shenpan Anli Yaolan (知识产权审判案例要览) [Review of the Key Cases of Intellectual Property] (Cheng Yongshun (程永顺) eds.1999). 151–159 Cheng Yongshun (程永顺), Zhuanli Qinquan Panding Shiwu (专利侵权判定实务) [The Practice of Patent Infringement Determination] (2001) 154–158.

287 Cheng Yongshun (程永顺) & Luo Lihua (罗李华), Zhuanli Qinquan Panding: Zhongmei Fatiao yu Anli Bijiao Yanjiu (专利侵权判定:中美法条与案例比较研究) [Cheng Yongshun, Luo Lihua, Deciding Patent Infringement: Comparative Study on Chinese and U.S. Law and Cases] 137 (2002).

288 Art.17, Guanyu Shenli Zhuanli Jiufen Anjian Shiyong Falü Wenti de Ruouan Guiding (关于审理专利纠纷案件适用法律问题的若干规定) [Several Provisions on Issues Concerning Applicable Laws to the Trial of Patent Controversies] (Promulgated by Sup. People's Ct., 2001, amended in 2013, 2015 & 2020), (Chinalawinfo) (China).

289 Ibid.

290 Ibid.

1990s used the phrase "no substantial difference", it does not make any difference in practice, since both terms are flexible and leave room for judges' discretion.

Some cases after 2001 provided detailed and clear reasoning to explain how the equivalents were determined. This was partially due to the clarity provided by the 2001 Judicial Interpretation, and partially due to the requirements set by the SPC to improve the drafting of judicial opinion.[291] However, there are still a substantive number of cases which did not discuss all of the elements provided in the 2001 Judicial Interpretation when finding infringement under the doctrine of equivalents. The lack of conformity in judicial practice increased the uncertainty of infringement litigation.

Ningbo, decided by the Jiangsu High People's Court, is a good example of a case which fully implemented the 2001 Judicial Interpretation. First, it discussed all-elements listed in the 2001 Judicial Interpretation including function, effect, means, and the PHOSITA standard. Second, it provided a very detailed explanation about how the court determined whether the replacement was "basically the same" and could be found by "a person with ordinary skills in the art without any creative effort" by relying on technical experts. The court classified "whether the replacement is an equivalent" as a question of fact, while "whether the equivalents constitutes infringement under the doctrine of equivalents" contains questions of law. Thus, it is appropriate to rely on technical experts to determine equivalents. The court selected five experts with help from the China Technology Law Association. Three of them were professors of mechanical engineering, one was a law professor and one was a previous examiner. Both the plaintiff and the defendant agreed with the selection of the experts. The report written by the expert panel was cross-examined during oral argument and some of the experts attended the oral arguments to respond to the questions by the judges and litigators. In the judicial opinion, the court also addressed the defendant's questioning of the credibility of the expert report. For example, the defendant argued that the report said that "both the patented device and the accused infringing device implemented the same law of nature"[292] and that this could not be a basis to find infringement. In the judicial opinion, the court pointed out that the expert report also analyzed the specific differences and similarities between the two technical solutions, and that therefore it provided a sufficient basis for finding equivalents.

Ningbo's judicial opinion is creditable, demonstrates the full implementation of the 2001 Judicial Opinion, and employed transparent procedures in using technical experts. It is helpful for potential plaintiffs and defendants to understand and assess their own cases. It is also helpful for peer judges to take this case as a reference and thus streamline the approach in determining infringement.

---

[291] Sifa Gaige Wunian Jihua (司法改革五年计划) (Five Years' Plan of Judicial Reform), Supreme People's Court.

[292] Ningbo Shi Dongfang Jixin Zongchang v. Jiangyin Jinling Wujin Zhipin Youxian Gongsi (宁波市东方机芯总厂与江阴金铃五金制品有限公司) [Ningbo Dongfang Jixin Zongchang v. Jiangyin Jinling Wujin Zhipin Youxian LL.C], ipr. Chinacourt (Sup. People's Ct. Mar. 6, 2002).

However, not all cases achieved the same level of compliance with the Judicial Interpretation, nor do they contain an equal level of clear legal reasoning as the *Ningbo* opinion. One example is a survey conducted by a high court judge.[293] This survey collected 20 cases from 2001 to 2005 which found infringement under the doctrine of equivalents, and listed the elements discussed in the judicial opinions. Only 11 cases discussed all-elements provided by the 2001 Judicial Interpretation. The other 9 cases missed at least one element in their reasoning; 5 cases merely concluded infringement under the doctrine of equivalents by finding similar function and effect, without discussing the "means." And 4 cases did not use the PHOSITA standard when determining that the accused infringing device was "basically the same" as the patented invention.

The split views increase uncertainty in infringement litigation. Finding equivalents merely by function and effect would unfairly broaden the scope of patent protection. Without the PHOSITA standard, determining whether two technical solutions are basically the same would be more subjective. The legal certainty issue of patent scope in China is not merely determined by the clarity of the rule, but also determined by the level of compliance among the more than fifty high people's courts and hundreds of intermediate courts.

4.5.2 *Limitation of Doctrine Equivalents: Dedication Principle*

Article 5 of the 2009 Judicial Interpretation introduces the dedication principle. If the technical solutions are described in the patent description but not included in the patent claims, the technical solutions are considered to be dedicated and excluded from the equivalents.[294] The purpose of this provision is to prevent tricks in patent application.[295] Some patentees use narrower terms in claims in order to obtain a patent and later expand the meaning of the patent terms by description.[296] In infringement litigation, the patentee would argue that the technical solution in the description is an

---

[293] Yan Wenjun (闫文军), Zhuanliquan de Baohu Fanwei: Quanli Yaoqiu Jieshi he Dengtong Yuanze Shiyong (专利权的保护范围:权利要求解释和等同原则适用) [Yan Wenjun, Scope of Patent Protection: Interpretation of Claim and Application of Doctrine of Equivalents] (2007).

[294] Guanyu Shenli Qinfan Zhuanliquan Jiufen Anjian Yingyong Falü Ruogan Wenti de Jieshi (关于审理侵犯专利权纠纷案件应用法律若干问题的解释) [Explanations of Issues regarding to Application of Law on Patent Infringement Trial] (Promulgated by Sup. People's Ct., Dec. 29, 2009, effective Jan.1, 2010), (Chinalawinfo) (China).

[295] Zuigao Renmin Fayuan Zhishi Chanquanting Fuzeren Jiu ⟨Guanyu Shenli Qinfan Zhuanliquan Jiufen Anjian Yingyong Falü Ruogan Wenti de Jieshi > Da Jizhe Wen (最高人民法院知识产权庭负责人就《关于审理侵犯专利权纠纷案件应用法律若干问题的解释》答记者问) [Public Interview with the Chief of the Intellectual Property Tribunal of Sup. People's Ct. Explanations of Issues regarding to Application of Law on Patent Infringement Trial, with Respect to ⟨Explanations of Issues regarding to Application of Law on Patent Infringement Tria⟩], Chinacourt (Sep.18, 2010, 19: 40 pm); http://rmfyb.chinacourt.org/public/detail.php?id=134762

[296] Ibid.

equivalent to the technical feature in the claim.[297] The establishment of the dedication principle emphasized the notice function of the patent.[298] The dedication principle is new in Chinese patent law and its application will be illustrated by future cases.

4.5.3 *Limitation to the Doctrine of Equivalents: Estoppel Principle*

The Chinese Estoppels Principle is applied to both of the literal interpretation of a patent scope and the expanded patent scope by the doctrine of equivalents. In the United States, prosecution history estoppel functions merely as a limitation to the doctrine of equivalents. Although prosecution history is also used in the United States to limit the literal scope of a patent, it is not covered under the scope of prosecution history.

If a technical solution was discarded during a patent prosecution procedure or invalidation procedure, it cannot be included in the scope of the patent under the doctrine of equivalents.[299] A party can discard a technical solution by amendment to the claim or description, or by a statement,[300] regardless of the reason for making the statement or amendment.[301] The Estoppel Principle can be established by the record of either the prosecution or the invalidation procedure.[302] It is unclear whether the prosecution and invalidation records of a related patent can also trigger the Estoppel Principle. A recent SPC opinion referred to a related patent prosecution in order to reject patentee's argument on establishing the doctrine of equivalents.[303]

---

[297] Ibid.

[298] Ibid.

[299] Guanyu Shenli Qinfan Zhuanliquan Jiufen Anjian Yingyong Falü Ruogan Wenti de Jieshi (关于审理侵犯专利权纠纷案件应用法律若干问题的解释) [Explanations of Issues regarding to Application of Law on Patent Infringement Trial] Art 6 (Promulgated by Sup. People's Ct., Dec. 29, 2009, effective Jan.1, 2010), (Chinalawinfo) (China).

[300] Ibid., Art 6.

[301] Zuigao Renmin Fayuan Zhishi Chanquanting Fuzeren Jiu < Guanyu Shenli Qinfan Zhuanliquan Jiufen Anjian Yingyong Falü Ruogan Wenti de Jieshi > Da Jizhe Wen (最高人民法院知识产权庭负责人就《关于审理侵犯专利权纠纷案件应用法律若干问题的解释》答记者问) [Public Interview with the Chief of the Intellectual Property Tribunal of Sup. People's Ct. Explanations of Issues regarding to Application of Law on Patent Infringement Trial, with Respect to < Explanations of Issues regarding to Application of Law on Patent Infringement Tria〉], Chinacourt (Sep.18, 2010, 19: 40 pm); http://rmfyb.chinacourt.org/public/detail.php?id=134762.

[302] Guanyu Shenli Qinfan Zhuanliquan Jiufen Anjian Yingyong Falü Ruogan Wenti de Jieshi (关于审理侵犯专利权纠纷案件应用法律若干问题的解释) [Explanations of Issues regarding to Application of Law on Patent Infringement Trial] Art 6 (Promulgated by Sup. People's Ct., Dec. 29, 2009, effective Jan.1, 2010), (Chinalawinfo) (China).

[303] Aonuo Zhongguo Zhiyao Youxian Gongsi v. Hubei Wushi Yaoye Gufen Youxian Gongsi (澳诺 (中国) 制药有限公司与湖北午时药业股份有限公司) Min Ti Zi di 20 Hao (民提字第20号), Supreme People's Court (2009).

Article 6 of the 2009 Judicial Interpretation defines an Estoppel Principle[304]; this is the first time that the principle is provided by an official source of law in China and clarified several disputed issues. Article 6 provides that in patent infringement litigation, the scope of a patent cannot include "the technology solution which was abandoned by patentee or applicant during patent prosecution or invalidation procedure, by amending claims or description or making a statement."[305] Although the text of the Judicial Interpretation does not use the wording of the Estoppel Principle, the official interpretation by the Third Tribunal of the SPC clarifiedthat Article 6 shall define the Estoppel Principle.[306] In the official interpretation of the 2009 Judicial Interpretation, the Third Tribunal of the SPC further found that the purpose of the statement and the amendment is irrelevant to the establishment of the Estoppels Principle.[307] It is also irrelevant if the statement and amendment are related to patentability or adopted by examiners.[308] The official interpretation also stated that excluding a technical solution can be "an amendment which sets limitations". This raised a question of whether emphasizing a technical feature instead of abandoning a technical solution also constitutes an estoppel.

a. The Origins of the Estoppel Principle

The earliest record of the Estoppel Principle in China was a SPC judicial opinion in 2001, *Wang Chuan*.[309] The disputed issue in the case was whether the term "discharge gap" in the claim should be interpreted to cover a discharge gap with a parallel resistance or explosion prevention device.[310] The SPC answered the issue in the negative since the patentee admitted during prosecution that the discharge gap was one without any parallel resistance or explosion prevention devices.[311] The SPC declared that its finding was based on the "Estoppel Principle" and defined the principle as follows: the scope of a patent cannot include any technology which was excluded by patentee

---

304 Guanyu Shenli Qinfan Zhuanliquan Jiufen Anjian Yingyong Falü Ruogan Wenti de Jieshi (关于审理侵犯专利权纠纷案件应用法律若干问题的解释) [Explanations of Issues regarding to Application of Law on Patent Infringement Trial] Art 6 (Promulgated by Sup. People's Ct., Dec. 29, 2009, effective Jan.1, 2010), (Chinalawinfo) (China).

305 Ibid.

306 "Zuigao Renmin Fayuan Zhishi Chanquanting Fuzeren Jiu < Guanyu Shenli Qinfan Zhuanliquan Jiufen Anjian Yingyong Falü Ruogan Wenti de Jieshi > Da Jizhe Wen"(最高人民法院知识产权庭负责人就《关于审理侵犯专利权纠纷案件应用法律若干问题的解释》答记者问) [Public Interview with the Chief of the Intellectual Property Tribunal of Sup. People's Ct. Explanations of Issues regarding to Application of Law on Patent Infringement Trial, with Respect to < Explanations of Issues regarding to Application of Law on Patent Infringement Tria〉], Chinacourt (Sep.18, 2010, 19: 40 pm); http://rmfyb.chinacourt.org/public/detail.php?id=134762.

307 Ibid.

308 Ibid.

309 Zuigao Renmin Fayuan Minshi Shenpanting Guanyu Wangchuan yu Hefei Jichu Maoyi Youxian Zeren Gongsi deng Zhuanli Qinquan Jiufen An de Han (最高人民法院民事审判第三庭关于王川与合肥继初贸易有限责任公司等专利侵权纠纷案的函) [Wangchuan v. Hefei Jichu Trade LL.C], ipr. Chinacourt (Sup. People's Ct. Feb. 2, 2001).

310 Ibid.

311 Ibid.

or public authority during a prosecution or invalidity procedure.[312] According to the definition, the records which can establish estoppel also include the statements made by an administrative authority (State Intellectual Property Office) or a judicial authority (court).

In *Wang Chuan* (2001), the SPC admitted that the Estoppel Principle was not provided by any statute or regulation. Instead, it is an application of the "Good Faith Principle" found in the Civil Law, and aims to balance the interests of patentee and the public.[313]

The SPC stated that this principle has been broadly applied in courts. However, there is no record to confirm this statement since the full texts of judicial opinions were rarely published before 2001. A book edited by Judge Yongshun Cheng published two cases involving the Estoppel Principle.[314] One was decided in 2000 by an intermediate court in Shandong.[315] Although the editor labeled this case as an application of the Estoppel Principle, it did not include any issues related to prosecution history or invalidation history. The only discussion in the case which comes close to the Estoppel Principle was that the court found that the patentee could not argue that the technology recorded in the claim and supported by the description was not a necessary technical feature.[316] This discussion is actually an application of the rule that a "claim defines the scope of a patent," not of the Estoppel Principle as defined in *Wang Chuan*. Another case involving the Estoppel Principle, *Wang Mou*, was summarized in a case note.[317] But the case note does not mention if the case was decided before 2001.[318] In *Wang Mou*, the court actually provided an understanding of the Estoppel Principle, which is different from that found in the SPC's *Wang Chuan* ruling.[319] According to the case note, the communication records to be considered

---

[312] Ibid.

[313] Ibid.

[314] Cheng Yongshun (程永顺), Zhuanli Qinquan Panding Shiwu (专利侵权判定实务) [The Practice of Patent Infringement Determination] 146 (2001).

[315] Liu Wanqing yu Weifang Zhongshi Zhiyao Youxian Gongsi (刘万庆与潍坊中狮制药有限公司实用新型专利纠纷案) [Liu Wanqing yu Weifang Zhongshi Zhiyao Youxian Gongsi],ipr.chinacourt. (Jinan Interm. People's Ct. 1999) see comments in Cheng Yongshun (程永顺), Zhuanli Qinquan Panding Shiwu (专利侵权判定实务) [The Practice of Patent Infringement Determination] 311 (2001).

[316] Ibid.

[317] Wangxiu v. Beijing Shenmo Kegongmao Youxian Gongsi (王秀诉北京深陌科工贸有限公司),Beijing 1s intermediate high people's court (北京市第一中级人民法院 (1999) 中知初字第104号案), cited in Yan Wenjun (闫文军), Zhuanliquan de Baohu Fanwei: Quanli Yaoqiu Jieshi he Dengtong Yuanze Shiyong (专利权的保护范围:权利要求解释和等同原则适用) [Yan Wenjun, Scope of Patent Protection: Interpretation of Claim and Application of Doctrine of Equivalents] (2007).).

[318] The Case number is 1999 Ji Zhi Chu zi Di 64 Hao, which indicated the case was accepted in 1999. There was no information about when the case was decided.

[319] Wangxiu v. Beijing Shenmo Kegongmao Youxian Gongsi (王秀诉北京深陌科工贸有限公司),北京市第一中级人民法院 (1999) 中知初字第104号案。Cheng Yongshun (程永顺), Zhuanli Qinquan Panding Shiwu (专利侵权判定实务) [The Practice of Patent Infringement Determination] 146 (2001).

under the Estoppels Principle only include the patent examination or re-examination procedures and do not include judicial invalidation procedures.[320] Also, technology abandonment can only be made by patentee, not by a public authority.[321]

Wang Chuan is the first case where the SPC explicitly adopted the Estoppel Principle. As a limitation to the doctrine of equivalents, adopting the Estoppels Principle means strict interpretation of patent claims. In the years following *Wang Chuan*, the SPC oscillated between strict and lax requirements to establish estoppel.

b. Development of the Estoppel Principle in the Supreme People's Court

Before the 2009 Judicial Interpretation, the SPC addressed the Estoppel Principle in other forms of judicial documents. One instance was in 2002; another instance was in 2009, a few months before the 2009 Judicial Interpretation was issued.

In 2001, the Supreme People's Court issued a Judicial Interpretation with respect to patent infringement litigation but did not mention the Estoppel Principle.[322] In 2002, the Third Tribunal of the SPC published an official interpretation of the 2001 Judicial Interpretation to define the Estoppel Principle.[323] Compared to the simple and broad definitions in *Wang Chuan* (2001), the 2002 official interpretation added more conditions. The manner of excluding technical solutions is through amendment. Making a statement is not explicitly mentioned. The historical documents are limited to the documents submitted by the applicant and do not include statements made by public authorities. The timeframe for inclusion is limited to that necessary for the prosecution procedure. Those requirements impose a strict limitation over establishing estoppel and consequently give patentees more opportunity to succeed under the doctrine of equivalents. The only negative aspect for the patentee is that the rule clarified that both "abandoning technical solutions" and "explicitly setting limitations" can later be considered as evidence of estoppel.

Also, in 2002, the SPC further clarified its understanding of the Estoppel Principle in *Ningbo*[324] by adding one additional requirement to establish estoppel. In this case, the SPC rejected the defense made under the Estoppel Principle because the amendment made by patentee had not resulted from the examiner's request.[325] In this judicial opinion, judges made "the purpose of the amendment" a necessary

---

320 Ibid.

321 Ibid.

322 Guanyu Shenli Qinfan Zhuanliquan Jiufen Anjian Yingyong Falü Ruogan Wenti de Jieshi (关于审理侵犯专利权纠纷案件应用法律若干问题的解释) [Explanations of Issues regarding to Application of Law on Patent Infringement Trial] (Promulgated by Sup. People's Ct., 2001), (Chinalawinfo) (China).

323 Zuigao Renmin Fayuan Minsanting, Ruhe Lijie Zuigao Renmin Fayuan Guanyu Zhuanli Fa 2001 Fa Shi Zi Di 21 Hao Sifa Jieshi (最高人民法院民三庭, 如何理解最高人民法院关于专利法 (2001) 法释字第21号司法解释) [Sup. People's Court, Understanding 2001 Judicial Interpertation], http://www.chinaiprlaw.cn/file/200201281245.html.

324 Ningbo Shi Dongfang Jixin Zongchang v. Jiangyin Jinling Wujin Zhipin Youxian Gongsi (宁波市东方机芯总厂与江阴金铃五金制品有限公司) [Ningbo Dongfang Jixin Zongchang v. Jiangyin Jinling Wujin Zhipin Youxian LL.C], ipr. Chinacourt (Sup. People's Ct. Mar. 6, 2002).

325 Ibid.

element.[326] Notably, the SPC discussed the Estoppel Principle, even though the accused infringer did not claim it. But this judicial opinion did not influence the lower courts to adopt the same approach.[327] Most courts would not examine estoppel unless the accused infringer claimed it.[328]

In early 2009, immediately after amending the Patent Law and before issuing the 2009 Judicial Interpretation, the SPC restated the Estoppel Principle in a Notice which instructed the lower courts on trial procedures concerning intellectual property cases, and expanded the scope of estoppel from prosecution to invalidation.[329] As in the 2002 official interpretation, the technical solution can only be excluded by patentee, not by public authority.[330] The manner of excluding technical solutions can be either through "abandoning" or "setting limitations."[331] But the scope was expanded to both the prosecution and invalidation procedures, and the requirement of "purpose of amending a claim" in Ningbo was not mentioned.[332]

The 2009 Judicial Interpretation defined the conditions of estoppel again as an official source of law and hopefully this definition will be sustained for a long time. The definition is similar to that in the 2009 Notice.[333]

c. The Impact of the 2009 Judicial Interpretation

Article 6 of the 2009 Judicial Interpretation, as well as the SPC's official interpretation of it clarified several questions while leaving many other issues unresolved.[334] It was clarified that both the amendment and statement can constitute estoppel.[335] The amendment or statement can be made by either patentee or applicant, but not by

---

[326] Ibid.

[327] Yan Wenjun (闫文军), Zhuanliquan de Baohu Fanwei: Quanli Yaoqiu Jieshi he Dengtong Yuanze Shiyong (专利权的保护范围:权利要求解释和等同原则适用) [Yan Wenjun, Scope of Patent Protection] 361 (2007).

[328] Supra Note 23.

[329] Supreme Court Conference Document: Zuigao Renmin Fayuan Guanyu Dangqian Jingji Xingshi Xia Zhishi Chanquan Shenpan Daju Ruogan Wenti de Yijian (最高人民法院关于当前经济形势下知识产权审判大局若干问题的意见), April. 4, 2009.

[330] Ibid.

[331] Ibid.

[332] Ibid.

[333] Guanyu Shenli Qinfan Zhuanliquan Jiufen Anjian Yingyong Falü Ruogan Wenti de Jieshi (关于审理侵犯专利权纠纷案件应用法律若干问题的解释) [Explanations of Issues regarding to Application of Law on Patent Infringement Trial]art.6 (Promulgated by Sup. People's Ct., 2001), (Chinalawinfo) (China).

[334] Zuigao Renmin Fayuan Minsanting, Ruhe Lijie Zuigao Renmin Fayuan Guanyu Zhuanli Fa 2001 Fa Shi Zi Di 21 Hao Sifa Jieshi (最高人民法院民三庭, 如何理解最高人民法院关于专利法 (2001) 法释字第21号司法解释) [Sup. People's Court, Understanding 2001 Judicial Interpertation],http://www.chinaiprlaw.cn/file/200201281245.html.

[335] Guanyu Shenli Qinfan Zhuanliquan Jiufen Anjian Yingyong Falü Ruogan Wenti de Jieshi (关于审理侵犯专利权纠纷案件应用法律若干问题的解释) [Explanations of Issues regarding to Application of Law on Patent Infringement Trial] (Promulgated by Sup. People's Ct., 2001), (Chinalawinfo) (China).

a public authority.[336] An amendment or statement may be made during either the prosecution procedure or the invalidation procedure.[337] The purpose of making a statement or amendment is irrelevant to establish estoppel.[338] The 2009 Judicial Interpretation provides that the purpose of making an amendment or statement is irrelevant, but it does not to clarify whether emphasizing a technical feature may trigger estoppel.

Some of the clarifications offered in the Judicial Interpretation of 2009 merely confirmed the widespread post 2001 practices, and thus did not make any substantive changes. For example, several lower courts' cases applied the Estoppel Principle based on either amendment or statement.[339] In a case appealed to the Shandong High People's Court, the patentee narrowed the claim by making a revision during re-examination.[340] The previous claim read, "design and produce plastic head of toy animal based on the shape of head" while the revised claim read, "first, design the model based on the skull die of animal, then use the model and a machine which injects plastic material into the model to produce the plastic head of toy animal."[341] The court held that what was covered by the previous claim but not covered by the revised claim could not be equivalents.[342] In another case appealed to the Jiang Su High People's Court, *Zhu Yuzhen*, the patentee made a statement during re-examination and emphasized the technical feature that "the air outlet of the ventilator is located outside the house" is a "new technology compared to prior

---

[336] Ibid.

[337] Ibid.

[338] Zuigao Renmin Fayuan Minsanting, Ruhe Lijie Zuigao Renmin Fayuan Guanyu Zhuanli Fa 2001 Fa Shi Zi Di 21 Hao Sifa Jieshi (最高人民法院民三庭, 如何理解最高人民法院关于专利法 (2001) 法释字第21号司法解释) [Sup. People's Court, Understanding 2001 Judicial Interpretation], http://www.chinaiprlaw.cn/file/200201281245.html.

[339] E.g. Liu Jingchang v. Zibo Youcheng Maorong Zhipin Youxian Gongsi (刘敬昌诉淄博友诚毛绒制品有限公司,山东省高级人民法院 (2003) 鲁民三终字第35号) [Liu Jingchang v. Zibo Youcheng Maorong Zhipin LL.C. Company] *in* Yan Wenjun (闫文军), Zhuanliquan de Baohu Fanwei: Quanli Yaoqiu Jieshi he Dengtong Yuanze Shiyong (专利权的保护范围:权利要求解释和等同原则适用) [Yan Wenjun, Scope of Patent Protection: Interpretation of Claim and Application of Doctrine of Equivalents] 354 (2007).

Zhu Yuzhen v. Ningbo Fangtai Chuju Youxian Gongsi deng [Zhu Yuzhen v. Ningbo Fangtai Chuju Youxian Gongsi] (朱玉振诉宁波方太厨具有限公司等,江苏省高级人民法院2004苏民三终字第017号案), *in* Yan Wenjun (闫文军), Zhuanliquan de Baohu Fanwei: Quanli Yaoqiu Jieshi he Dengtong Yuanze Shiyong (专利权的保护范围:权利要求解释和等同原则适用) [Yan Wenjun, Scope of Patent Protection: Interpretation of Claim and Application of Doctrine of Equivalents] 355 (2007)).

[340] Liu Jingchang v. Zibo Youcheng Maorong Zhipin Youxian Gongsi (刘敬昌诉淄博友诚毛绒制品有限公司,山东省高级人民法院 (2003) 鲁民三终字第35号) [Liu Jingchang v. Zibo Youcheng Maorong Zhipin LL.C. Company] *in* Yan Wenjun (闫文军), Zhuanliquan de Baohu Fanwei: Quanli Yaoqiu Jieshi he Dengtong Yuanze Shiyong (专利权的保护范围:权利要求解释和等同原则适用) [Yan Wenjun, Scope of Patent Protection: Interpretation of Claim and Application of Doctrine of Equivalents] 354 (2007).

[341] Ibid.

[342] Ibid.

art."[343] The court held that the statement "a ventilator of which the air outlet is inside of the house and connected to a tube extended to outside" is not an equivalent.[344]

The purpose of making either a statement or an amendment is no longer relevant, as explained by the SPC.[345] This is a significant change to the past practice. In the past, the general judicial practice was that the amendment or statement had to be relevant to patentability in order to trigger the Estoppel Principle.[346] If the amendment or statement was made in response to an examiner's question or rejection, or the examiner accepted the amendment or statement and granted a patent, the court would hold that the amendment or statement was relevant to patentability.[347] For example, in *Ning Bo*, decided in 2002, the SPC held that the Estoppel Principle was not triggered since the revision was not made in order to respond to an examiner's question.[348] In *Zhu Yuzhen*, the Jiang Su High People's Court held that the Estoppel Principle was triggered because the examiner accepted the statement which emphasized that an "air outlet is located outside the house."[349] Thus, before the 2009 Judicial Interpretation, if the accused infringer failed to find evidence of an examiner's question or acceptance, estoppel would not be triggered and the infringement under the DOE (doctrine of equivalents) would have a greater opportunity to be established. However, patentee did not have much to do in this situation. There is no rule establishing how a patentee can find positive evidence to rebut an estoppel claim. Patentee can only hope that

---

343 Zhu Yuzhen v. Ningbo Fangtai Chuju Youxian Gongsi deng [Zhu Yuzhen v. Ningbo Fangtai Chuju Youxian Gongsi] (朱玉振诉宁波方太厨具有限公司等,江苏省高级人民法院2004苏民三终字第017号案), *in* Yan Wenjun (闫文军), Zhuanliquan de Baohu Fanwei: Quanli Yaoqiu Jieshi he Dengtong Yuanze Shiyong (专利权的保护范围:权利要求解释和等同原则适用) [Yan Wenjun, Scope of Patent Protection: Interpretation of Claim and Application of Doctrine of Equivalents] 355 (2007).

344 Ibid.

345 Zuigao Renmin Fayuan Minsanting, Ruhe Lijie Zuigao Renmin Fayuan Guanyu Zhuanli Fa 2001 Fa Shi Zi Di 21 Hao Sifa Jieshi (最高人民法院民三庭, 如何理解最高人民法院关于专利法 (2001) 法释字第21号司法解释) [Sup. People's Court, Understanding 2001 Judicial Interpretation], http://www.chinaiprlaw.cn/file/200201281245.html.

346 Yan Wenjun (闫文军), Zhuanliquan de Baohu Fanwei: Quanli Yaoqiu Jieshi he Dengtong Yuanze Shiyong (专利权的保护范围:权利要求解释和等同原则适用) [Yan Wenjun, Scope of Patent Protection: Interpretation of Claim and Application of Doctrine of Equivalents] 359 (2007).

347 Zhu Yuzhen v. Ningbo Fangtai Chuju Youxian Gongsi deng [Zhu Yuzhen v. Ningbo Fangtai Chuju Youxian Gongsi] (朱玉振诉宁波方太厨具有限公司等,江苏省高级人民法院2004苏民三终字第017号案), *in* Yan Wenjun (闫文军), Zhuanliquan de Baohu Fanwei: Quanli Yaoqiu Jieshi he Dengtong Yuanze Shiyong (专利权的保护范围:权利要求解释和等同原则适用) [Yan Wenjun, Scope of Patent Protection: Interpretation of Claim and Application of Doctrine of Equivalents] 355 (2007).

348 Ningbo Shi Dongfang Jixin Zongchang v. Jiangyin Jinling Wujin Zhipin Youxian Gongsi (宁波市东方机芯总厂与江阴金铃五金制品有限公司) [Ningbo Dongfang Jixin Zongchang v. Jiangyin Jinling Wujin Zhipin Youxian LL.C], ipr. Chinacourt (Sup. People's Ct. Mar. 6, 2002).

349 See. e.g. [Zhu Yuzhen v. Ningbo Fangtai Chuju Youxian Gongsi] (朱玉振诉宁波方太厨具有限公司等,江苏省高级人民法院2004苏民三终字第017号案), *in* Yan Wenjun (闫文军), Zhuanliquan de Baohu Fanwei: Quanli Yaoqiu Jieshi he Dengtong Yuanze Shiyong (专利权的保护范围:权利要求解释和等同原则适用) [Yan Wenjun, Scope of Patent Protection: Interpretation of Claim and Application of Doctrine of Equivalents] 355 (2007); see also Yan, at 359.

the record fails to show an examiner's request or acceptance of an amendment or statement.

Since January 2010 when the 2009 Judicial Interpretation became effective, the standard became clearer. The SPC explained that reforms were implemented in order to simplify the patent litigation.[350] As a consequence, it is now less burdensome for accused infringers to establish evidence of estoppel. An accused infringer only has to find evidence in the prosecution or invalidation that narrows the scope of the patent, without needing additional evidence involving relevance to patentability. This reform reduced uncertainty in litigation. Certainly, this also means that patentees have one fewer opportunity to do away with the limitations of the Estoppel Principle. But since the amendment or statement is made by the patentee, it is reasonable to require patentee to be bound to his/her own statement. The new rule does not disadvantage patentee in infringement litigation. Instead, it merely urges patentee or patentee's agent to carefully consider the scope of the patent when making an argument of patentability.

What remains unclear is whether a statement which merely emphasizes a technical feature should be understood to be an exclusion of alternative technical solutions and thus trigger estoppel. The Judicial Interpretation did not address this question, and there is no consensus among the High People's Courts. Some courts have held that estoppel can only be triggered when a patentee explicitly states which technical solutions are abandoned. In one case, patentee revised the phrase "organic binder" to "organic binder, which is either acrylonitrile-butadiene, Chloroprene, or Acetic acid ethenyl ester".[351] The accused infringing technology includes Water-Soluble Acrylic Polymers. The defendant argued that Water-Soluble Acrylic Polymers was not listed in the claim, which meant that it was abandoned by patentee. Thus, it cannot be an equivalent to "organic binder". The appellate court rejected this argument and found infringement under DOE. The court found that only explicitly excluding a technical solution triggers estoppel; merely listing examples does not.[352] Some courts have used an opposite approach. In Zhu Yuzhen, the patentee made a statement emphasizing that the location of a ventilator air outlet was a key technical equivalent, which distinguished the patented invention from a prior art. The court held that this statement triggered an estoppel. The accused infringing product was an air outlet

[350] Zuigao Renmin Fayuan Minsanting, Ruhe Lijie Zuigao Renmin Fayuan Guanyu Zhuanli Fa 2001 Fa Shi Zi Di 21 Hao Sifa Jieshi (最高人民法院民三庭, 如何理解最高人民法院关于专利法 (2001) 法释字第21号司法解释) [Sup. People's Court, Understanding 2001 Judicial Interpertation], http://www.chinaiprlaw.cn/file/200201281245.html.

[351] Difang Guoying Xiangjiang Cixi Mifeng Cailiao Factory v. Xiaoshan Mifeng Jian Factory (地方国营湘江慈溪密封材料厂诉萧山市密封件厂),Comments on Intellectual Property Cases (知识产权判案评述),40 (Zhaohong Dong ed., 2003). Accord Yan Wenjun (闫文军), Zhuanliquan de Baohu Fanwei: Quanli Yaoqiu Jieshi he Dengtong Yuanze Shiyong (专利权的保护范围:权利要求解释和等同原则适用) [Yan Wenjun, Scope of Patent Protection: Interpretation of Claim and Application of Doctrine of Equivalents] 360 (2007).

[352] Ibid.

located at the top of a ventilator, which was different from the patented invention. The court held that "an air outlet on the top" was a prior art, which had been excluded by patentee's statement. Thus, it was not an infringing patent under the doctrine of equivalents.[353]

[353] Zhu Yuzhen v. Ningbo Fangtai Chuju Youxian Gongsi] (朱玉振诉宁波方太厨具有限公司等,江苏省高级人民法院2004苏民三终字第017号案), *in* Yan Wenjun (闫文军), Zhuanliquan de Baohu Fanwei: Quanli Yaoqiu Jieshi he Dengtong Yuanze Shiyong (专利权的保护范围:权利要求解释和等同原则适用) [Yan Wenjun, Scope of Patent Protection: Interpretation of Claim and Application of Doctrine of Equivalents] 355 (2007).

Chapter 5
Comparative Analysis

5.1 Policy

5.1.1 United States

In the United States, the courts have addressed two competing interests: (1) fair protection, which emphasizes patentee's interest and thus supports broader claim interpretation; and (2) legal certainty, which emphasizes the public notice function of the claim and thus requires narrower claim interpretation. One example of the court's concern to balance these two conflicting interests is found in the dissenting opinion in *Pennwalt Corp.*

On the one hand, there is the historic right of affording the public fair notice of what the patentee regards as his claimed invention in order to allow competitors to avoid actions which infringe that patent and to permit 'designing around' the patent. On the other hand, equally important to the statutory purpose of encouraging progress in the useful arts, is the policy of affording the patent owner complete and fair protection of what was invented.[1]

In *Graver Tank* (1950),[2] the U.S. Supreme Court emphasized fair protection for patentee and the importance of creating incentives for innovation. In *Warner-Jenkinson* (1997), the U.S. Supreme Court shifted its policy and emphasized public notice and the function of the claim to define the patent right.[3]

In recent years, the U.S. Supreme Court and the Federal Circuit have emphasized legal certainty and restricted claim interpretation by a series of decisions, with respect to both the literal scope of a patent and extended protection under the doctrine of equivalents.

[1] *Pennwalt Corp. v. Durand-Wayland, Inc.*, 833 F.2d 931, 945 (Fed. Cir. 1987) (Bennett, J., dissenting in part) (1988).

[2] *Graver Tank & Mfg. Co. v. Linde Air Prods.* Co., 339 U.S. 605. (1950).

[3] *Warner-Jenkinson Company, Inc. v. Hilton Davis Chemical Co.*, 520 U.S. 17 (1997).

© Intellectual Property Publishing House 2025

Z. Peng, *Comparative Study on Patent Claim Interpretation: The United States and China*, https://doi.org/10.1007/978-981-96-0836-2_5

a. Phillips: Narrowing the Literal Scope of Patents

Phillips resulted in narrowing the literal scope of patents. *Phillips* resolved the Federal Circuit split regarding intrinsic and extrinsic evidence. Some judges in the Federal Circuit gave more weight to intrinsic evidence (claims, specification/drawings and the prosecution history),[4] while other Federal Circuit judges gave more weight to extrinsic evidence.[5] Intrinsic evidence favors a focus on legal certainty and thus tends to support a narrow claim interpretation.[6] *Phillips en banc* agreed that intrinsic evidence should be given greater deference than extrinsic evidence, thus effectively eliminates using of extrinsic evidence.[7]

b. *Warner-Jenkinson* requires All-Elements to Establish the Doctrine of Equivalents

Warner-Jenkinson[8]is an unanimous decision, greatly enhanced legal certainty concerning the doctrine of equivalents.[9] *Warner-Jenkinson* held that the application of the doctrine of equivalents must be determined element by element ("all-elements rule"), rather than "as a whole." When the as a whole approach was practiced, a patent's scope could be extended to an accused device or process even though an element was completely missing. Under the all-elements rule, a patent's scope cannot be extended as broadly as before.

c. *Festo*: Limiting the Doctrine of Equivalents to After-Arising Technology

The standard applied by the Federal Circuit *en banc* decision in Festo to find prosecution history estoppel, resulted in a subsequent finding that the doctrine of equivalents mainly applies to the after-arising technology which was unknown at the time of invention.[10] The Federal Circuit en banc decision attempted to enhance legal

---

[4] See *Vitronics Corp. v. Conceptronic, Inc.*, 90 F.3d 1576, 39 U.S.P.Q. 1573 (Fed. Cir. 1996). E.g.

[5] *Pitney Bowes, Inc. v. Hewlett-Packard Co.*, 182 F.3d 1298, 51 U.S.P.Q.2d 1161 (Fed. Cir. 1999).

[6] Toshiko Takenaka, *Claim construction and the extend of patent protection: a comparative analysis of the Phillips en banc Federal Circuit decision*, 1 Journal of Intellectual Property Law 119, 120 (2006).

[7] Toshiko Takenaka, *Extent of patent protection in the United States, Germany, The United Kingdom and Japan: examination through the concept of 'person having ordinary skill in the art of the invention, in* PATENT LAW AND THEORY: A HANDBOOK OF CONTEMPORARY RESEARCH 350 (TOSHIKO TAKENAKA ed, 2008).

[8] For a discussion of impact of *Warner-Jenkinson*, see Toshiko Takenaka, *Claim Construction and the Extent of Patent Protection: A Comparative Analysis of the Phillips En Banc Federal Circuit Decision*, 1 Journal of Intellectual Property Law & Practice 119–130 (2006). KIMBERLY P MOORE PAUL R. MICHEL RAPHAEL V. Lupo, Patent Litigation And Strategy (2008); Timothy R. Holbrook, *The Supreme Court's Complicity in Federal Circuit Formalism*, 20 Santa Clara Computer & High Technology Law Journal 1 (2003); John R. Thomas, *Formalism at the Federal Circuit*, 52 American University Law Review 771 (2003); Christina Y. Lai, Comments, *A Dysfunctional Formalism: How Modern Courts Are Undermining the Doctrine of Equivalents*, 44 UCLA Law Review 2031 (1997).

[9] Donald S. Chisum, *The Scope of Protection for Patents After the Supreme Court's Warner-Jenkinson Decision: The Fair Protection-Certainty Conundrum*, 14 Santa Clara Computer & High Technology Law Journal 1, 3 (1998).

[10] Takenaka, *supra* note 8 at 126. See also John R. Thomas, *Claim Re-Construction: The Doctrine Of Equivalents In The Post-Markman Era*, 9 Lewis & Clark Law Review 153 (2005).

certainty through a complete bar, which means that an amendment would completely prevent extending patent scope under the doctrine of equivalents if the amendment narrows the scope of a patent claim. The Supreme Court rejected the Federal Circuit's complete bar approach, but did not return to the old flexible bar.[11] The new flexible approach determined in the Supreme Court's holding in Festo supports a narrower patent scope than the scope under the previous flexible approach prior to the Federal Circuit *en banc* decision.[12]

5.1.2 China

Chinese judicial opinions contain little policy discussion. The major sources of policy analysis are contained in the documents issued by the government or Supreme People's Court. The attitude of the Chinese government in the patent policy documents has become more and more positive. The landmark document, The Outline of National Intellectual Property Strategies, announced the goal to establish an "innovation-based" country.

In the past, the Chinese courts' policy documents mainly addressed incentives for innovation without discussing the legal certainty concerns in claim interpretation. After the U.S. courts gave more weight to legal certainty in claim interpretation, the SPC has also started to address legal certainty and the public notice function of claim interpretation in its policy documents in recent years.

The attitude of the Chinese government toward patents has become more and more positive, and the reason is obvious. The Chinese government previously accepted the patent system as a condition to participate in the global market.[13] As the number of Chinese patent application increases and the manufacture-based industry began to evolve into an innovation-based industry, the Chinese government started to consider the patent system as a tool to accelerate economic development.[14] By 2005, the number of patent litigation cases filed in China exceeded the number filed in the United States.[15] In more than 95% of the cases filed in China, Chinese patentees

---

[11] See Lawrence B. Ebert, *Meet the New Festo: Same as the Old Festo?*, available at http://www.nyipla.org/Bulletin/June2002.pdf (last visited November 2, 2002). See also Kenneth R. Adamo, *Back to the Future: Festo, Equivalents and Presumptive Prosecution History Estoppel*, 716 Pli/Pat 147 (2002).

[12] Mark R. Hull, *Festo Corp. v. Shoketsu Kinzoku Kogyo Kabushiki Co.: A Fog Between the Bars*, 37 Akron Law Review 339, 377 (2004).

[13] Zhuan Yuanguo (赵元果), Zhongguo Zhuanli Fa de Yunyu yu Dansheng (中国专利法的孕育与诞生) [The birth of Chinese Patent Law] 37 38 (2003).

[14] Jintao Hu (胡锦涛), Jianchi Zou Zhongguo Tese Zizhu Chuangxin Daolu Wei Jianshe Chuangxinxing Guojia er Nuli Fendou—Zai Quanguo Kexue Jishu Dahui shang de Jianghua (坚持走中国特色自主创新道路为建设创新型国家而努力奋斗——在全国科学技术大会上的讲话) [speech note regarding to innovation based country] 2006. (emphasizing enhancing IP system).

[15] *The China We Hardly Know–Revealing the New China's Intellectual Property Regime*, 55 St. Louis University Law Journal 773. "There were more patent litigation cases filed in China from

enforced their patents against Chinese competitors.[16] There is a strong domestic incentive in China for patent protection. Because of the domestic incentive, Chinese government's perspective of patent became more positive. Evidence of this new perspective can be found in the Notice of the State Council on Issuing the Outline of the National Intellectual Property Strategy in 2008, which is also a landmark document in Chinese patent policy.[17]

However, one may wonder why SPC started to emphasize on legal certainty in addition to fair protection. There are several factors that may possibly have influenced this policy decision: the concern that foreign patents may suppress the growth of the domestic industry, the change of the U.S. patent policy, and the shifted focus of academic patent law studies.

One possible factor is the Chinese government's concern that foreign patentees will dominate the Chinese market and reduce the space for domestic industry to grow. From 2001 to 2007, the number of IP cases involving a foreign party increased every year by 57.96%.[18] Also, the non-practicing entities,[19] have entered the Chinese market, and caused a serious concern to the public interest as well as further innovation.[20]

Another possible factor is the influence from the United States. Through a series of cases, the United States has changed its pro-patent policy with an emphasis on incentives for inventors to a policy which keeps a balance between incentives for inventors and legal certainty for the public since *Warner-Jenkinson*.

Academic discussions also significantly impact judges' understanding of the law, which is somtimes reflected in judicial opinions. In the patent field, some Chinese judges were actively involved in academic research and publications. The majority of the literature published on claim interpretation in China was written by judges. Thus, the academic discussion directly reflects the judges' understanding of claim interpretation. The academic discussion on patent law reflects the challenges that China faced during certain periods and impacted other judges' understanding of patent law.

The major research questions posed by intellectual property law studies changed from issues of "whether" and "how" to those considering "to what extent." In the later 1970s, 1980s and early 1990s, the main research question was "whether the

---

2005 through 2007—10,184 cases, compared to 8,391 cases filed in the United States during the same three years".

[16] *Ibid.*

[17] Guowuyuan Guanyu Yinfa Zhishi Chanquan Guojia Zhanlüe Gangyao de Tongzhi (国务院关于印发国家知识产权战略纲要的通知)[Notice of the State Council on Issuing the Outline of the National Intellectual Property Strategy] (No. 18 [2008] of the State Council).

[18] http://news.xinhuanet.com/legal/2008-02/19/content_7632383.htm.

[19] Non-practicing entities are sometimes referred as patent troll in the United States http://en.wikipedia.org/wiki/Patent_troll#Non-practicing_entity.

[20] Qi Yang (杨琪), Zhongguo Zhuanli Yu Lang Gong Wu (中国专利与"狼"共舞), in Zhongguo Kexue Bao (中国科学报), April 28, 2012. http://news.sciencenet. cn/sbhtmlnews/2012/4/257394.shtm, http://news.sciencenet.cn/sbhtmlnews/2012/4/257394.shtm.

patent system should be established in China".[21] During that time, it was not well recognized that a country can make its own policy choice regarding to the extent of patent protection. After the patent law system was essentially established, the academic community gradually accepted patent law as a fact. During the 1990s, the main research question became "how patents should be protected". By discussing the law and cases in China, the studies in the 1990s became more detailed and examined how the law impacts the scope of patent protection.[22] Also, comparative patent law studies revealed the variety of levels of protection and approaches.[23] However, research during this period gave little attention to the public interest or the reasonable limit of patent protection. Since 2001, the scholars advocating for public rights became stronger and many scholars emphasized that protection of innovation must be reasonable rather than too strong.[24] The academic community started to focus on a new research question: "to what extent should patent rights be protected?" The legislators and judges had a chance to reconsider the level of patent protection which complies with TRIPS and strikes a policy balance.

5.2 Rules

5.2.1 Procedure

U.S. and Chinese procedural laws are similar in some aspects of claim interpretation, although the text of laws appears very different. In both countries, claim interpretation is determined by a judge of first instance, and reviewed without deference by the second instance court. Although China does not officially adopt the concepts of intrinsic and extrinsic evidence, the Judicial Interpretation 2009 has similar provisions to the U.S. *Phillips* case.

In China, there is no separate procedure for claim interpretation. In U.S. law, claim interpretation and comparing a claim to an accused device involve two steps. There is a separate hearing for claim interpretation, and claim interpretation can be

[21] See representative works in Zheng Chengsi (郑成思), Zhishi Chanquan Fa: Xinshiji Chu de Ruogan Yanjiu Zhongdian (知识产权法:新世纪初的若干研究重点) 7 (2001).

[22] E. g. Cheng Yongshun (程永顺), Zhuanli Susong (专利诉讼)[Patent Litigation] (1993); Cheng Yongshun (程永顺), Zhuanli Qinquan Panding Shiwu (专利侵权判定实务) [The Practice of Patent Infringement Determination] (2001). see other representative works in Zheng, Supra Note 23.

[23] E.g. Cheng Yongshun (程永顺)& Luo Lihua (罗李华), Zhuanli Qinquan Panding: Zhongmei Fatiao yu Anli Bijiao Yanjiu (专利侵权判定:中美法条与案例比较研究) [Cheng Yongshun, Luo Lihua, Deciding Patent Infringement: Comparative Study on Chinese and U.S. Law and Cases] (2002).

[24] Ibid. See also Xu Xuan (徐萱), Zhishi Chanquan de Zhengdangxing –Lun Zhishi Chanquan Fa zhong de Duijia Yu Hengping (知识产权的正当性——论知识产权法中的对价与衡平), 4 Zhongguo Shehui Kexue (中国社会科学) (2003); Zhang Ping (张平), Wu Jiaoshou Bi Tui Feilipu Zhengyi Zhuanli (五教授逼退飞利浦争议专利) [five professors fights against Phillips patent]http://gzjaxxz.blog.hexun.com/6929267_d.html.

decided by summary judgment. In China there is no separate hearing, or opportunity for summary judgment.

The appellate procedure involving review of a district court's finding on the issue of claim interpretation in China does not raise an issue of whether claim interpretation is a question of law or fact. Appellate judges review both findings of fact and law without deference to the district court. Unlike U.S. judges, appellate judges in China have the power to find facts. The Chinese appellate review standard of claim interpretation is similar to the de novo review standard in U.S. law. The general civil procedure law applies to all patent infringement cases. According to China's Civil Procedure Law, the appellate court reviews both factual and legal issues.[25] The review standard is "the facts are clear" and "the application of law is correct", which does not give any deference to lower courts.[26] Since *Teva* case, the appellate review standard on the factual findings in the claim interpretation had become "clear-error". This made U.S. law slightly different from Chinese law on the appellate review standard with respect to claim interpretation.[27]

There are substantial differences between the U.S. law and the Chinese procedure law concerning the application of the doctrine of equivalents. In the United States, the application of the doctrine of equivalents is decided by a jury. In China, the application of the doctrine of equivalents is decided by a judge, since China as a civil law country and does not have a jury. In the United States, infringement under the doctrine of equivalents is reviewed under the substantial evidence standard if the infringement is decided by a jury. If infringement under the doctrine of equivalents is decided by a district court, infringement is reviewed under the clearly erroneous standard. In China, the appellate courts apply the "no deference" standard to review infringement under the doctrine of equivalents.

In the United States, claim interpretation is a question of law. In China, there are no provisions addressing this issue, but some judges believe it is a question of law. Chinese judges do not have to distinguish factual and legal issues for a judge/jury trial purpose. Some judges advocate that claim interpretation is a question of law, in order to limit the use of forensic reports as claim interpretation aids.[28]

With respect to sources for interpreting claims, U.S. case law distinguishes between "intrinsic evidence" and "extrinsic evidence". Intrinsic evidence includes claims, specification, and prosecution history. Extrinsic evidence means any other evidence besides intrinsic evidence, such as dictionaries and expert testimonies. Chinese law has not officially adopted the term "intrinsic evidence" and "extrinsic evidence". However, the 2009 Judicial Interpretation in China did treat claims,

---

[25] Article 151, Minshi Susong Fa (民事诉讼法) [Civil Procedure Law Court], (promulgated by the Standing Comm. Nat'l People's Cong., Apr. 7,1991, effective Apr. 7,1991, June 27 Amended 2017) 1991 STANDING COMM. NAT'L PEOPLE'S CONG. GAZ. (China).

[26] *Ibid.*

[27] *Teva Pharms. USA, Inc. v. Sandoz,* Inc., 135 S. Ct. 831, 835 (2015).

[28] Zheng, *Supra* note 21 at 7.

description and drawing, and prosecution history as one category, and the other evidence as another category.[29]

Both U.S. law and Chinese law provide a hierarchy[30] of different kinds of evidence in claim interpretation. The Chinese rule on this issue offers flexible guidance rather than a rigid framework, while U.S. law provides a mandatory hierarchy requirement. U.S. case law made it clear in *Phillips* that intrinsic evidence (claims, specification, prosecution history) is superior to extrinsic evidence (e.g., dictionaries, expert testimonies).[31] *Phillips* also emphasized that the hierarchy of the evidence means the weight instead of the sequence.

Compared to the U.S. law, Chinese law does not have a rigid rule on this issue. Judges are allowed to consult both intrinsic and extrinsic evidence, but are not obligated to consult extrinsic evidence. The 2009 Judicial Interpretation provides that claim interpretation can be made based on claims, description and drawings, and prosecution history, which would constitute intrinsic evidence in the United States.[32] The other kinds of evidence, which would be extrinsic evidence in the United States, "may" be used in claim interpretation, "if the meaning of a claim cannot be clarified" by the intrinsic evidence. The condition that the intrinsic evidence must be insufficient makes this rule focus more on the sequence rather than the weight of the evidence. However, the language in judicial interpretations use a permissive term "may", which grants permission to use extrinsic evidence instead without needing to satisfy a mandatory requirement. The judicial interpretations do not explicitly forbid the use of extrinsic evidence even if the intrinsic evidence is sufficient. In an official announcement, a judge in the SPC further clarified that if the intrinsic evidence is sufficient, a judge does not have to consult extrinsic evidence. This clarification confirmed that the Judicial Interpretation allows judges to exercise their discretion to decide whether to use extrinsic evidence.

Although in both countries the specification is viewed as the most important evidence in claim interpretation, Chinese judges are divided on whether it is always necessary to consult the specification in claim interpretation. Some judges argue that when the claim itself is clear, consulting the specification may result in an inappropriately narrow interpretation. In the United States, the case law requires that the specification must always be reviewed. U.S. courts emphasize that "claims cannot be clear and unambiguous at their faces."[33] The nature of language makes it impossible to capture the essence of invention in a patent application because the invention is a three dimensional device or a series of actions in a process and some inventions are so novel that a dictionary may not provide terms to describe such

---

[29] Interpretation of the Supreme People's Court on Several Issues concerning the Application of Law in the Trial of Patent Infringement Dispute Cases 2009 article 3.

[30] Robert L. Harmon, Cynthia A. Homan, and Charles M. McMahon, Patents and the Federal Circuit (2011).

[31] *Phillips v. AWH Corp.*, 415 F.3d 1303 (Fed. Cir. 2005).

[32] Interpretation of the Supreme People's Court on Several Issues concerning the Application of Law in the Trial of Patent Infringement Dispute Cases 2009, article 3.

[33] *Autogiro Co. of America v. United States,* 384 F.2d 391, 155 USPQ 697 (1967).

inventions.[34] Therefore, the doctrine of inventor as lexicographer makes it possible for inventors to define their inventions freely by clarifying their own definitions of claim terms in their specifications.

5.2.2 Substantive Law

a. Defining Literal Claim Scope

i. Fundamental Rules

In the current U.S. and Chinese law, most fundamental rules in substantive law on claim interpretation are similar. In both countries, claims define the scope of a patent. All-elements of claims limit the scope of a patent. The PHOSITA standard is an important tool in claim interpretation.

Although Chinese patent law has a much shorter history than U.S. patent law, some fundamental Chinese claim interpretation rules have gone through a similar evolutionary path as the U.S. rules. For example, in the past, in both the United States and China, some judges did not define a patent's scope based on its claim language. Instead, courts used commercialized embodiments to determine the patent scope. Both countries also have old cases that permitted omitting an element or technical feature as a limitation to claim scope.

(a) The central role of claims

U.S. patent law started to increase the significance of the claim to define the scope of a patent since the end of nineteenth century.[35] Before the 1836 Patent Act, the claim system was not established.[36] Even after the Patent Act came into effect, judges did not require an inventor to define his or her invention with any degree of specificity until 1870.[37] As a consequence, the judges adopted a liberal interpretation of the scope of patent protection.[38]

Since the Chinese Patent Law was promulgated 1984, the Patent Law statute provides rules explaining that claims define the scope of patents. However, some judges inevitably experimented with other approaches to define a patent's scope. For example, in one case, a trial judge used the patentee's product to define the scope of the patent, and then compared the patentee's device to the accused infringer's products.[39]

---

[34] *Festo Corp. v. Shoketsu Kinzoku Kogyo Kabushiki Co., Ltd*., 344 F.3d 1359 (Fed. Cir. 2003).

[35] See *Merrill v. Yeomans*, 94 U.S. 568, 570 (1876).

[36] Toshiko Takenaka, *Interpreting Patent Claims: The United States, Germany and Japan, 17* IIC Studies 6 (1995).

[37] Ibid., at 6–11.

[38] Ibid.

[39] Qianrushi Zhengfaqi Yian (嵌入式蒸发器一案) [In Re Embedded evaporator], *in* Zhuanli Shangbiao Jishu Hetong Yinan Anli Pingxi (专利、商标、技术合同疑难案例评析) [Review

In the past, some Chinese judges emphasized the technical features; specifically, the purpose and effect of the technical idea in the invention, which was an influence from Japanese and German patent law practice. In Japan and Germany, the courts emphasize the object and result of the technical idea in claim interpretation and thus undermine the role of claim language.[40] Japanese courts take this approach to restrict the scope of a patent to the features disclosed in the specification.[41] German courts use the principle to expand the literal claim scope to all alternative means to attain the same result.[42] Both the Japanese narrow interpretation approach and the German broad interpretation approach were formerly used by Chinese judges, but have been eliminated.

In the 1980s, Chinese judges adopted the German approach to expand the literal scope of patents.[43] This approach was later eliminated when Chinese courts adopted the doctrine of equivalents and the dedication to the public principle.

A case decided in 1990, adopted the German approach by using the description to interpret a claim term broadly. The disputed word was overlapped.[44] The claims stated that after a particular manufacturing step, edge No. 1 and edge No. 3 should be overlapped to close the product.[45] According to the accused infringing technical solution, after a similar manufacturing step, edge No. 1 and edge No. 3 were not connected together. Instead, there was a gap of 4 mm.[46] Literally, the meaning of "overlapping" is reclosing or matching together. Two dictionaries explain "overlapping" as "two geometric figures that occupy the same space."[47] Since there is a gap between edges No. 1 and No. 3, they neither match together nor occupy the same space.[48] They do not literally overlap.[49] However, the court still found infringement based on the description. The court examined the description, analyzed the purpose

---

of Patent, Trademark and Technology Transfer Contract] 111 (Yang Jinqi (杨金琪) eds., 1995). See comments in Cheng Yongshun (程永顺)& Luo Lihua (罗李华) Zhuanli Qinquan Panding: Zhongmei Fatiao yu Anli Bijiao Yanjiu (专利侵权判定:中美法条与案例比较研究) [Cheng Yongshun, Luo Lihua, Deciding Patent Infringement: Comparative Study on Chinese and U.S. Law and Cases] 107 (2002).

[40] TAKENAKA, *supra* note 36, at 202–203.

[41] Ibid., 67, 203.

[42] Ibid., 203.

[43] Ibid.

[44] Zhang Yuejin (张跃进), Shuoming Shu Zai Zhuanli Qinquan Panduan zhong de Zuoyong. (说明书在专利侵权判断中的作用) [The function of Claims in Patent Infringement Determination], Zhongguo Zhuanli Bao, Jan.19, 1990. See discussion in Yan Wenjun (闫文军), Zhuanliquan de Baohu Fanwei: Quanli Yaoqiu Jieshi he Dengtong Yuanze Shiyong (专利权的保护范围:权利要求解释和等同原则适用) [Yan Wenjun, Scope of Patent Protection: Interpretation of Claim and Application of Doctrine of Equivalents] 326 327 (2007). Cheng Yongshun (程永顺), *in* Zhuanli Qinquan Panding Shiwu (专利侵权判定实务) [The Practice of Patent Infringement Determination]28,29 (2001).

[45] Ibid.

[46] Ibid.

[47] Ibid.

[48] Ibid.

[49] Ibid.

of invention, and the overall technical solution. The court concluded that the key to this patented technical solution was that the two edges needed to have the same size and shape. Thus, the two edges could be connected when the manufacturing process was completed. According to the court's understanding, it was not important whether the two edges were connected together in one particular step, as long as they could be connected later. Consequently, the court interpreted "overlapped" as "having the same shape and length," and found infringement.[50]

In contrast, a recent case decided by the Zhejiang High People's court exemplifies how other Chinese judges followed the Japanese approach to restrict the literal scope of patents. The overturned this case to eliminate the practice of importing a limitation from the specification into the claim scope. The disputed patent involved a flashlight with a solar panel. On appeal, the Zhejiang High People's Court found that "removable" in the claim language means that the lid at the end has to be removable from the body of the flashlight, because one of the purposes of the invention was to make it easier to take off the solar panel by having a removal lid at the end of the body. The rejected the appellate court's decision and found that "removable" does not require the lid at the end to be removable. The SPC emphasized that the claim language did not include "the lid at the end". As long as the cover of the solar panel, the solar panel, and the body could be separated, it fell within the patent scope. The SPC rejected the appellate court's analysis and criticized the appellate court for importing the limitation from the embodiment.

(b) All-Elements Rule and Exceptions

Current law in both the United States and China requires that all-elements/ technical features in the claim are relevant to limit the claim scope. Therefore, China is now more similar to the United States than Japan or Germany. A technical feature is the Chinese counterpart to the U.S. element. Currently, neither the United States nor China has an exception to the all-elements/technical feature rule. However, U.S. case law has found that some terms in claim language are not relevant to qualify as a limitation or element.[51] In China, every word in the claim is relevant without exception.

The Chinese "all technical feature rule" is equivalent to the U.S. "all-elements rule." "Technical feature" is the same concept as the U.S. "element." Sometimes, jishu tezheng' is translated as "element". However, in the official English version of the Patent Law of the People's Republic of China and Implementing Regulations of the Patent Law of the People's Republic of China, it is always literally translated as "technical feature."[52]

---

[50] Ibid.

[51] *Syntex (U.S.A.) LLC v. Apotex, Inc.*, 407 F.3d 1371 (Fed. Cir. 2005); *Altiris, Inc. v. Symantec Corp.* 318 F.3d 1363 (2003);*Storage Technology Corp. v. Cisco Systems*, Inc. 329 F.3d 823 (2003)*;IMS Technology Inc. v. Haas Automation Inc.* 206 F.3d 1422 (2000);*Vaupel Textilmaschinen KG v. Meccanica Euro Italia S.P.A.* 944 F.2d 870 (1991);*Am. Med. Sys., Inc. v. Biolitec, Inc.*, 618 F.3d 1354, 1358 (Fed. Cir. 2010).

[52] See English version of patent statutes and regulations on State Intellectual Property Office of People's Republic of China website. http://english.sipo.gov.cn/laws/.

The United States and China went through a similar legal evolution of the all-elements/technical feature rule. In the United States, the old rule adopted the "as a whole" approach,[53] which was replaced by the "all-elements rule" with an emphasis on the "element-by-element" analysis.[54] In China, the old rule was the "redundant feature principle," which was an exception to the technical feature rule and has now been replaced by the "technical feature rule without exception". Although the names of the rules and the theoretical frameworks are different, the legal evolutionary process is the same. In both countries, the old rule allowed omitting an element or technical feature when defining the scope of a patent. The current rule prohibits that practice.

Although in both countries the current rule does not allow omitting an element or technical feature, the United States and China have different rules with respect to what constitutes an element or technical feature. In the United States, the terms in the preamble do not necessarily count as elements.[55] The Federal Circuit has set forth some general principles to determine when a preamble limits the claim scope.[56] However, in China, the technical features in the preamble are also "essential technical features" and always limit the scope of protection of the independent claim.[57]

(c) Specification (Description and Drawings)

In both the United States and China, the specification is the most frequently used reference in claim interpretation. The U.S. case law provides that the specification is the single best reference in claim interpretation. Claim construction begins with, and remains focused on, the language of the claims.[58] In China, descriptions and

---

[53] "Apply the doctrine of equivalents to the claimed invention as a whole" *Hughes Aircraft Co. v. United States*, 717 F.2d 1351, 219 USPQ 473 (Fed. Cir. 1983). *Pennwalt Corp. v. Durand-Wayland*, Inc. 833 F.2d 931, 961 (Fed. Cir. 1987) reviewed the history that Supreme Court applied doctrine of equivalents as a whole, citing *Winans v. Denmead,* 56 U.S. (15 How.) 330, 14 L.Ed. 717 (1853) McCormick v. Talcott, 61 U.S. 402(1857) and Burr v. Duryee, 68 U.S. 531, 572, 17 L. Ed. 650 (1863).

[54] *Warner-Jenkinson Co. v. Hilton Davis Chem. Co.* held that the doctrine of equivalents must be applied to each element in a patent claim, not to the invention as a whole. 520 U.S. 17, 19 (1997) Supreme Court rejected the as a whole approach in Warner-Jenkinson, although did not refer to Hughes Aircraft. See Donald S. Chisum, *Chisum on Patents § 18.04.*

[55] *Syntex (U.S.A.) LLC v. Apotex, Inc.*, 407 F.3d 1371 (Fed. Cir. 2005); *Altiris, Inc.*. 318 F.3d at 1363; *Storage Technology Corp. v. Cisco Systems*, Inc. 329 F.3d 823 (2003);*IMS Technology Inc. v. Haas Automation Inc.* 206 F.3d 1422 (2000);*Vaupel Textilmaschinen KG v. Meccanica Euro Italia S.P.A.* 944 F.2d 870 (1991);*Am. Med. Sys., Inc. v. Biolitec*, Inc., 618 F.3d 1354, 1358 (Fed. Cir. 2010).

[56] *Am. Med. Sys., Inc.*, 618 F.3d at 1358.

[57] Zhuanli Fa Shishi Xize (专利法实施细则) [Detailed Rules for the Implementation of the Patent Law] arts.21, (promulgated by the St. Council., Jun.15, 2001, effective Jul. 1,2001, amended Jan.09., 2010) (Chinalawinfo) (China). Guanyu Shenli Qinfan Zhuanliquan Jiufen Anjian Yingyong Falü Ruogan Wenti de Jieshi (Er) (关于审理侵犯专利权纠纷案件应用法律若干问题的解释(二)) [Explanations of Issues regarding to Application of Law on Patent Infringement Trial II] (Promulgated by Sup. People's Ct., Jan. 25, 2016, effective April.1, 2016, amended on Dec. 29, 2020), (Chinalawinfo) (China).

[58] *Innova/Pure Water, Inc. v. Safari Water Filtration Sys., Inc.*, 381 F.3d 1111, 1116 (Fed.Cir.2004). reaffirmed in *phllips.*

drawings are the only evidence permitted by the statute: the description and the appended drawings may be used to interpret the claims.[59]

In the United States, patentee can act as his own lexicographer.[60] Similarly, in China, judicial interpretation provides that "if the specification defines any particular wording of a claim, such particular definition shall apply."[61]

(d) PHOSITA

PHOSITA is an important tool used in both U.S. and Chinese claim interpretation. U.S. courts frequently use PHOSITA as a conceptual tool in claim interpretation.[62] US courts justify this approach by stating that inventors are typically PHOSITAs and patents are addressed to and intended to be read by PHOSITAs.[63] PHOSITA has been used by Chinese courts to determine infringement under the doctrine of equivalents only since the 1990s. Applying the PHOSITA standard in literal claim interpretation only began in 2009 by the SPC's Judicial Interpretation.[64]

In the United States, the knowledge level of PHOSITA is determined by the time of invention,[65] except in determining of doctrine of equivalents, the timing would be when the infringement happens.[66] In China, the time to determine doctrine of equivalents is based on infringement time.[67] There is no judicial interpretation clarify that or official guidance to determine at what point the knowledge level of a PHOSITA is established with respect to claim interpretation, but this does not mean that we have no clue about the answer to this question. In China, there is no separate procedure for claim interpretation. Instead, claim interpretation and infringement analysis are considered as one step in patent litigation procedure. Thus, it seems that the way Chinese judges use PHOSITA in claim interpretation is the same as how

---

59 Patent Law Article 59.

60 *Phillips v. AWH Corp.*, 415 F.3d 1303 (Fed. Cir. 2005).

61 Interpretation of the Supreme People's Court on Several Issues concerning the Application of Law in the Trial of Patent Infringement Dispute Cases.

62 See *Multiform Desiccants, Inc. v. Medzam, Ltd.*, 133 F.3d 1473, 1477, 45 USPQ2d 1429, 1432 (Fed.Cir.1998) ("It is the person of ordinary skill in the field of the invention through whose eyes the claims are construed."). *Cybor Corp. v. FAS Technologies, Inc.*, 138 F.3d 1448, 1475 (Fed. Cir. 1998) The objective of claim interpretation is to discern the meaning of the claim terms to one of ordinary skill in the art at the time of invention.

63 *Phillips v. AWH Corp.*,415 F.3d 1303, 75 USPQ. 2d 1321 (Fed. Cir. 2005). Takenaka, Patent Protection, 444.

64 Guanyu Shenli Qinfan Zhuanliquan Jiufen Anjian Yingyong Falü Ruogan Wenti de Jieshi (关于审理侵犯专利权纠纷案件应用法律若干问题的解释) [Explanations of Issues regarding to Application of Law on Patent Infringement Trial] (Promulgated by Sup. People's Ct., Dec. 29, 2009, effective Jan.1, 2010), (Chinalawinfo) (China).

65 *Phillips v. AWH Corp.*, 415 F.3d 1303, 1313 (Fed. Cir. 2005).

66 *Warner-Jenkinson Co. v. Hilton Davis Chem. Co.*, 520 U.S. 17, 37 (1997).

67 Guanyu Shenli Zhuanli Jiufen Anjian Shiyong Falü Wenti de Ruogan Guiding (关于审理专利纠纷案件适用法律问题的若干规定) [Several Provisions on Issues Concerning Applicable Laws to the Trial of Patent Controversies] (Promulgated by Sup. People's Ct., 2001, amended in 2013, 2015 & 2020), (Chinalawinfo) (China).

they use it in determining infringement. Thus, the time to determine the knowledge level of PHOSITA in claim interpretation would be the time of infringement.

ii. Canons

The United States has developed a series of rules for claim interpretation. The literature refers to those rules as "canons." Chinese statutes and cases do not have corresponding counterparts for most the U.S. canons of claim interpretation. The legal reasoning in Chinese cases is similar to the U.S. doctrine of claim differentiation, but the rule is not explicitly established by statute or judicial interpretation.

Chinese courts have not explicitly adopted cannons for claim interpretation. This difference is likely due to the different approaches Chinese and U.S. judges apply to claim interpretation. The legal reasoning in Chinese judicial opinions usually focuses on the technological solutions for the invention instead of merely focusing on the text of the claims.[68] As a result, the reasoning in Chinese opinions heavily reply on the technological facts in a case, rather than applying a specific rule.

iii. Special Types of Claims

(a) Functional Technical Features

35 U.S.C. 112(f) limits the scope of a means-plus-function claim to the disclosed embodiments and their equivalents. The Federal Circuit has been working on finding a "solid test"[69] to determine whether a particular claim element is a means-plus-function element. The solid test consists of two presumptions which can be rebutted. If the word of "means" is used in the claim, the presumption is that this is a means-plus-function claim and it will be interpreted narrowly, unless the presumption is rebutted with evidence of sufficient structure. If the word of "means" is not used in the claim, the presumption is that this is not a means-plus-function claim and embodiments should not be interpreted as limitations, unless the presumption is rebutted with evidence that the claim does not contain sufficient structure.

In China, a means-plus-function element is referred to as a functional technical feature. Similar to the United States, there is a rebuttable "positive presumption" in Chinese patent law: if a technical feature is defined by its function or effect, it is a functional feature and its interpretation should be limited to its embodiments.[70] This presumption can be rebutted, but the standard is higher than that in the United States. In the United States, both claim and description can be used to rebut the presumption. However, in China, the presumption can be rebutted if "by merely reading the claims, a PHOSITA can directly and explicitly determine the specific means for achieving the

[68] See discussion in supra "the central role of claims".

[69] ROBERT L. HARMON, CYNTHIA A. HOMAN, AND CHARLES M. MCMAHON, PATENTS AND THE FEDERAL CIRCUIT 410 (2011).

[70] Article 4, Guanyu Shenli Qinfan Zhuanliquan Jiufen Anjian Yingyong Falü Ruogan Wenti de Jieshi (关于审理侵犯专利权纠纷案件应用法律若干问题的解释) [Explanations of Issues regarding to Application of Law on Patent Infringement Trial] (Promulgated by Sup. People's Ct., Dec. 29, 2009, effective Jan.1, 2010), (Chinalawinfo)art.4 (China), art 4.

aforesaid functions or effects".[71] Higher standard to rebut the positive presumption is bad news for patent holders. But the good news is there is nothing about rebutting the negative presumption in Chinese patent law. As long as you don't define your claim by function or effect, your claim is safe from functional technical feature.

(b) Product-by-Process Claim

It is a uniform rule in the United States that "process terms in product-by-process claims serve as limitations in determining infringement".[72] In *Pan Luli*, decided by the Shanghai High People's Court,[73] the court held that in a product-by-process claim, the process is a necessary technical feature, which is very similar to the U.S. rule. This rule was confirmed in 2016 Judicial Interpretation.[74]

(c) Combination of Chemistry Components

In the United States, a frequently litigated issue in claims involving a combination of chemistry compounds is whether a patent scope is limited to the recited components. The U.S. Federal Circuit has found that the phrase "consisting of" is a term of art in patent law signifying restriction and exclusion; while, in contrast, the term "comprising" indicates an open-ended construction.[75] However, the restriction implied by "consisting of" has exceptions. The limiting phrase "consisting of" does not exclude impurities.

Similarly, in Chinese patent law there are open-ended and closed-ended claims for chemistry component claims.[76] Open-ended claims are identified by their wording and description.[77] If the description does not explain other components, the claim is considered a close-ended claim and is therefore interpreted narrowly,[78] but "impurities" are permitted.[79] The practice was confirmed in 2016 Judicial Interpretation.[80]

---

[71] Article 8, Guanyu Shenli Qinfan Zhuanliquan Jiufen Anjian Yingyong Falü Ruogan Wenti de Jieshi (Er) (关于审理侵犯专利权纠纷案件应用法律若干问题的解释(二)) [Explanations of Issues regarding to Application of Law on Patent Infringement Trial II] (Promulgated by Sup. People's Ct., Jan. 25, 2016, effective April.1, 2016, amended on Dec. 29, 2020), (Chinalawinfo) (China).

[72] *Abbott Laboratories* 566 F.3d at 1293 (Fed. Cir. 2009).

[73] Pan Luli v. Shanghai Gaoyu Yiliao Qixie Chang (潘璐莉与上海高宇医疗器材厂) [Pan Luli v. Shanghai Gaoyu Medical Device Factory], ipr. Chinacourt (Shanghai High People's Ct., 2004).

[74] Guanyu Shenli Qinfan Zhuanliquan Jiufen Anjian Yingyong Falü Ruogan Wenti de Jieshi (Er) (关于审理侵犯专利权纠纷案件应用法律若干问题的解释(二)) [Explanations of Issues regarding to Application of Law on Patent Infringement Trial II] (Promulgated by Sup. People's Ct., Jan. 25, 2016, effective April.1, 2016, amended on Dec. 29, 2020), (Chinalawinfo) (China).

[75] *Vehicular Technologies Corp. v. Titan Wheel Int'l, Inc.*, 212 F.3d 1377, 1382 (Fed. Cir. 2000).

[76] Zhuanli Shencha Zhinan (专利审查指南) [Patent Examination Guideline]part 2, chapter10, 4.2.1, art. 26.4 (promulgated by the St. Intellectual Property Office, Jan.1, 2010, effective Feb. 1, 2010) (SIPO) (China).

[77] Ibid.

[78] Ibid.

[79] Ibid.

[80] Guanyu Shenli Qinfan Zhuanliquan Jiufen Anjian Yingyong Falü Ruogan Wenti de Jieshi (Er) (关于审理侵犯专利权纠纷案件应用法律若干问题的解释(二)) [Explanations of Issues regarding to

(d) Dependent Claims

In the United States, it is expressly provided by statute that dependent claims should be interpreted to include all of the limitations of the independent claim to which it refers: "A claim in dependent form shall be construed to incorporate by reference all the limitations of the claim to which it refer."[81] The Chinese Judicial Interpretation 2009, similarly provides that the limitations of independent claims should be read into dependent claims.[82]

b. The Doctrine of Equivalents

i. Elements to establish the Doctrine of Equivalents

Although the U.S. law and Chinese law use different terms to define the elements of the doctrine of equivalents, there is no practical difference in the rule as applied by the two countries. In both countries, the doctrine of equivalents is determined on an element-by-element basis. The Chinese standard of determining claim interpretation involves a combination of standards used by U.S. courts. In both countries, the PHOISTA standard is used in determining the doctrine of equivalents but the knowledge level of PHOSITA is rarely defined in the cases. Both U.S. case law and Chinese Judical Interpretation clarifies that the knowledge level of PHOSITA at the time of infringement is used to determine infringement under the doctrine of equivalents.

The test that U.S. courts most frequently use for determining infringement under the doctrine of equivalents is the function-way-result test: "if it performs substantially the same function in substantially the same way to obtain the same result", infringement will be found.[83] The Federal Circuit in the Hilton David *en banc* decision (1995) emphasized that the "substantiality of the differences" between the claimed and accused products or processes is the ultimate question for determining infringement under the doctrine of equivalents.[84] The Federal Circuit en banc has also stressed "the importance of evidence of known interchangeability to show the substantiality of the differences."[85]

Application of Law on Patent Infringement Trial II] (Promulgated by Sup. People's Ct., Jan. 25, 2016, effective April.1, 2016, amended on Dec. 29, 2020), (Chinalawinfo) (China).

[81] 35 U.S.C § 112, ¶ 4 (2000).

[82] Guanyu dui Dangshiren Nengfou Xuanze Congshu Quanli Yaoqiu Queding Zhuanliquan Baohu Fanwei de Qingshi de Dafu (关于对当事人能否选择从属权利要求确定专利权保护范围的请示的答复) [In Re the dependent claims], ipr. Chinacourt. (Sup. People's Ct. 2007) Guanyu Shenli Qinfan Zhuanliquan Jiufen Anjian Yingyong Falü Ruogan Wenti de Jieshi (关于审理侵犯专利权纠纷案件应用法律若干问题的解释) [Explanations of Issues regarding to Application of Law on Patent Infringement Trial] (Promulgated by Sup. People's Ct., Dec. 29, 2009, effective Jan.1, 2010), (Chinalawinfo) (China).

[83] *Sanitary Refringerator Co. v. Winter*s 280 US 30, 42 (1929).

[84] *Hilton Davis Chem. Co. v. Warner-Jenkinson Co., Inc.*, 62 F.3d 1512 (Fed. Cir. 1995) supplemented, 64 F.3d 675 (Fed. Cir. 1995) and rev'd, 520 U.S. 17, 117 S. Ct. 1040, 137 L. Ed. 2d 146 (1997) and adhered to, 114 F.3d 1161 (Fed. Cir. 1997) In.

[85] *Hilton Davis Chem. Co.* 62 F.3d at 1519. See also *Corning Glass Works v. Sumitomo Elec. U.S.A., Inc.*, 868 F.2d 1251, 1261, 9 USPQ2d 1962, 1969 (Fed.Cir.1989); *Thomas & Betts Corp. v. Litton*

Chinese law has combined all of the above U.S. standards to establish its own doctrine of equivalents. According to Judicial Interpretation 2001, the technical feature of an accused infringing technology is equivalent to the technical feature in the patent claim if: (a) they perform basically the same function, and (b) they achieve basically the same effect, (c) through basically the same technical means, and (d) the technical feature in the accused infringing technology can be found by a person with ordinary skills in the art without any creative effort.[86] The first three elements are similar to the U.S. court's classic test, the function-way-result test: "if it performs substantially the same function in substantially the same way to obtain the same result", infringement will be found.[87] Also, the last element is similar to the U.S. interchangeability standard.

The U.S. case law provides that the timing for determining infringement under the doctrine of equivalents is the time of infringement rather than the time of invention (or effective filing date.)[88] Chinese judges used to have conflicting views. The SPC attempted to clarify this issue but failed. In the draft 2001 judicial interpretation, the SPC originally proposed that the doctrine of equivalents shall be determined at the time of infringement.[89] When the proposal was circulated and discussed by various judges, there were disputes between the judges who believed the timing should be the infringement date and those who believed that the timing should be the application date.[90] Because the dispute was never resolved, the final version of the 2011 Judicial Interpretation did not address the timing issue. Justice Jianming Chao, who was the Vice Chief Justice of the SPC at that time, nevertheless explained his opinion in a book that the knowledge level of PHOSITA in the doctrine of equivalents should be determined at the time of infringement.[91] The disagreements among judges were finally resolved by 2016 Judicial Interpretation, which clarified that the knowledge

Sys., Inc., 720 F.2d 1572, 1579, 220 USPQ 1, 6 (Fed.Cir.1983), *Interactive Pictures Corp. v. Infinite Pictures, Inc.*, 274 F.3d 1371 (Fed. Cir. 2001).

[86] Guanyu Shenli Qinfan Zhuanliquan Jiufen Anjian Yingyong Falü Ruogan Wenti de Jieshi (关于审理侵犯专利权纠纷案件应用法律若干问题的解释) [Explanations of Issues regarding to Application of Law on Patent Infringement Trial] art.17 (Promulgated by Sup. People's Ct., 2001), (Chinalawinfo) (China).

[87] *Sanitary*, 280 U.S. 30 (1929).

[88] *Warner-Jenkinson Co., Inc. v. Hilton Davis Chem. Co.*, 520 U.S. 17, 37 (1997).

[89] Yan Wenjun (闫文军), Zhuanliquan de Baohu Fanwei: Quanli Yaoqiu Jieshi he Dengtong Yuanze Shiyong (专利权的保护范围:权利要求解释和等同原则适用) [Yan Wenjun, Scope of Patent Protection: Interpretation of Claim and Application of Doctrine of Equivalents] 352 (2007).

[90] Ibid. Zhang Xiaodu (张晓都), Shanghai High Court judge's books Zhang Xiaodu, Zhuanli Qinquan Panding: Lilun Tantao Yu Shenpan Shijian (专利侵权判定:理论探讨与审判实践) [Deciding Patent Infringement: Theoretical Discussion and Practice in Trial] (Falü Chubanshe 2008).

[91] Zuigao Renmin Fayuan Guanyu Shenli Zhuanli Jiufen Anjian Shiyong Falü Wenti de Ruogan Guiding Tiaowen Shiyi (最高人民法院《关于审理专利纠纷案件适用法律问题的若干规定》条文释义), in Jianming Cao (曹建明) ed., Xin Zhuan Ii FA Si Fa Jie Shi Jing Jie (新专利法司法解释精解) [The Explanation of New Patent Law Judicial Interpretation] (2002).

level of PHOSITA in finding doctrine of equivalents is the time of infringement.[92] Eventually, Chinese law became the same as the U.S. law on this issue.

ii. Limitations to Doctrine of Equivalents

(a) Dedication to the Public

It is a rule in the United States that a patentee cannot assert the doctrine of equivalents to cover a disclosed but unclaimed subject matter.[93] In China, Article 5 of the 2009 Judicial Interpretation introduces a similar dedication principle: "if a technical solution is described in the patent description but not included in the patent claim, the technical solutions are considered to be dedicated and excluded from the equivalents".[94]

(b) Prosecution History Estoppel /Principle of Estoppel

The Principle of Estoppel is the Chinese counterpart to the U.S. prosecution history estoppel rule. In both countries, this rule serves as a limitation for the doctrine of equivalents. However, in the Chinese law, it is unclear whether the presumption of estoppel is rebuttable.

In China, the principle of estoppel applies in both claim interpretation and the doctrine of equivalents. In United States, although prosecution history estoppel only applies to limit the doctrine of equivalents, prosecution history can also be used to interpret claims to exclude some embodiments from the literal scope if the prosecution supports a surrender of such embodiments.[95] In the U.S. law, the "prosecution history estoppel" and "narrowing literal interpretation of claims by prosecution history" are two concepts. The weights given by U.S. judges to prosecution history for literal interpretation of claims may vary on a case-by-case basis.[96]

---

[92] Art. 17 Guanyu Shenli Qinfan Zhuanliquan Jiufen Anjian Yingyong Falü Ruogan Wenti de Jieshi (Er) (关于审理侵犯专利权纠纷案件应用法律若干问题的解释(二)) [Explanations of Issues regarding to Application of Law on Patent Infringement Trial II] (Promulgated by Sup. People's Ct., Jan. 25, 2016, effective April.1, 2016, amended on Dec. 29, 2020), (Chinalawinfo) (China).

[93] See e.g., *Johnson & Johnston Associates Inc. v. R.E. Serv. Co., Inc.*, 285 F.3d 1046, 1055 (Fed. Cir. 2002).

[94] Guanyu Shenli Qinfan Zhuanliquan Jiufen Anjian Yingyong Falü Ruogan Wenti de Jieshi (关于审理侵犯专利权纠纷案件应用法律若干问题的解释) [Explanations of Issues regarding to Application of Law on Patent Infringement Trial] (Promulgated by Sup. People's Ct., Dec. 29, 2009, effective Jan.1, 2010), (Chinalawinfo) (China).

[95] Robert L. Harmon, Cynthia A. Homan, and Charles M. McMahon, Patents and the Federal Circuit (2011).

[96] *AquaTex v. Techniche* 419 F.3d 137,476 U.S.P.Q.2d 1213 (Fed. Cir. 2005) (quotint Phillips for the conclusion that the prosecution history is an ongoing negotiation that "often lacks the clarity of the specification and thus is less useful for claim construction.").

(c) Practicing Prior Art

The U.S. courts have developed a doctrine to limit the doctrine of equivalents in the context of the prior art. If an accused device is merely practicing the prior art and the technology used in the device has already been in the public domain, it cannot be found to be an infringement.[97] In China, the judicial interpretation of 2009 adopted this limitation.

[97] *Wilson,* 904 F.2d. 677, 683.

Conclusion

In contrast to the long-held view that China is reluctant to protect intellectual property rights, including patents,[1] this comparative study on claim interpretation shows that claim interpretation rules on China function similarly to the U.S. rules in most aspects. Regardless of the different conceptual frameworks in procedural laws and different terminologies in substantive laws, the legal reasoning and factual analysis in the cases illustrate that the law of China and the United States functions similarly. Besides the similarity in the current practice, the evolution process of Chinese claim interpretation is also similar to the U.S. law.[2,3]

Procedure law is where Chinese law on claim interpretation looks very different from the U.S. law. However, it is unnecessary to amend the procedural laws just because the conceptual frameworks are different. The difference in trial procedures and appellate standards is due to the fact that the United States belongs to the common law system and China follows the civil law tradition. In order to seek possible improvements to the procedure law, it would be more practical for China to look into other civil law countries' experiences. Following a common law approach runs the risk that the Chinese patent judicial process may depart from the overall legal system, which may cause more problems than it resolves.

---

[1] Xuan-Thao Nguyen, The China We Hardly Know–Revealing the New China's Intellectual Property Regime, 55 St. Louis University Law Journal 773 (Lead Article) (2011).

[2] E.g., on the issue of whether patent scope is defined by the claim, whether one element can be completely excluded.

[3] Chinese history of claim interpretation starts from 1984, when the first patent statute was issued and required claims to define the scope of patent. U.S. claim interpretation starts from the 1836 Patent Act which first time requires claims in patent.

© Intellectual Property Publishing House 2025

Z. Peng, *Comparative Study on Patent Claim Interpretation: The United States and China*, https://doi.org/10.1007/978-981-96-0836-2

Table of Cases and Other Authorities

The United States: Cases

Abbott Laboratories v. Sandoz, Inc., 566 F.3d 1282 (Fed. Cir. 2009).
Acoustical Design, Inc. v. Control Electronics Co., Inc., 932 F.2d 939 (Fed. Cir. 1991).
Allen Eng'g Corp. v. Bartell Indus., Inc., 299 F.3d 1336, 1346 (Fed.Cir.2002).
Altiris, Inc. v. Symantec Corp., 318 F.3d 1363 (Fed. Cir. 2003).
Am. Med. Sys., Inc. v. Biolitec, Inc., 618 F.3d 1354 (Fed. Cir. 2010).
Amegan Inc. V. Hoechst Marion Roussel, Inc., 126 F. Supp.2d 69 (D. Mass. 2001).
AquaTex v. Techniche 419 F.3d 1374 (Fed. Cir. 2005).
Aspex Eyewear, Inc. v. E'Lite Optik, Inc., No. Civ.A. 398CV2996, 2002 WL 1751381 (N.D.Tex. Apr.4, 2002).
Astrazeneca AB v. Mutual Pharmaceutical Co., Inc., 384 F.3d 1333 (Fed. Cir. 2004).
Athletic Alternatives, Inc. v. Prince Mfg., Inc., 73 F.3d 1573, 1581 (Fed. Cir. 1996).
Atl. Thermoplastics Co., Inc. v. Faytex Corp., 970 F.2d 834, 846 (Fed. Cir. 1992).
Atlas Powder Co. v. E.I. duPont de Nemours & Co., 750 F.2d 1569 (Fed. Cir. 1984).
Autogiro Co. of Am. v. United States, 384 F.2d 391 (Ct. Cl. Oct. 13, 1967)Burr v.
Aventis Pharmaceuticals, Inc. v. Barr Laboratories, Inc., 335 F. Supp. 2d 558 (D.N.J. 2004).
Bausch & Lomb Inc. v. Moria S.A., 222 F. Supp. 2d 616 (E.D. Pa. 2002).
Becton Dickinson and Co. v. C.R. Bard, Inc., 922 F.2d 792 (Fed.Cir.1990).
Belll Atl. Network Servs., Inc. v. Covard Commc'ns Group Inc., 262 F.3d 1258 (Fed. Cir. 2001).
Brosnan v. Rollerblade, Inc., No. C97-0782, C97-3258, 1998 WL 209155 (N.D.Cal. Apr.27, 1998).
Burke, Inc. v. Bruno Indep. Living Aids, Inc., 183 F.3d 1334 (Fed. Cir. 1999).
Burrv. Duryee, 68 U.S. 531 (1863).
C.R. Bard, Inc. v. U.S. Surgical Corp., 388 F.3d 858, 862 (Fed. Cir.2004).
Astrazeneca AB v. Mutual Pharm. Co., 384 F.3d 1333 (Fed.Cir.2004).
Capon v. Eshhar, 418 F.3d 1349 (Fed. Cir. 2005).
Catalina Mktg. Int'l, Inc. v. Coolsavings.com, Inc., 289 F.3d 801 (Fed.Cir.2002).

© Intellectual Property Publishing House 2025

Z. Peng, *Comparative Study on Patent Claim Interpretation: The United States and China*, https://doi.org/10.1007/978-981-96-0836-2

CCS Fitness, Inc. v. Brunswick Corp., 288 F.3d 1359 (Fed.Cir.2002).
Christianson v. Colt Indus. Operating Corp., 486 U.S. 800 (1988).
Cole v. Kimberly-Clark Corp., 102 F.3d 524 (Fed. Cir. 1996).
Comark Commc'ns, Inc. v. Harris Corp., 156 F.3d 1182 (Fed.Cir.1998)).
Commissioner v. Duberstein, 363 U.S. 278 (1960).
Computer Docking Station v. Dell, Inc., 519 F.3d 1366 (Fed.Cir.2008).
Conoco, Inc. v. Energy & Envtl. Int'l, L.C., 460 F.3d 1349 (Fed. Cir. 2006).
Corning Glass Works v. Sumitomo Elec. U.S.A., Inc., 868 F.2d 1251 (Fed. Cir. 1989).
Curtiss-Wright Flow Control Corp. v. Velan, Inc., 438 F.3d 1374 (Fed. Cir. 2006).
CVI/Beta Ventures, Inc. v. TuraLP, 112 F.3d 1146 (Fed.Cir.1997).
Cybor Corp. v. FAS Technologies, Inc., 138 F.3d 1448 (Fed. Cir. 1998).
DeMarini Sports, Inc. v. Worth, Inc., 239 F.3d 1314 (Fed. Cir. 2001).
Eastman Kodak Co. v. Goodyear Tire & Rubber Co., 114 F.3d 1547 (Fed.Cir.1997).
Eldon Industries, Inc. v. Vanier Mfg., Inc., 14 U.S.P.Q.2d (BNA) 1075 (C.D. Cal. 1990).
Electronic Planroom, Inc. v. McGraw-Hill Cos., 135 F.Supp.2d 805 (E.D.Mich.2001).
Elf Atochem North America, Inc. v. Libbey –Owens-Ford Co. 894 F. Supp. 850 (D. Del. 1995).
Envirco Corp. v. Clestra Cleanroom, Inc., 209 F.3d 1360 (Fed.Cir.2000).
Ex Parte Davis & Tuukkanen, 1949 WL 3555 (Feb. 15, 1949).
Fantasy Sports Props. v. Sportsline.com, 287 F.3d 1108 (Fed.Cir.2002).
Festo Corp. v. Shoketsu Kinzoku Kogyo Kabushiki Co., Ltd., 344 F.3d 1359 (Fed. Cir. 2003).
General Am. Transp. v. Cryo-Trans, Inc., 93 F.3d 766 (Fed.Cir.1996).
Generation II Orthotics, Inc. v. Med. Tech., Inc., 263 F.3d 1356 (Fed. Cir. 2001).
Gould v. Rees, 82 U.S. 187 (1872).
Gill v. Wells, 89 U.S. 1 (1874).
Graver Tank & Mfg. Co. v. Linde Air Prods. Co., 339 U.S. 605 (1950).
Hilton Davis Chem. Co. v. Warner-Jenkinson Co., Inc., 62 F.3d 1512 (Fed. Cir. 1995). supplemented, 64 F.3d 675 (Fed. Cir. 1995) and rev'd, 520 U.S. 17 (1997) and adhered.
Hilton Davis Chem. Co. v. Warner-Jenkinson Co., Inc., 62 F.3d 1512, 1530 (Fed. Cir. 1995). supplemented, 64 F.3d 675 (Fed. Cir. 1995) and rev'd, 520 U.S. 17, 117 S. Ct. 1040, 137 L. Ed. 2d 146 (1997) and adhered to, 114 F.3d 1161 (Fed. Cir. 1997).
Hoechst Celanese Corp. v. BP Chems. Ltd., 78 F.3d 1575 (Fed. Cir. 1996)).
Holmes Group v. Vornado Air Circulation Sys., Inc., 535 U.S. 826 (2002).
Housey Pharms., Inc. v. Astrazeneca UK Ltd., 366 F.3d 1348 (Fed. Cir. 2004).
Hughes Aircraft Co. v. United States, 717 F.2d 1351 (Fed. Cir. 1983).
Hughes Aircraft Co. v. United States, 717 F.2d 1351 (Fed. Cir. 1983).
IMS Tech., Inc. v. Haas Automation, Inc., 206 F.3d 1422 (Fed.Cir.2000).
In re Bridgeford, 53 C.C.P.A. 1182 (1966).
In re Fout, 675 F.2d 297 (CCPA 1982).

Innova/Pure Water, Inc. v. Safari Water Filtration Sys., Inc., 381 F.3d 1111 (Fed.Cir.2004). reaffirmed in Phllips.
Inpro II Licensing, S.A.R.L. v. T-Mobile USA, Inc., 450 F.3d 1350 (Fed. Cir. 2006).
Insituform Techs., Inc. v. Cat Contracting, Inc., 99 F.3d 1098 (Fed.Cir.1996).
Interactive Gift Express, Inc. v. Compuserve Inc., 95 Civ. 6871 (S.D.N.Y. May 15, 1998), vacated on other grounds, 256 F.3d 1323 (Fed.Cir.2001).
Interactive Pictures Corp. v. Infinite Pictures, Inc., 274 F.3d 1371 (Fed. Cir. 2001).
Inventio AG v. ThyssenKrupp Elevator Americas Corp., 2011 WL 2342744 (Fed. Cir. June 15, 2011).
Inventio AG v. ThyssenKrupp Elevator Americas Corp., 2011 WL 2342744 (Fed. Cir. 2011).
Johns Hophins Univ. v. CellPro, Inc., 894 F. Supp. 819 (D.Del 1995).
Johnson & Johnston Associates Inc. v. R.E. Service Co., Inc., 285 F.3d 1046, 62 USPQ2d 1046 (Fed. Cir. 2002) (en banc).
Johnston v. IVAC Corp., 885 F.2d 1574, 12 U.S.P.Q.2d 1382, 1384 (Fed. Cir. 1989).
Kraft Foods, Inc. v. International Trading Co., 203 F.3d 1362 (Fed.Cir.2000).
Kraft Foods, Inc. v. International Trading Co., 203 F.3d 1362 (Fed.Cir.2000).
Kraus v. Bell Atlantic Corp., 716 F.Supp. 182, 184 (E.D.Pa.1989).
Laitram Corp. v. Rexnord, Inc., 939 F.2d 1533, 1538 (Fed.Cir.1991).
LG Electronics, Inc. v. Bizcom Electronics, Inc. 453 F.3d 1364 (2006).
Liebel-Flarsheim Co. v. Medrad, Inc., 358 F.3d 898, 910 (Fed.Cir.2004).
Loral Fairchild Corp. V. Victor Co. of Japan, Ltd, 906 F.Supp. 789 (E.D.N.Y. 1995).
LRC Elec., Inc. v. John Mezzalingua Assocs., Inc., 974 F.Supp. 171 (N.D.N.Y.1997).
Lupin Ltd. v. Abbott Laboratories, 484 F.Supp.2d 448 (E.D.Va.2007).
Markman v. Westview Instruments, Inc., 517 U.S. 370 (1996) (Marman II).
Markman v. Westview Instruments, Inc., 52 F.3d 967 (Fed.Cir.1995) (in banc) (Markman I) .
Mas-Hamilton Group v. LaGard Inc., 156 F.3d 1206 (Fed. Cir. 1998).
Maxwell v. J. Baker, Inc., 86 F.3d 1098 (Fed. Cir. 1996).
Maxwell v. J. Baker, Inc., 86 F.3d 1098, 39 USPQ2d 1001 (Fed. Cir. 1996) , cert. denied, 520 U.S. 1115 (1997).
McCormick v. Talcott, 61 U.S. 4 (20) (1857).
Merrill v. Yeomans, 94 U.S. 568 (1876).
Metaullics Sys. Co. v. Cooper, 100 F.3d 938 (Fed.Cir.1996).
Micro Motion, Inc. v. Exac Corp., 741 F. Supp. 1426 (1990).
Miller v. Fenton, 474 U.S. 104, 114, 106 S.Ct. 445 (1985).
Modine Mfg. Co. v. U.S. Int'l Trade Comm'n, 75 F.3d 1545 (Fed. Cir. 1996).
Monsanto Co. v. Syngenta Seeds, Inc., 503 F.3d 1352 (Fed. Cir. 2007).
Multiform Desiccants, Inc. v. Medzam, Ltd., 133 F.3d 1473 (Fed.Cir.1998).
National Presto Industries, Inc. v. West Bend Co., 76 F.3d 1185, 1190, 37 U.S.P.Q.2d (Fed. Cir. 1996).
Nazomi Commc'ns, Inc. v. Arm Holdings, PLC., 403 F.3d 1364 (Fed.Cir.2005).
Norian Corp. v. Stryker Corp., 363 F.3d 1321 (Fed.Cir.2004).
Norian Corp. v. Stryker Corp., 363 F.3d 1321 (Fed.Cir.2004).
Ortho-McNeil Pharms. Inc. v. Mylan Labs., Inc. (Fed. Cir. 2008).

Overhead Door Corp. v. Chamberlain Group, Inc., 194 F.3d 1261 (Fed. Cir. 1999).
Parker v. Hulme, 18 F. Cas. 1138 (C.C.E.D. Pa. 1849).
PC Connector Solutions LLC v. SmartDisk Corp., 406 F.3d 1359 (Fed.Cir.2005).
Pennwalt Corp. v. Durand-Wayland, Inc., 833 F.2d 931 (Fed. Cir. 1987).
Phillips v. AWH Corp., 415 F.3d 1303 (Fed. Cir. 2005) (en banc), cert. denied, 126 S. Ct. 1332 (2006).
Pitney Bowes, Inc. v. Hewlett-Packard Co., 182 F.3d 1298 (Fed. Cir. 1999).
Playtex Prods., Inc. v. Procter & Gamble Co., 400 F.3d 901 (Fed. Cir. 2005).
Renishaw PLC v. Marposs Societa' per Azioni, 158 F.3d 1243 (Fed.Cir.1998).
Retractable Technologies, Inc. v. Becton, Dickinson & Co., 659 F.3d 1369 (Fed. Cir. 2011).
Revlon Consumer Products Corp. v. Estee Lauder Companies, Inc., 00 CIV.5960 RMB AJP, 2003 WL 21751833 (S.D.N.Y. July 30, 2003).
Rodime PLC v. Seagate Tech., Inc., 174 F.3d 1294 (Fed. Cir. 1999).
Rogers v. Desa Int'l, Inc., 166 F.Supp.2d 1202 (E.D.Mich.2001).
Sage Prods. v. Devon Indus., Inc., 126 F.3d 1420 (Fed. Cir. 1997).
Salem v. U. S. Lines Co., 370 U.S. 31 (1962).
Sanitary Refrigerator Co. v. Winters, 280 U.S. 30 (1929).
Schinzing v. Mid-States Stainless, Inc., 415 F.3d 807 (8th Cir. 2005).
Scripps Clinic & Research Foundation v. Genentech, Inc., 927 F.2d 1565 (Fed.Cir.1991).
Serrano v. Telular Corp., 111 F.3d 1578 (Fed.Cir.1997); Alpex Computer Corp. v. Nintendo Co., 102 F.3d 1214, 40 USPQ2d 1667 (Fed.Cir.1996).
Siemens Med. Solutions USA, Inc. v. Saint-Gobain Ceramics & Plastics, Inc., 647 F.3d 1373 (Fed. Cir. 2011).
Southwall Techs., Inc. v. Cardinal IG, Co., 54 F.3d 1570 (Fed.Cir.1995).
Storage Tech. Corp. v. Cisco Sys., Inc., 329 F.3d 823, 831 (Fed.Cir.2003).
Storage Technology Corp. v. Cisco Systems, Inc. 329 F.3d 823 (2003).
Sunrace Roots Enter. Co. v. SRAM Corp., 336 F.3d 1298 (Fed.Cir.2003).
Superguide Corp. v. DirecTV Enterprises, Inc., 358 F.3d 870 (Fed. Cir. 2004).
Symantec Corp. v. Computer Assocs. Int'l, Inc., 522 F.3d 1279 (Fed. Cir. 2008).
Syntex (U.S.A.) LLC v. Apotex, Inc., 407 F.3d 1371 (Fed. Cir. 2005).
Tandon Corp. v. United States Int'l Trade Comm'n, 831 F.2d 1017 (Fed.Cir.1987).
Teleflex, Inc. v. Ficosa North America Corp., 299 F.3d 1313 (Fed. Cir. 2002).
Teva Pharmaceuticals USA, Inc. v. Sandoz, Inc., 135 S. Ct. 831 (2015).
Texas Instruments Inc. v. United States Int'l Trade Comm'n, 805 F.2d 1558 (Fed.Cir.1986).
Thomas & Betts Corp. v. Litton Sys., Inc., 720 F.2d 1572 (Fed.Cir.1983).
Toro Co. v. White Consol. Indus., Inc., 199 F.3d 1295(Fed.Cir.1999).
TriMed, Inc. v. Stryker Corp., 514 F.3d 1256 (Fed. Cir. 2008).
Ultra-Tex Surfaces, Inc. Hill Bros. Chemical Co. 204 F3d 1360 (Feb. Cir. 2000).
Unique Concepts, Inc. v. Brown, 939 F.2d 1558 (Fed. Cir. 1991).
United States v. McConney, 728 F.2d 1195 (C.A.9 1984) (en banc).
Vaupel Textilmaschinen KG v. Meccanica Euro Italia S.P.A. 944 F.2d 870 (1991).
Versa Corp. v. Ag-Bag Int'l Ltd., 392 F.3d 1325 (Fed.Cir.2004).

Vitronics Corp. v. Conceptronic, Inc., 90 F.3d 1576 (Fed. Cir. 1996). E.g.
Vanderlande Indus. Nederland BV v. Int'l Trade Comm'n, 366 F.3d 1311 (Fed.Cir.2004).
Warner-Jenkinson Co., Inc. v. Hilton Davis Chem. Co., 520 U.S. 17 (1997).
Wiener v. NEC Elecs. Inc., 102 F.3d 534 (Fed.Cir.1996).
Winans v. Denmead, 56 U.S. 330 (1853).
YBM Magnex, Inc. v. Int'l Trade Comm'n, 145 F.3d 1317 (Fed. Cir. 1998).
York Prods., Inc. v. Central Tractor, 99 F.3d 1568 (Fed. Cir. 1996).

The United States: The Other Authorities

Federal Rules of Civil Procedure (2010).
Federal Rules of Evidence (2011).
H.R. 1249: Leahy-Smith America Invents Act.
H.R. 628, 111th Cong. (2011).
Manual of Patent Examining Procedure (MPEP) (2010).
Title 28 of the United States Code (Judiciary and Judicial Procedure).
Title 35o of the United States Code (Patents).

China: Cases

Aonuo Zhongguo Zhiyao Youxian Gongsi v. Hubei Wushi Yaoye Gufen Youxian Gongsi (澳诺 (中国) 制药有限公司与湖北午时药业股份有限公司) Min Ti Zi di 20 Hao (民提字第20号), Supreme People's Court (2009).
Beijing Nanchen Touzi Youxian Gongsi, Beijing Weihao Lüye Youxian Gongsi v. Wujiang Feile Dianzi Youxian Gongsi (北京南辰投资有限公司 北京伟豪铝业有限公司诉吴江飞乐电子有限公司), (Shanghai Hig. People's Ct., 2004).
Chong Yang Dongtai Fajiaoji [充氧动态发酵机], Beijing High People's Court (1992) (离经终字第16号), in Cheng Yongshun (程永顺)& Luo Lihua (罗李华) Zhuanli Qinquan Panding: Zhongmei Fatiao yu Anli Bijiao Yanjiu (专利侵权判定:中美法条与案例比较研究) [Cheng Yongshun, Luo Lihua, Deciding Patent Infringement: Comparative Study on Chinese and U.S. Law and Cases] 163 (2002).
Ningbo Shi Dongfang Jixin Zongchang v. Jiangyin Jinling Wujin Zhipin Youxian Gongsi (宁波市东方机芯总厂与江阴金铃五金制品有限公司) [Ningbo Dongfang Jixin Zongchang v. Jiangyin Jinling Wujin Zhipin Youxian LL.C],ipr. Chinacourt (Sup. People's Ct. Mar. 6, 2002).
Difang Guoying Xiangjiang Cixi Mifeng Cailiao Factory v. Xiaoshan Mifeng Jian Factory (地方国营湘江慈溪密封材料厂诉萧山市密封件厂),in Comments on Intellectual Property Cases (知识产权判案评述),40 (Zhaohong Dong ed., 2003). Accord Yan Wenjun (闫文军), Zhuanliquan de Baohu Fanwei: Quanli Yaoqiu Jieshi he Dengtong Yuanze Shiyong (专利权的保护范围:权利要求解释和等同原则适用) [Yan Wenjun, Scope of Patent Protection: Interpretation of Claim and Application of Doctrine of Equivalents] 360 (2007).
Guandong Sheng Jiangling v. Yuanda (广东省阳江陵岛(集团)公司与元大金属实业(深圳)有限公司), Guangdong Hig. People's Ct. Feb.1 2004) Yuanda Jinshu v.

Guanyu dui Henansheng Gaoji Renmin Fayuan Qingshi Zhengzhou Shi Zhenzhong Dianronggaoye Youxian Gongsi yu Zhengzhou Jiansong Naihuo Cailiao Youxian Gongsi Zhuanli Qinquan Jiufen Zaishen Yian Youguan Wenti De Dafu (关于对河南省高级人民法院请示郑州市振中电熔锆业有限公司与郑州建嵩耐火材料有限公司专利侵权纠纷再审一案有关问题的答复) [In re Henan Hig. People's Ct.'s request on Zhengzhou Zhengzhong Dianronggaoye LL.C v. Zhengzhou Jiansong Naihuo Cailiao LL.C.], ipr.chinacourt (Sup. People's Ct. Mar.7, 2006) (China).

Haodeng Jituan Gongsi v. Shanghai Kesheng (豪登集团公司诉上海科盛) [Howden Group Limited v. Shanghai Kesheng], ipr.Chinacourt. (2005). See commentsin Zhang Xiaodu, Zhuanli Qinquan Panding : Lilun Tantao Yu Shenpan Shijian [张晓都,专利侵权判定:理论探讨与审判实践,2008. Zhang Xiaodu, Deciding Patent Infringement: Theoretical Discussion and Practice in Trial] (e 2008).

Jiguang Tance Yi case (激光探测仪案), in Zhishi Chanquan Anli Pingxi (知识产权案例评析) 175 (Chengsi Zheng es., 1994).

Kunming Zhiyao Jituan Gufen Youxian Gongsi yu Kunming Longjin Yaoye Youxian Gongsi Zhuanli Qinquan Jiufen Yian de Dafu (关于昆明制药集团股份有限公司与昆明龙津药业有限公司专利侵权纠纷一案的答复) [In Re Kunming Zhiyao LL.C. v. Kunming Longjin LL.C], ipr. chinacourt. (Sup. People's Ct. 2005) 2005.

Liang Jinshui v. Li Changzhong etc. (梁锦水诉李昌众等) [Liang Jinshui v. Li Changzhong ect] ipr. Chinacourt. (Shanghai Hig. People's Ct.) ipr. Chincout. (July10, 2006).

Liang Jinshui v. Li Changzhong etc. (梁锦水诉李昌众等) [Liang Jinshui v. Li Changzhong ect] ipr. Chinacourt. (Zhejiang Hig. People's Ct.) ipr. Chincout. (July10, 2008).

Liu Jingchang v. Zibo Youcheng Maorong Zhipin Youxian Gongsi (刘敬昌诉淄博友诚毛绒制品有限公司,山东省高级人民法院 (2003) 鲁民三终字第35号) [Liu Jingchang v. Zibo Youcheng Maorong Zhipin LL.C. Company] in Yan Wenjun (闫文军), Zhuanliquan de Baohu Fanwei: Q uanli Yaoqiu Jieshi he Dengtong Yuanze Shiyong (专利权的保护范围:权利要求解释和等同原则适用) [Yan Wenjun, Scope of Patent Protection: Interpretation of Claim and Application of Doctrine of Equivalents] 354 (2007).

Liu Wanqing yu Weifang Zhongshi Zhiyao Youxian Gongsi (刘万庆与潍坊中狮制药有限公司实用新型专利纠纷案) [Liu Wanqing yu Weifang Zhongshi Zhiyao Youxian Gongsi], ipr.chinacourt. (Jinan Interm. People's Ct. 1999).

Motuo Che Wuji Biansu Pidai Lun Shiyong Xinxing Zhuanli Qinquan An (摩托车无级变速皮带轮实用新型专利侵权案), in Zhuanli Shangbiao Jishu Hetong Yinan Anli Pingxi (专利、商标、技术合同疑难案例评析) [Review of Patent, Trademark and Technology Transfer Contract] 111 (Yang Jinqi (杨金琪) ed., 1995).

Ningbo Shi Dongfang Jixin Zongchang v. Jiangyin Jinling Wujin Zhipin Youxian Gongsi (宁波市东方机芯总厂与江阴金铃五金制品有限公司) [Ningbo Dongfang Jixin Zongchang v. Jiangyin Jinling Wujin Zhipin Youxian LL.C],ipr. Chinacourt [Sup. People's Ct. Mar. 6, 2002].

Pan Luli v. Shanghai Gaoyu Yiliao Qixie Chang (潘璐莉与上海高宇医疗器材厂) [Pan Luli v. Shanghai Gaoyu Medicial Device Facotory], ipr. Chinacourt (Shanghai High People's Ct., 2004).

Qianrushi Zhengfaqi Yian (嵌入式蒸发器一案) [In Re Embedded evaporator], Zhuanli Shangbiao Jishu Hetong Yinan Anli Pingxi (专利、商标、技术合同疑难案例评析) [Review of Patent, Trademark and Technology Transfer Contract] 111 (Yang Jinqi (杨金琪) eds., 1995).

Qinghua Daxue v. Jixie Dianzi Gongye Shejiyuan, Beijing Weiken Jixie Dianzi Shebei Youxian Gongsi (清华大学诉机械电子工业设计院,北京威肯机械电子设备有限公司) [Qinghua University v. Mechenical & Electornic Industry Design Institute, Beijing Weiken Mechincl & Electronical Device LL.C.], in Zhishi Chanquan Mingan Pingxi (知识产权名案评析) [Review of Famous Intellectual Property Cases] 413-420 (Sun Jian (孙建), Luo Dongchuan (罗东川) ed., 1998). See discussion in Yan Wenjun (闫文军), Zhuanliquan de Baohu Fanwei: Quanli Yaoqiu Jieshi he Dengtong Yuanze Shiyong (专利权的保护范围:权利要求解释和等同原则适用) [Yan Wenjun, Scope of Patent Protection: Interpretation of Claim and Application of Doctrine of Equivalents]329 (2007).

Renda Jiancai Chang v. Xinyi Gongsi (仁达建材厂诉新益公司) [Renda Construction Material Factory v. Xinyi Company], ipr.Chinacourt (Sup. People's Ct. Aug. 22, 2005).

Shanghai cases Yuanda v. Changzhou Heli (元大金属实业 (深圳) 有限公司与常州合力电器有限公司), Shanghai Hig. People's Ct., Feb.25, 2003.Yuanda v. Jiangsu Chunlan (元大金属实业 (深圳) 有限公司与江苏春兰进出口有限公司) Shanghai Hig. People's Ct., Feb.25, 2003. (Yuanda v. Ningbo Jixian)元大金属实业 (深圳) 有限公司与宁波市鄞县对外贸易有限责任公司)Shanghai Hig. People's Ct., Feb.25, 2003.

Shuitao Q unuan Lu (水套取暖炉) [In Re Residential heating furnace], (Shandong High People's Court), see summary and comments in Yan Wenjun (闫文军), Zhuanliquan de Baohu Fanwei: Quanli Yaoqiu Jieshi he Dengtong Yuanze Shiyong (专利权的保护范围:权利要求解释和等同原则适用) [Yan Wenjun, Scope of Patent Protection: Interpretation of Claim and Application of Doctrine of Equivalents] 327 (2007).

Supreme Court case Zuigao Renmin Fayuan Minshi Shenpanting Guanyu Wangchuan yu Hefei Jichu Maoyi Youxian Zeren Gongsi deng Zhuanli Qinquan Jiufen An de Han (最高人民法院民事审判第三庭关于王川与合肥继初贸易有限责任公司等专利侵权纠纷案的函) [Wangchuan v. Hefei Jichu Trade LL.C], ipr. Chinacourt (Sup. People's Ct. Feb. 2, 2001).

Wangxiu v. Beijing Shenmo Kegongmao Youxian Gongsi (王秀诉北京深陌科工贸有限公司),Beijing 1s intermediate high people's court (北京市第一中级人民法院 (1999) 中知初字第104号案), cited in Yan Wenjun (闫文军), Zhuanliquan de Baohu Fanwei: Quanli Yaoqiu Jieshi he Dengtong Yuanze Shiyong (专利权的保护范围:权利要求解释和等同原则适用) [Yan Wenjun, Scope of Patent Protection: Interpretation of Claim and Application of Doctrine of Equivalents] (2007).

Zhanchi v. Zhenyu Gongsi (展翅诉珍誉公司) [Zhanchi v. Zhenyu Company], ipr. Chinacourt, (Beijing Hig. People's Ct., Jun. 13, 2006)) http://www.panjueshu.com/beijing/gaoyuan/m200606132006367.html.

Zhejiang Bosuer Yundong Qixie Youxian Gongsi v. Hangzhou Qike Zhineng Keji Youxian Gongsi(浙江波速尔运动器械有限公司与杭州骑客智能科技有限公司), (2018) Zui Gao Fa Min Shen 2345 Hao (Sup. People's Ct. 2020) (China).

Zhongguo Dongnan Jishu Maoyi Zonggongsi v. Beijing Shi Wangma Diannao Zonggongsi (中国东南技术贸易总公司与北京市王码电脑总公司)[China Dongnan Technology Trade Company v. Beijing Wangma Computer Company], ipr.chinacourt (Beijing Hig. People's Ct. Jul. 18, 1997) (China).

Zhoulin v. Beijing Aomei Guang Jidian Lianhe Kaifa Gongsi, Beijing Huaao Dianzi Yiliao Yiqi Youxian Gongsi (周林诉北京奥美光机电联合开发公司,北京华奥电子医疗仪器有限公司) [Zhoulin v. Beijing Aomei Guangjidian Lianhe Kaifa LL.C., Beijing Huaoa Electronic Medical Device LL.C.], ipr. Chinacourt (Beijing Hig. People's Ct., Mar. 22, 1996) See summary and comments in Zhishi Chanquan Shenpan Anli Yaolan (知识产权审判案例要览) [Review of the Key Cases of Intellectual Property] 151-159 (Cheng Yongshun (程永顺) eds.1999).

Zhoulin v. Xingyun Shiye (Chengdu) Youxian Gongsi Deng (周林诉兴运实业) [Zhoulin v. Xingyun Shiye LL.C. etc.] ipr. Chinacourt (Beijing Intermediate Court. Jun. 24, 2005).

Zhu Yuzhen v. Ningbo Fangtai Chuju Youxian Gongsi deng [Zhu Yuzhen v. Ningbo Fangtai Chuju Youxian Gongsi] (朱玉振诉宁波方太厨具有限公司等,江苏省高级人民法院2004苏民三终字第017号案), in Yan Wenjun (闫文军), Zhuanliquan de Baohu Fanwei: Quanli Yaoqiu Jieshi he Dengtong Yuanze Shiyong (专利权的保护范围:权利要求解释和等同原则适用) [Yan Wenjun, Scope of Patent Protection: Interpretation of Claim and Application of Doctrine of Equivalents] 355 (2007).

Zhuanli Qinquan Panding Ruogan Wenti de Yijian (专利侵权判定若干问题的意见) [The opinion on several issues of deciding patent infringement] (Promulgated by Beijing High People's Court., 2001), (Chinalawinfo) (China).

Zuhe Yichu Shiyong Zhuanli (组合衣橱实用新型专利) [In Re Zhuhe Yichu Utility Patent] Xiaodu Zhang 17-34.

Zuhe Yichu Shiyong Zhuanli (组合衣橱实用新型专利) [In Re Zhuhe Yichu Utility Patent] in Zhang Xiaodu, Zhuanli Qinquan Panding : Lilun Tantao Yu Shenpan Shijian [张晓都,专利侵权判定:理论探讨与审判实践,2008.Zhang Xiaodu, Deciding Patent Infringement: Theoretical Discussion and Practice in Trial] (2008), and Haodeng Jituan Gongsi v. Shanghai Kesheng (豪登集团公司诉上海科盛) [Howden Group Limited v. Shanghai Kesheng], ipr.Chinacourt. (2005).

Zuigao Renmin Fayuan Minshi Shenpanting Guanyu Wangchuan yu Hefei Jichu Maoyi Youxian Zeren Gongsi deng Zhuanli Qinquan Jiufen An de Han (最高人民法院民事审判第三庭关于王川与合肥继初贸易有限责任公司等专利侵权纠纷案的函) [Wangchuan v. Hefei Jichu Trade LL.C], ipr. Chinacourt (Sup. People's Ct. Feb. 2, 2001).

China: Other Authorities

The Third Civil Divison of Beijing High People's Court (北京市高级法院民三庭), Suggestions and Thoughts on Intellectual Property Judicial Protection (关于知识产权司法保护机制中有关主要问题及其意见和建议), China Intellectual Property Judicial Protection Website (中国知识产权司法保护网) (2005), http://www.chinaiprlaw. cn/file/200510105865.html.).

Fayuan Zuzhi Fa (法院组织法) [Court Organization Law], 2006 (P.R.C.).

Guangdong Sheng Gaoji Renmin Fayuan Q uansheng Zhishi Chanquan Shenpan Gongzuo Huiyi (广东省高级人民法院全省知识产权审判工作会议), May 2004. (strict application of DOE. Factors including pioneer invention should be considered. The application of DOE in untitlity patent should be limited. DOE does not apply to design patent).

GuangDong High Court Conference Documents: Guangdong High People's Court Conference Documents, Guangdong Sheng Gaoji Renmin Fayuan Q uansheng Zhishi Chanquan Shenpan Gongzuo Huiyi (广东省高级人民法院全省知识产权审判工作会议), May 2004. (strict application of DOE. Factors including pioneer invention should be considered. The application of DOE in untitlity patent should be limited. DOE does not apply to design patent).

Guanyu Jinyibu Jiaqiang Heyiting Zhize de Ruogan Guiding (关于进一步加强合议庭职责的若干规定) [several rules about enhancing the trial panel], (Sup. People's Ct., Dec. 14, 2009, Feb. 1, 2010), art. 7.

Guanyu Kaizhan Zhuanli Shenpan Gongzuo de Jige Wenti de Tongzhi (关于开展专利审判工作的几个问题的通知) [Announcement on several issues in patent trial work] (Sup. People's Ct., Feb. 16, 1985) Zhonghua Renmin Gongheguo Falü Q uanshu (中华人民共和国法律全书) (P.R.C.).

Guanyu Shenli Zhuanli Jiufen Anjian Shiyong Falü Wenti de Ruogan Guiding (关于审理专利纠纷案件适用法律问题的若干规定) [Several Provisions on Issues Concerning Applicable Laws to the Trial of Patent Controversies] (Promulgated by Sup. People's Ct., 2001,amended in 2013, 2015 & 2020), (Chinalawinfo) (China).

Guanyu Renmin Peishenyuan Canjia Shenpan Huodong Ruogan Wenti de Guiding (关于人民陪审员参加审判活动若干问题的规定) [Several rules about the jurors' participate in trial] (Sup. People's Ct., Nov. 23, 2009) Zhonghua Renmin Gongheguo Falü Q uanshu (中华人民共和国法律全书) (P.R.C.), art 2.

Guanyu Shenli Qinfan Zhuanliquan Jiufen Anjian Yingyong Falü Ruogan Wenti de Jieshi (关于审理侵犯专利权纠纷案件应用法律若干问题的解释) [Explanations of Issues regarding to Application of Law on Patent Infringement Trial] (Promulgated by Sup. People's Ct., Dec. 29, 2009, effective Jan.1, 2010), (Chinalawinfo) (China).

Guanyu Shenli Qinfan Zhuanliquan Jiufen Anjian Yingyong Falü Ruogan Wenti de Jieshi (Er) (关于审理侵犯专利权纠纷案件应用法律若干问题的解释(二)) [Explanations of Issues regarding to Application of Law on Patent Infringement Trial II] (Promulgated by Sup. People's Ct., Jan. 25, 2016, effective April.1, 2016, amended on Dec. 29, 2020), (Chinalawinfo) (China).

Guanyu Tiaozheng Difang Geji Renmin Fayuan Guanxia Diyishen Zhishi Chanquan Minshi Anjian Biaozhun de Tongzhi (最高人民法院, 关于调整地方各级人民法院管辖第一审知识产权民事案件标准的通知) [The announcement on adjusting the standard of local courts' jurisdiction over the first instance civil intellectual property cases] (Sup. People's Ct, Jan 28, 2010, Feb.1, 2010) Zhonghua Renmin Gongheguo Falü Q uanshu (中华人民共和国法律全书) (P.R.C.).

Guanyu Wanshan Renmin Peishenyuan Zhidu de Jueding (关于完善人民陪审员制度的决定) [the decision of improving institution of juror] [Standing Comm. Nat'l People's Cong.,May 1st, 2005], art 18.

Guanyu dui Dangshiren Nengfou Xuanze Congshu Q uanli Yaoqiu Q ueding Zhuanliquan Baohu Fanwei de Qingshi de Dafu (关于对当事人能否选择从属权利要求确定专利权保护范围的请示的答复) [In Re the dependent claims], ipr. Chinacourt. (Sup. People's Ct. 2007) .

"Guojia Zhishi Chanquan Zhanlüe" (国家知识产权战略) [Outline of the National Intellectual Property Strategy] (St. Council, June 5th, 2008), Zhonghua Renmin Gongheguo Falü Q uanshu (中华人民共和国法律全书) (P.R.C.).

Guowuyuan Guanyu Yinfa Zhishi Chanquan Guojia Zhanlüe Gangyao de Tongzhi (国务院关于印发国家知识产权战略纲要的通知)[Notice of the State Council on Issuing the Outline of the National Intellectual Property Strategy] (No. 18 [2008] of the State Council).

IANG MINCAO, Vice director, Supreme People's Court, "Zai Quanguo Fayuan Zhishi Chanquan Shenpan Gongzuo Huiyi Shang de Jianghua" (在全国法院知识产权审判工作会议上的讲话) [The Speech at National Intellectual Property Trial Conference] (2003), in Zhishi Chanquan Nianjian (CNIPA ed., 2004).

Jiang Zhipei (蒋志培), "Zai Quanguo Fayuan Zhishi Chanquan Shenpan Gongzuo Huiyi Shang de Jianghua" (在全国法院知识产权审判工作会议上的讲话) [The Speech at National Intellectual Property Trial Conference], (guo jia zhi shi chan quan ju bian ji., Zhishi Chanquan Chubanshe 2003).

Jiangming Cao (曹建明), "Zai Quanguo Fayuan Zhishi Chanquan Shenpan Gongzuo Huiyi Shang de Jianghua" (在全国法院知识产权审判工作会议上的讲话) [The Speech at National Intellectual Property Trial Conference] , (National Intellectual Property Office ed., Intellectual Property Press) [载知识产权年鉴, 国家知识产权局编] (2006).

Jintao Hu (胡锦涛),"Jianchi Zou Zhongguo Tese Zizhu Chuangxin Daolu Wei Jianshe Chuangxinxing Guojia er Nuli Fendou—Zai Quanguo Kexue Jishu Dahui shang de Jianghua (坚持走中国特色自主创新道路为建设创新型国家而努力奋斗——在全国科学技术大会上的讲话) [speech note regarding to innovation based country] 2006. (emphasizing enhancing IP system).

Lifa Fa (立法法) [Law on Legislation] (promulgated by the Standing Comm. Nat'l People's Cong., Mar. 15, 2000, effective July 1, 2000) 2000 STANDING COMM. NAT'L PEOPLE'S CONG. GAZ. (China).

Minshi Susong Fa (民事诉讼法) [Civil Procedure Law Court], (promulgated by the Standing Comm. Nat'l People's Cong., Apr. 7,1991, effective Apr. 7,1991, June 27 Amended 2017)1991 STANDING COMM. NAT'L PEOPLE'S CONG. GAZ. (China).

Sifa Gaige Wunian Jihua (司法改革五年计划) (Five Years' Plan of Judicial Reform), Supreme People's Court.

Sup. People's Court, Understanding 2001 Judicial Interpertation 最高人民法院民三庭,如何理解最高人民法院关于专利法 (2001) 法释字第21号司法解释,http://www.chinaiprlaw.cn/file/200201281245.html .

Sup. People's Ct, The Rules on Citing Normative Documents (关于裁判文书引用法律、法规等规范性法律文件的规定), (2009).

Supreme Court Conference Document: Zuigao Renmin Fayuan Guanyu Dangqian Jingji Xingshi Xia Zhishi Chanquan Shenpan Daju Ruogan Wenti de Yijian (最高人民法院关于当前经济形势下知识产权审判大局若干问题的意见), April. 4, 2009.

Zhuanli Fa Shishi Xize (专利法实施细则) [Detailed Rules for the Implementation of the Patent Law] arts.19, (promulgated by the St. Council., Jun.15, 2001, effective Jul. 1,2001, amended Jan.09., 2010) (Chinalawinfo) (China).

Zhishichanquan Susong Anjian Jianding Guize (知识产权诉讼案件技术鉴定规则) [Forensic rule of intellectual property cases] (Jiangsu High People's Ct., 2001) , art 3, 7, 29.

Zhuanli Shencha Zhinan (专利审查指南) [Patent Examination Guideline] part II Chapter 2. (promulgated by the St. Intellectual Property Office, Jan.1, 2010, effective Feb. 1, 2010) (CNIPA) (China).

Zhuanli Fa (专利法)[Patent Law], (promulgated by the Standing Comm. Nat'l People's Cong., Mar.12, 1984, effective Apr. 1, 1985)1984 Standing Comm. Nat'l People's Cong. Gaz. (China). English version is available in lawinfochina.

Zhuanli Qinquan Panding Ruogan Wenti de Yijian (专利侵权判定若干问题的意见) [The opinion on several issues of deciding patent infringement] (Promulgated by Beijing Hig. People's Ct., 2001), (Chinalawinfo) (China). Beijing High People's Court ruled that abstract cannot be used to interpret patent claims.

Zuigao Renmin Fayuan Guanyu Dangqian Jingji Xingshi Xia Zhishi Chanquan Shenpan Daju Ruogan Wenti de Yijian (最高人民法院关于当前经济形势下知识产权审判大局若干问题的意见), April. 4, 2009. (strict application of DOE). Guangdong High People's Court Conference Documents.

Zuigao Renmin Fayuan Minsanting, Ruhe Lijie Zuigao Renmin Fayuan Guanyu Zhuanli Fa 2001 Fa Shi Zi Di 21 Hao Sifa Jieshi (最高人民法院民三庭, 如何理解最高人民法院关于专利法 (2001) 法释字第21号司法解释) [Sup. People's Court, Understanding 2001 Judicial Interpertation] ,http://www.chinaiprlaw.cn/file/200201281245.html.

Zuigao Renmin Fayuan Zhishi Chanquanting Fuzeren Jiu < Guanyu Shenli Qinfan Zhuanliquan Jiufen Anjian Yingyong Falü Ruogan Wenti de Jieshi > Da Jizhe Wen (最高人民法院知识产权庭负责人就《关于审理侵犯专利权纠纷案件应用法律若干问题的解释》答记者问) [Public Interview with the Chief of the Intellectual Property Tribunal of Sup. People's Ct. Explanations of Issues regarding to Application of Law on Patent Infringement Trial, with Respect to < Explanations of Issues regarding to Application of Law on Patent Infringement Trial >], Chinacourt (Sep.18, 2010, 19: 40pm); http://rmfyb.chinacourt.org/public/detail.php?id=134762.

Zuigao Renmin Fayuan Zhishi Chanquanting Fuzeren Jiu < Zuigao Renmin Fayuan Guanyu Shenli Zhuanli Jiufen Anjian Shiyong Falü Ruouan Wenti de Guiding > Da Jizhe Wen [最高人民法院民三庭负责人就《最高人民法院关于审理专利纠纷案件适用法律问题的若干规定》答记者问] (Public Interview with the Chief of the Intellectual Property Tribunal of Sup. People's Ct. , with Respect to Supreme People's Court Rules regarding to Application of Law on Trialing Patent Disputes >) (June 13, 2001)http://www.fsou.com/html/text/bnew/6039821/603982162.html.

Zuigao Renmin Fayuan Guanyu Shenli Zhuanli Jiufen Anjian Shiyong Falü Ruouan Wenti de Guiding (最高人民法院关于审理侵犯专利权纠纷案件应用法律若干问题的解释征求意见稿) [The Proposal of upreme People's Court Rules regarding to Application of Law on Trialing Patent Disputes] , in Yan Wenjun(闫文军), Zhuanliquan de Baohu Fanwei: Quanli Yaoqiu Jieshi he Dengtong Yuanze Shiyong (专利权的保护范围:权利要求解释和等同原则适用) [Yan Wenjun, Scope of Patent Protection: Interpretation of Claim and Application of Doctrine of Equivalents] (2007).

Bibliography

United States

Amy L. Landers, Understanding Patent Law (2008).

James R. Barney, An Empirical Analysis of District Court Claim Construction Decisions, 2011 Stanford Technology Law Review 1 (2011).

Christina Y. Lai, Comments, A Dysfunctional Formalism: How Modern Courts Are Undermining the Doctrine of Equivalents, 44 UCLA Law Review 2031 (1997).

Dave Schwartz, Practice Makes Perfect? An Empirical Study of Claim Construction Reversal Rates in Patent Cases, 107 Michigan Law Review 223, 265 (2008).

Dolly Wu, Patent Litigation: What About Qualification Standards for Court Appointed Experts? 2010 Boston College Intellectual Property and Technology Forum, (2010).

Donald S. Chisum, Chisum on Patent (2012).

Giles S. Rich, The Extent of the Protection and Interpretation of Claims-American Perspectives, 21 The International Review of Intellectual Property and Competition Law, 497 (1990).

John R. Thomas, Claim Re-Construction: The Doctrine of Equivalents In The Post-Markman Era, 9 Lewis & Clark Law Review 153 (2005).

janice m. muller, An Introduction to Patent Law (2006).

Janice Muller, Federal circuit 2004: Eight Significant Patent Law Developments Every Ip Litigator Must Understand, 11 Ip Litigator 27–38 (2005).

John Gladstone Mills, Donald Cress Reiley, III, Robert Clare Highley, Patent Law Fundamentals (2012).

John R. Thomas, Formalism at the Federal Circuit, 52 American University Law Review 771 (2003).

Kenneth R. Adamo, Back to the Future: Festo, Equivalents and Presumptive Prosecution History Estoppel, 716 Pli/Pat 147 (2002).

Kimberly P. Moore Paul R. Michel Raphael V. Lupo, Patent Litigation and Strategy (2008).

Kristen Osenga, Linguistics and Patent Claim Construction, 38 Rutgers Law Journal 61 (2006).

Learned Hand, Historical and Practical Considerations Regarding Expert Testimony, 15 Harvard Law Review 40 (1901).

Lawrence B. Ebert, Meet the New Festo: Same as the Old Festo?, http://www.nyipla.org/Bulletin/June2002.pdf (last visited November 2, 2002).

Mark R. Hull, Festo Corp. v. Shoketsu Kinzoku Kogyo Kabushiki Co.: A Fog Between the Bars, 37 Akron Law Review 339 (2004).

Michael H. Davis, Patent Policies, 56 Cleveland State University Law Review 337 (2004).

Patrick J. Flinn, Claim Construction Trends in the Federal Circuit, 572 PLI/PAT 317 (1999).

Robert L. Harmon, Cynthia A. Homan, and Charles M. McMahon, Patents and the Federal Circuit (2011).

© Intellectual Property Publishing House 2025

Z. Peng, *Comparative Study on Patent Claim Interpretation: The United States and China*, https://doi.org/10.1007/978-981-96-0836-2

Robert W. Gomulkiewicz, The Federal Circuit's Licensing Law Jurisprudence: Its Nature and Influence, 84 Washington Law Review 199 (2009).
Rochelle Cooper Dreyfuss, The Federal Circuit: A Case Study in Specialized Courts, 64 New York University Law Review 1 (1989).
Rochelle Cooper Dreyfuss, The Federal Circuit: A Continuing Experiment in Specialization, 54 Case Western Reserve Law Review 769 (2004).
Timothy R. Holbrook, The Supreme Court's Complicity in Federal Circuit Formalism, 20 Santa Clara Computer & High Technology Law Journal 1 (2003).
Toshiko Takenaka ed., Patent Law and Theory: A Handbook of Contemporary Research (2008).
Toshiko Takenaka, Claim Construction and the Extent of Patent Protection: A Comparative Analysis of the Phillips En Banc Federal Circuit Decision, 1 Journal of Intellectual Property Law & Practice 119 (2006).
Toshiko Takenaka, Doctrine of Equivalents After Hilton Davis: A Comparative Law Analysis, 22 Rutgers Computer & Technology Law Journal 479 (1996).
Toshiko Takenaka, Interpreting Patent Claims: The United States, Germany and Japan, 17 IIC Studies (1995).
Toshiko Takenaka, IP Boom or IP Bashing? Current Trends in IP Legislation and Case Law, 21 Japan Spotlight 23 (2006).
Toshiko Takenaka, The Doctrine of Equivalents in Japan, 6 CASRIP Symposium Publications 125(2001).
Webster's Ninth New Collegiate Dictionary (1990).
William Redin Woodward, Definiteness and Particularity in Patent Claims, 46 Michigan Law Review 755 (1948).

China

Zhishi Chanquan Ban'an Cankao(知识产权办案参考) [Reference for Intellectual Property Trial], (Zhognguo Shehui Kexue Yuan Zhishi Chanquan Zhongxin & Beijingshi Gaoji Renmin Fayuan Zhishi Chanquan Ting (中国社会科学院知识产权中心,北京市高级人民法院知识产权庭) [Intellectual Property Law Center of China Social Academy & Beijing High People's Court Intellectual Property] ed. 2001).
Bing Liang, The Changing Chinese Legal System, 1978-Present: Centralization of Power and Rationalization of The Legal System 45 (2008).
Cheng Yongshun (程永顺)& Luo Lihua (罗李华), Zhuanli Qinquan Panding: Zhongmei Fatiao Yu Anli Bijiao Yanjiu(专利侵权判定:中美法条与案例比较研究) [Deciding Patent Infringement: Comparative Study on Chinese and U.S. Law and Cases] (2002).
Cheng Yongshun (程永顺), Zhuanli Qinquan Panding Shiwu (专利侵权判定实务) [The Practice of Patent Infringement Determination] (2001).
David T. Wang, Judicial Reform in China: Improving Arbitration Award Enforcement by Establishing a Federal Court System ,48 Santa Clara Law Review. 649, 652 (2008).
Fang Dongxing (方东兴), Lun Zhongguo Ruanjian Zhishi Chanquan Baohu de Shida Guanxi(论中国软件知识产权保护的十大关系)[The Ten Relationships in China's Software Intellectual Property Protection],http://tech.sina.com.cn/it/e/2001-12-23/97035.shtml.
Sun Hailong (孙海龙) & Yao Jianjun (姚建军), Qinquan Wenti Wanqua Bu Yinggai Jianding (侵权问题完全不应该鉴定) [Forensic Certificate should absolutely not be used in Infringement Determination], 02 China Patent and Trademark (中国专利与商标) 57(2010).
He Weifang (贺卫方), Zhongguo Sifa Guanli Zhidu de Liangge Wenti (中国司法管理制度的两个问题) [China Two Issues of China's Judicial administration], Zhongguo Shehui Kexue (中国社会科学) [Social Sciencesin Chias], (1997).

Interview with Cheng Yongshun, Chief Justice, Intellectual Property Tribunal of Beijing High People's Court. (Dec. 20, 2006), (Sep. 18, 2010, 20:37 pm), http://www.sipo.gov.cn/sipo2008/mtjj/2006/200804/t20080401_362467.html.

Jessica Zoe Renwald, Foreign Investment Law in the People's Republic of China: What to Expect from Enterprise Establishment to Dispute Resolution, 16 Indiana International & Comparative Law Review 453, (2006).

Yang Jiancheng (杨建成), Zhishi Chanquan Shenpan zhong Zhuanli Jianding Wenti Yanjiu (知识产权审判中专利鉴定问题研究) [Patent Forensic Report in Intellectual Property Trial], 2Zhishi chanquan banan cankao(知识产权办案参考) (2001).

Jiang Zhipei (蒋志培), Zuigao Renmin Fayuan Zhishi Chanquan Ting de Sheli he Fazhan (最高人民法院知识产权庭的设立和发展) [The Establishment and The Development of The Intellectual Property Tribunal of Supreme People's Court], in Zhishi Chanquan yu Gaige Kaifang Sanshi Nian (知识产权与改革开放三十年)[Intellectual Property and 30 Years of Reform and Opening-up], (State Intellectual Property Office ed. 2008).

Wang Jing (王静), Tui er Buxiu Xinxi Zhishi Chanquan Zeren Buyiyang de Faguan Jiang Zhipei—Jianzheng Gaige Kaifang Yilai Zhongguo Zhishi Chanquan Shenpan (退而不休心系知识产权责任不一样的法官蒋志培——见证改革开放以来中国知识产权审判) [Retirement But Not Laying Back: Judge Zhipei Jiang Witnessed The History of China Intellectual Property Trial], Fa zhi wang (法制网)[Legal Daily](2009), at http://www.legaldaily.com.cn/2007fxy/2009-03/19/content_1056467.htm.

C. Fred Bergsten , Bates Gill, Nicholas R. Lardy & Derek Mitchell ed.China: The Balance Sheet: What the World Needs to Know Now About the Emerging Superpower (2006).

Kandishka Jayasuriya, Corporatism and Judicial Independence within Statist Legal Institutions in East Asia, in Law, Capitalism and Power in East Asia: The Rule of Law and Legal Institutions 195 (Kandishka Jayasuriya ed. 1999).

Li Guochang (李国昌), Panduan Qinquan Yingyi Duli Q uanli Yoqiu Weizhun (判断侵权应以独立权利要求为准) [Determining Infringements Should be Based on Independent Claim], Zhongguo Jishu Shichang Bao (中国技术报) [China Technology Newspaper], Feb.7th 1994.

Wang Liming (王利明), Sifa Gaige Yanjiu (司法改革研究) [Research on Judical Reform] 201-203 (Falü Chuban She 2000).

Ming Chang (常鸣), Beijing Yizhongyuan Yinru Zhuanjia Peishenyuan Duiwu Chengxiao Xianzhu (北京一中院引入专家陪审员队伍成效显著) [Experts jurors work well in Beijing First Intermediate People's Court](2010),at http://www.chinacourt.org/html/article/201002/22/396132.shtml.

Qi Yang (杨琪), Zhongguo Zhuanli Yulang-gongwu(中国专利与"狼"共舞)[Dancing with Wolves], in Zhongguo Kexue Bao (中国科学报)[China Science Newspaper], April 28, 2012. http://news.sciencenet.cn/sbhtmlnews/2012/4/257394.shtm.

Renmin Fayuan Jianjie (人民法院简介)[The Introduction of People's Courts], Zuigao Renmin Fayuan Wang (最高人民法院网) [The Website of the Supreme People's Court] (2010), at http://www.court.gov.cn/jgsz/rmfyjj/.

Robert Slate, Judicial Copyright Enforcement in China: Shaping World Opinion on TRIPS Compliance, 31 North Carolina Journal of International Law and Commercial Regulation 665 (2006).

Ronald S. Fernando, Understanding Judicial Patent Enforcement in China, 2 China Patents & Trademarks 24 (2008).

Shanghai Shi Gaoyuan Jianli Zhishi Chanquan ZhuanJia Ku (上海市高院建立知识产权专家库) [Shanghai High People's Eourt Established IP Expert Group], Wenhui Bao (文汇报)[Wenhui Daily], Dec. 2, 2009.

Sida Liu, Beyond Global Convergence: Conflicts of Legitimacy in a Chinese Lower Court, 31 Law & Social Inquiry 75 (2006).

Guojia Zhishi Chanquan Ju Tiafa Si(国家知识产权局条法司)[China National Intellectual Property Administration], Zhuanli Fa ji Zhuanli Fa Shishi Xize Disan Ci Xiugai Zhuanti

Yanjiu Baogao (专利法及专利法实施细则第三次修改专题研究报告)[Research Report on The Third Amendment to The Patent Law and The Implementing Rule], (2006).

Susan Trevaskes, Courts on the Campaign Path in China: Criminal Court Work in the "Yanda 2001" Anti-Crime Campaign, 42 Asian Survey 673 (2002).

Tan Xiaoqing (谭筱清), Dui Dengtong Yuanze Shiyong Xianzhi Tiaojian de Tantao (对等同原则适用限制条件的探讨), 2 Zhishi ChanQ uan (知识产权) [Intellectual Property] (2004).

Jining Shi Zhongji Renmin Fayuan (济宁市中级人民法院)[The Intermediate People's Court of Jining], Guanyu Shandong Sheng Zhishi Chanquan Sifa Baohu de Diaoyan—yi Zhishi Chanquan Minshi Shenpan wei Shijiao (关于山东省知识产权司法保护的调研——以知识产权民事审判为视角)[A Research on Intellectual Property Judicial Enforcement in Shandong Province: from A Civil Litigation Perspective], 22 Shandong Shenpan (山东审判) [Shandong Trial] 44 (2006).

Tu Jianhua (涂建华), Zouchu Pianju (走出骗局)[See Through the Scam] (1999).

Wei Huang (黄伟), Yiwushi Fayuan Chengwei Quanguo Shouge Ke Shenli Zhuanli Jiufen An Jiceng Fayuan (义乌市法院成为全国首个可审理专利纠纷案基层法院) [The Yiwu Court Becomes the First Basic Court Which Trails Patent Disputes], Zhongguo Zhishi Chanquan Bao (中国知识产权报)[China Intellectual Property Newspaper], Jul. 17th 2009.

Zhang Xiaodu (张晓都), Zhuanli Qinquan Panding--Lilun Tantao yu Shenpan Shijian (专利侵权判定——理论探讨与审判实践) [Determination of patent infringement--Theoretical discussion and judicial practice] (2008).

Yin Xintian (尹新天), Zhuanjia Dianping (专家点评)[Expert Commentary], in Beijing Zhishi Chanquan Shenpan Anli Yanjiu (北京知识产权审判案例研究)[Study on Beijing Intellectual Property Cases] (Beijing Gaoji Renmin Fayuan Minsan Ting (北京高级人民法院民三庭) [Beijing High People's Court, Tribunal No.3] ed., 2000).

Xu Xuan (徐萱), Zhishi Chanquan de Zhengdang Xing — Lun Zhishi Chanquan Fa Zhong de Duijia yu Hengping(知识产权的正当性——论知识产权法中的对价与衡平)[Justification of Intellectual Property: Also on Consideration and Equity in the Law of Intellectual Property], Zhongguo Shehui Kexue (中国社会科学) [Social Science of Chian] (2003).

Xuan-Thao Nguyen, The China We Hardly Know–Revealing the New China's Intellectual Property Regime,55 St. Louis University Law Journal 773 (Lead Article) (2011).

Yalei Sun, A Comparative Study of the Chinese Patent Law Practice Part II: Patent Litigation and Case Studies, 7 Perspective 5 (2006).

Yan Wenjun(闫文军), Zhuanliquan de Baohu Fanwei: Quanli Yaoqiu Jieshi he Dengtong Yuanze Shiyong (专利权的保护范围:权利要求解释和等同原则适用) [Yan Wenjun, Scope of Patent Protection: Interpretation of Claim and Application of Doctrine of Equivalents] (2007).

Yin Xingtian (尹新天), Zhuanliquan de Baohu (专利权的保护) [Protection of Patent Rights] (2005).

Yonghui Chen(陈永辉)& Xiaoxi Xie(谢晓曦), Quanguo Fayuan Zhishi Chanquan Shenpan Gongzuo Q ude Xinjinzhan (全国法院知识产权审判工作取得新进展) [The New Improvement Of National Courts In Intellectual Property Trial], Renmin Fayuan Bao (人民法院报)[People's Court Newspaper] ,Dec. 1. 2008.

Chen Xiaofang & Li Mingxia(陈晓芳,李明霞), Wu Jiaoshou Bitui Feilipu Zhengyi Zhuanli (五教授逼退飞利浦争议专利)[Five Professors Fights Against Phillips Patent], in Fazhi Ribao (法制日报)[Legal Daily], Dec.12, 2006.

Zhang Qingqui (张清奎), Huaxue Lingyu Zhuanli Shenqing Wenjian de Zhuanxie yu Shencha [化学领域发明专利申请的文件撰写与审查] (2010).

Zhang Yuejin (张跃进), Shuoming Shu zai Zhuanli Qinquan Panduan Zhong de Zuoyong (说明书在专利侵权判断中的作用) [The function of Claims in Patent Infringement Determination], Zhongguo Zhuanli Bao(中国专利报)[China Patent Newspaper], Jan. 19, 1990.

Zhang Zewu (张泽吾), Duoyu Zhiding Yuanze zhi Q uexian Fenxi ji Sifa Duice (多余指定原则之缺陷分析及司法对策) [The Analysis of The Problems of Redundant Element Rule and Judicial Solutions],2 Xingzheng yu Fa(行政与法)[Administration and Law] 124 (2004).

Zheng Wei (郑伟), Zhishi Chanquan Jingan Pingxi (知识产权精案评析) [Review of Classic Intllectual Property Cases], (2004).

Zhipei Jiang (蒋志培), Patent Litigation in China, 9 Federal Circuit Bar Journal. 479 (1999—2000).

Zhishi Chanquan Shenpan Anli Yaolan (知识产权审判案例要览) [Review of the Key Cases of Intellectual Property] (Cheng Yongshun (程永顺) ed.1999).

Zhongguo Zhishi Chanquan Baohu Tixi Yanjiu (中国知识产权保护体系研究,[The Study on Chinese Intellectual Property Protection System] (Zhongguo Shehui Kexue Yuan Zhishi Chanquan Zhongxin (中国社会科学院知识产权中心)[Intellectual Property Law Center, China Social Science Academy] ed. 2008).

The manufacturer's authorised representative in the EU is Springer Nature Customer Service Centre GmbH, Europaplatz 3, 69115 Heidelberg, Germany. If you have any concerns regarding our products, please contact ProductSafety@springernature.com

Printed and bound by CPI Group (UK) Ltd, Croydon, CR0 4YY
30/09/2026
02225264-0017